ADMISSION TEST SERIES

MORRIS AUTOMATED INFORMATION NETWORK

0 1029 0714576 1

D1240456

THIS IS YOUR **PASSBOOK**® FOR ...

CATHOLIC HIGH SCHOOL ENTRANCE EXAMINATION (CHSEE)

NATIONAL LEARNING CORPORATION®
passbooks.com

PASSBOOK® SERIES

THE *PASSBOOK® SERIES* has been created to prepare applicants and candidates for the ultimate academic battlefield – the examination room.

At some time in our lives, each and every one of us may be required to take an examination – for validation, matriculation, admission, qualification, registration, certification, or licensure.

Based on the assumption that every applicant or candidate has met the basic formal educational standards, has taken the required number of courses, and read the necessary texts, the *PASSBOOK® SERIES* furnishes the one special preparation which may assure passing with confidence, instead of failing with insecurity. Examination questions – together with answers – are furnished as the basic vehicle for study so that the mysteries of the examination and its compounding difficulties may be eliminated or diminished by a sure method.

This book is meant to help you pass your examination provided that you qualify and are serious in your objective.

The entire field is reviewed through the huge store of content information which is succinctly presented through a provocative and challenging approach – the question-and-answer method.

A climate of success is established by furnishing the correct answers at the end of each test.

You soon learn to recognize types of questions, forms of questions, and patterns of questioning. You may even begin to anticipate expected outcomes.

You perceive that many questions are repeated or adapted so that you can gain acute insights, which may enable you to score many sure points.

You learn how to confront new questions, or types of questions, and to attack them confidently and work out the correct answers.

You note objectives and emphases, and recognize pitfalls and dangers, so that you may make positive educational adjustments.

Moreover, you are kept fully informed in relation to new concepts, methods, practices, and directions in the field.

You discover that you arre actually taking the examination all the time: you are preparing for the examination by "taking" an examination, not by reading extraneous and/or supererogatory textbooks.

In short, this PASSBOOK®, used directedly, should be an important factor in helping you to pass your test.

CONTENT OF THE EXAMINATION

Test 1 Sequences

This test measures the student's ability to comprehend a rule or principle implicit in a pattern or sequence of numbers, letters, or figures. The student must analyze the pattern or sequence established in the item stem and then select the part that would continue the pattern or sequence.

Test 2 Analogies

This test measures the student's ability to see concrete and abstract relationships and to classify objects or concepts according to common attributes. The student must recognize the nature of the relationship between two pictures and then choose a picture that is related to a third picture in the same way that the first two are related.

Test 3 Verbal Reasoning

This test measures the student's ability to discern relationships and reason logically. Some of the items require the student to infer relationships between separate but related sets of words. An additional item type requires the student to identify essential aspects of objects or concepts. A final type of item requires the student to draw logical conclusions from information given in short passages.

Test 4 Reading Vocabulary

This test measures same-meaning words, multimeaning words, and unfamiliar words in context.

Test 5 Reading Comprehension

This test contains items that measure comprehension of reading passages. Items test the student's ability to extract details, analyze characters, identify main ideas, and draw conclusions from passages. Items also test the ability to differentiate between writing techniques and between forms of writing.

Test 6 Mathematics Computation

This test measures the operations of addition, subtraction, multiplication, and division. Content covered includes whole numbers, decimals, fractions, and integers.

Test 7 Mathematics Concepts and Applications

This test measures understanding of mathematics concepts. Specific skills include numeration, number sentences, number theory, problem solving, measurement, and geometry.

Test 8 Language Mechanics

This test measures the skills of capitalization and punctuation.

Test 9 Language Expression

This test measures skills in language usage and sentence structure. The items measure skills in the use of various parts of speech, formation and organization of sentences and paragraphs, writing for clarity, and the appropriate use of various writing styles. All items in the test are based on rules of written standard English.

TIPS ON TAKING THE TEST

Before the test—

- To do your best, you need to be rested. Get a good night's sleep!
- Make sure you give yourself plenty of time to get to the admissions examination center so you can relax before taking the test.
- Bring your **admission card** with you.
- Bring **several No. 2 pencils** with you. Make sure that they are sharp and that the erasers are clean.
- Don't bring any notes, books, scratch paper, or a calculator with you. You won't be allowed to take them into the examination room.

When you take the test—

- An examiner will give directions. **Listen carefully!** Read all the directions in the examination itself so you know exactly what to do in each part. Studying this handbook will not give you all the information you need.
- Use your test book to do scratch work. Don't write on your answer sheet.
- Pay attention to how much time you have. Don't spend too long on any one question.
- If you think you know the answer, mark it. It is better to try than to leave the answer blank.
- If you don't know the answer, go on to the next question. Try to answer all the questions you can in the time you have. If there is time remaining, go back to the questions you omitted.
- Generally, the questions in each section of the test start with the easier ones and get harder. If you are running out of time, you may want to work on questions toward the beginning of each section.
- Make sure that you mark your answers in the correct section of the answer sheet. Mark only one answer for each question. If you mark more than one answer, the whole answer will be scored as incorrect. To change an answer, erase your first answer completely.
- Don't be careless or sloppy. It could lower your score. If you have extra time, check your work. Make sure that you have:
  - Marked your answers in the right spaces.
  - Made no stray marks on your answer sheet.
  - Erased any answer you changed as completely as possible.

HOW TO TAKE A TEST

You have studied long, hard and conscientiously.

With your official admission card in hand, and your heart pounding, you have been admitted to the examination room.

You note that there are several hundred other applicants in the examination room waiting to take the same test.

They all appear to be equally well prepared.

You know that nothing but your best effort will suffice. The "moment of truth" is at hand: you now have to demonstrate objectively, in writing, your knowledge of content and your understanding of subject matter.

You are fighting the most important battle of your life—to pass and/or score high on an examination which will determine your career and provide the economic basis for your livelihood.

What extra, special things should you know and should you do in taking the examination?

I. YOU MUST PASS AN EXAMINATION

A. WHAT EVERY CANDIDATE SHOULD KNOW

Examination applicants often ask us for help in preparing for the written test. What can I study in advance? What kinds of questions will be asked? How will the test be given? How will the papers be graded?

B. HOW ARE EXAMS DEVELOPED?

Examinations are carefully written by trained technicians who are specialists in the field known as "psychological measurement," in consultation with recognized authorities in the field of work that the test will cover. These experts recommend the subject matter areas or skills to be tested; only those knowledges or skills important to your success on the job are included. The most reliable books and source materials available are used as references. Together, the experts and technicians judge the difficulty level of the questions.

Test technicians know how to phrase questions so that the problem is clearly stated. Their ethics do not permit "trick" or "catch" questions. Questions may have been tried out on sample groups, or subjected to statistical analysis, to determine their usefulness.

Written tests are often used in combination with performance tests, ratings of training and experience, and oral interviews. All of these measures combine to form the best-known means of finding the right person for the right job.

II. HOW TO PASS THE WRITTEN TEST

A. BASIC STEPS

1) Study the announcement

How, then, can you know what subjects to study? Our best answer is: "Learn as much as possible about the class of positions for which you've applied." The exam will test the knowledge, skills and abilities needed to do the work.

Your most valuable source of information about the position you want is the official exam announcement. This announcement lists the training and experience qualifications. Check these standards and apply only if you come reasonably close to meeting them. Many jurisdictions preview the written test in the exam announcement by including a section called "Knowledge and Abilities Required," "Scope of the Examination," or some similar heading. Here you will find out specifically what fields will be tested.

2) Choose appropriate study materials

If the position for which you are applying is technical or advanced, you will read more advanced, specialized material. If you are already familiar with the basic principles of your field, elementary textbooks would waste your time. Concentrate on advanced textbooks and technical periodicals. Think through the concepts and review difficult problems in your field.

These are all general sources. You can get more ideas on your own initiative, following these leads. For example, training manuals and publications of the government agency which employs workers in your field can be useful, particularly for technical and professional positions. A letter or visit to the government department involved may result in more specific study suggestions, and certainly will provide you with a more definite idea of the exact nature of the position you are seeking.

3) Study this book!

III. KINDS OF TESTS

Tests are used for purposes other than measuring knowledge and ability to perform specified duties. For some positions, it is equally important to test ability to make adjustments to new situations or to profit from training. In others, basic mental abilities not dependent on information are essential. Questions which test these things may not appear as pertinent to the duties of the position as those which test for knowledge and information. Yet they are often highly important parts of a fair examination. For very general questions, it is almost impossible to help you direct your study efforts. What we can do is to point out some of the more common of these general abilities needed in public service positions and describe some typical questions.

1) General information

Broad, general information has been found useful for predicting job success in some kinds of work. This is tested in a variety of ways, from vocabulary lists to questions about current events. Basic background in some field of work, such as sociology or economics, may be sampled in a group of questions. Often these are principles which have become familiar to most persons through exposure rather than through formal training. It is difficult to advise you how to study for these questions; being alert to the world around you is our best suggestion.

2) Verbal ability

An example of an ability needed in many positions is verbal or language ability. Verbal ability is, in brief, the ability to use and understand words. Vocabulary and grammar tests are typical measures of this ability. Reading comprehension or paragraph interpretation questions are common in many kinds of civil service tests. You are given a paragraph of written material and asked to find its central meaning.

IV. KINDS OF QUESTIONS

1. Multiple-choice Questions

Most popular of the short-answer questions is the "multiple choice" or "best answer" question. It can be used, for example, to test for factual knowledge, ability to solve problems or judgment in meeting situations found at work.

A multiple-choice question is normally one of three types:
- It can begin with an incomplete statement followed by several possible endings. You are to find the one ending which *best* completes the statement, although some of the others may not be entirely wrong.
- It can also be a complete statement in the form of a question which is answered by choosing one of the statements listed.
- It can be in the form of a problem – again you select the best answer.

Here is an example of a multiple-choice question with a discussion which should give you some clues as to the method for choosing the right answer:

When an employee has a complaint about his assignment, the action which will *best* help him overcome his difficulty is to
  A. discuss his difficulty with his coworkers
  B. take the problem to the head of the organization
  C. take the problem to the person who gave him the assignment
  D. say nothing to anyone about his complaint

In answering this question, you should study each of the choices to find which is best. Consider choice "A" – Certainly an employee may discuss his complaint with fellow employees, but no change or improvement can result, and the complaint remains unresolved. Choice "B" is a poor choice since the head of the organization probably does not know what assignment you have been given, and taking your problem to him is known as "going over the head" of the supervisor. The supervisor, or person who made the assignment, is the person who can clarify it or correct any injustice. Choice "C" is, therefore, correct. To say nothing, as in choice "D," is unwise. Supervisors have and interest in knowing the problems employees are facing, and the employee is seeking a solution to his problem.

2. True/False

3. Matching Questions
Matching an answer from a column of choices within another column.

V. RECORDING YOUR ANSWERS

Computer terminals are used more and more today for many different kinds of exams.

For an examination with very few applicants, you may be told to record your answers in the test booklet itself. Separate answer sheets are much more common. If this separate answer sheet is to be scored by machine – and this is often the case – it is highly important that you mark your answers correctly in order to get credit.

VI. BEFORE THE TEST

YOUR PHYSICAL CONDITION IS IMPORTANT
If you are not well, you can't do your best work on tests. If you are half asleep, you can't do your best either. Here are some tips:

1) Get about the same amount of sleep you usually get. Don't stay up all night before the test, either partying or worrying—DON'T DO IT!
2) If you wear glasses, be sure to wear them when you go to take the test. This goes for hearing aids, too.
3) If you have any physical problems that may keep you from doing your best, be sure to tell the person giving the test. If you are sick or in poor health, you relay cannot do your best on any test. You can always come back and take the test some other time.

Common sense will help you find procedures to follow to get ready for an examination. Too many of us, however, overlook these sensible measures. Indeed, nervousness and fatigue have been found to be the most serious reasons why applicants fail to do their best on civil service tests. Here is a list of reminders:

- Begin your preparation early – Don't wait until the last minute to go scurrying around for books and materials or to find out what the position is all about.
- Prepare continuously – An hour a night for a week is better than an all-night cram session. This has been definitely established. What is more, a night a week for a month will return better dividends than crowding your study into a shorter period of time.
- Locate the place of the exam – You have been sent a notice telling you when and where to report for the examination. If the location is in a different town or otherwise unfamiliar to you, it would be well to inquire the best route and learn something about the building.
- Relax the night before the test – Allow your mind to rest. Do not study at all that night. Plan some mild recreation or diversion; then go to bed early and get a good night's sleep.
- Get up early enough to make a leisurely trip to the place for the test – This way unforeseen events, traffic snarls, unfamiliar buildings, etc. will not upset you.

- Dress comfortably – A written test is not a fashion show. You will be known by number and not by name, so wear something comfortable.
- Leave excess paraphernalia at home – Shopping bags and odd bundles will get in your way. You need bring only the items mentioned in the official notice you received; usually everything you need is provided. Do not bring reference books to the exam. They will only confuse those last minutes and be taken away from you when in the test room.
- Arrive somewhat ahead of time – If because of transportation schedules you must get there very early, bring a newspaper or magazine to take your mind off yourself while waiting.
- Locate the examination room – When you have found the proper room, you will be directed to the seat or part of the room where you will sit. Sometimes you are given a sheet of instructions to read while you are waiting. Do not fill out any forms until you are told to do so; just read them and be prepared.
- Relax and prepare to listen to the instructions
- If you have any physical problem that may keep you from doing your best, be sure to tell the test administrator. If you are sick or in poor health, you really cannot do your best on the exam. You can come back and take the test some other time.

VII. AT THE TEST

The day of the test is here and you have the test booklet in your hand. The temptation to get going is very strong. Caution! There is more to success than knowing the right answers. You must know how to identify your papers and understand variations in the type of short-answer question used in this particular examination. Follow these suggestions for maximum results from your efforts:

1) Cooperate with the monitor
The test administrator has a duty to create a situation in which you can be as much at ease as possible. He will give instructions, tell you when to begin, check to see that you are marking your answer sheet correctly, and so on. He is not there to guard you, although he will see that your competitors do not take unfair advantage. He wants to help you do your best.

2) Listen to all instructions
Don't jump the gun! Wait until you understand all directions. In most civil service tests you get more time than you need to answer the questions. So don't be in a hurry. Read each word of instructions until you clearly understand the meaning. Study the examples, listen to all announcements and follow directions. Ask questions if you do not understand what to do.

3) Identify your papers
Civil service exams are usually identified by number only. You will be assigned a number; you must not put your name on your test papers. Be sure to copy your number correctly. Since more than one exam may be given, copy your exact examination title.

4) Plan your time
Unless you are told that a test is a "speed" or "rate of work" test, speed itself is usually not important. Time enough to answer all the questions will be provided, but this

does not mean that you have all day. An overall time limit has been set. Divide the total time (in minutes) by the number of questions to determine the approximate time you have for each question.

5) Do not linger over difficult questions

If you come across a difficult question, mark it with a paper clip (useful to have along) and come back to it when you have been through the booklet. One caution if you do this – be sure to skip a number on your answer sheet as well. Check often to be sure that you have not lost your place and that you are marking in the row numbered the same as the question you are answering.

6) Read the questions

Be sure you know what the question asks! Many capable people are unsuccessful because they failed to *read* the questions correctly.

7) Answer all questions

Unless you have been instructed that a penalty will be deducted for incorrect answers, it is better to guess than to omit a question.

8) Speed tests

It is often better NOT to guess on speed tests. It has been found that on timed tests people are tempted to spend the last few seconds before time is called in marking answers at random – without even reading them – in the hope of picking up a few extra points. To discourage this practice, the instructions may warn you that your score will be "corrected" for guessing. That is, a penalty will be applied. The incorrect answers will be deducted from the correct ones, or some other penalty formula will be used.

9) Review your answers

If you finish before time is called, go back to the questions you guessed or omitted to give them further thought. Review other answers if you have time.

10) Return your test materials

If you are ready to leave before others have finished or time is called, take ALL your materials to the monitor and leave quietly. Never take any test material with you. The monitor can discover whose papers are not complete, and taking a test booklet may be grounds for disqualification.

VIII. EXAMINATION TECHNIQUES

1) Read the general instructions carefully. These are usually printed on the first page of the exam booklet. As a rule, these instructions refer to the timing of the examination; the fact that you should not start work until the signal and must stop work at a signal, etc. If there are any *special* instructions, such as a choice of questions to be answered, make sure that you note this instruction carefully.

2) When you are ready to start work on the examination, that is as soon as the signal has been given, read the instructions to each question booklet, underline any key words or phrases, such as *least, best, outline, describe*

and the like. In this way you will tend to answer as requested rather than discover on reviewing your paper that you *listed without describing*, that you selected the *worst* choice rather than the *best* choice, etc.

3) If the examination is of the objective or multiple-choice type – that is, each question will also give a series of possible answers: A, B, C or D, and you are called upon to select the best answer and write the letter next to that answer on your answer paper – it is advisable to start answering each question in turn. There may be anywhere from 50 to 100 such questions in the three or four hours allotted and you can see how much time would be taken if you read through all the questions before beginning to answer any. Furthermore, if you come across a question or group of questions which you know would be difficult to answer, it would undoubtedly affect your handling of all the other questions.

4) If the examination is of the essay type and contains but a few questions, it is a moot point as to whether you should read all the questions before starting to answer any one. Of course, if you are given a choice – say five out of seven and the like – then it is essential to read all the questions so you can eliminate the two that are most difficult. If, however, you are asked to answer all the questions, there may be danger in trying to answer the easiest one first because you may find that you will spend too much time on it. The best technique is to answer the first question, then proceed to the second, etc.

5) Time your answers. Before the exam begins, write down the time it started, then add the time allowed for the examination and write down the time it must be completed, then divide the time available somewhat as follows:
   - If 3-1/2 hours are allowed, that would be 210 minutes. If you have 80 objective-type questions, that would be an average of 2-1/2 minutes per question. Allow yourself no more than 2 minutes per question, or a total of 160 minutes, which will permit about 50 minutes to review.
   - If for the time allotment of 210 minutes there are 7 essay questions to answer, that would average about 30 minutes a question. Give yourself only 25 minutes per question so that you have about 35 minutes to review.

6) The most important instruction is to *read each question* and make sure you know what is wanted. The second most important instruction is to *time yourself properly* so that you answer every question. The third most important instruction is to *answer every question*. Guess if you have to but include something for each question. Remember that you will receive no credit for a blank and will probably receive some credit if you write something in answer to an essay question. If you guess a letter – say "B" for a multiple-choice question – you may have guessed right. If you leave a blank as an answer to a multiple-choice question, the examiners may respect your feelings but it will not add a point to your score. Some exams may penalize you for wrong answers, so in such cases *only*, you may not want to guess unless you have some basis for your answer.

7) Suggestions

   a. Objective-type questions

      1. Examine the question booklet for proper sequence of pages and questions
      2. Read all instructions carefully
      3. Skip any question which seems too difficult; return to it after all other questions have been answered
      4. Apportion your time properly; do not spend too much time on any single question or group of questions
      5. Note and underline key words – *all, most, fewest, least, best, worst, same, opposite*, etc.
      6. Pay particular attention to negatives
      7. Note unusual option, e.g., unduly long, short, complex, different or similar in content to the body of the question
      8. Observe the use of "hedging" words – *probably, may, most likely*, etc.
      9. Make sure that your answer is put next to the same number as the question
     10. Do not second-guess unless you have good reason to believe the second answer is definitely more correct
     11. Cross out original answer if you decide another answer is more accurate; do not erase until you are ready to hand your paper in
     12. Answer all questions; guess unless instructed otherwise
     13. Leave time for review

   b. Essay questions

      1. Read each question carefully
      2. Determine exactly what is wanted. Underline key words or phrases.
      3. Decide on outline or paragraph answer
      4. Include many different points and elements unless asked to develop any one or two points or elements
      5. Show impartiality by giving pros and cons unless directed to select one side only
      6. Make and write down any assumptions you find necessary to answer the questions
      7. Watch your English, grammar, punctuation and choice of words
      8. Time your answers; don't crowd material

8) Answering the essay question

Most essay questions can be answered by framing the specific response around several key words or ideas. Here are a few such key words or ideas:

M's: manpower, materials, methods, money, management
P's: purpose, program, policy, plan, procedure, practice, problems, pitfalls, personnel, public relations

   a. Six basic steps in handling problems:

      1. Preliminary plan and background development
      2. Collect information, data and facts
      3. Analyze and interpret information, data and facts
      4. Analyze and develop solutions as well as make recommendations

5. Prepare report and sell recommendations
6. Install recommendations and follow up effectiveness

b. Pitfalls to avoid
1. *Taking things for granted* – A statement of the situation does not necessarily imply that each of the elements is necessarily true; for example, a complaint may be invalid and biased so that all that can be taken for granted is that a complaint has been registered
2. *Considering only one side of a situation* – Wherever possible, indicate several alternatives and then point out the reasons you selected the best one
3. *Failing to indicate follow up* – Whenever your answer indicates action on your part, make certain that you will take proper follow-up action to see how successful your recommendations, procedures or actions turn out to be
4. *Taking too long in answering any single question* – Remember to time your answers properly

EXAMINATION SECTION

EXAMINATION SECTION
TEST 1

DIRECTIONS: Each question or incomplete statement is followed by several suggested answers or completions. Select the one that BEST answers the question or completes the statement. *PRINT THE LETTER OF THE CORRECT ANSWER IN THE SPACE AT THE RIGHT.*

Questions 1-9.

DIRECTIONS: Questions 1 through 9 each consists of a series of numbers which follow in sequence according to a certain rule. Determine the rule and use it to select the next number from among the four choices given on the right side of each row.

SAMPLE X:

						(A)	(B)	(C)	(D)
3	6	9	12	15	18	19	20	21	22

In Sample X above, the rule is to add 3 to each successive number in the series in order to get the next number. Therefore, since 18 plus 3 is 21, the CORRECT choice is C.

SAMPLE Y:

						(A)	(B)	(C)	(D)
4	6	9	13	18	24	27	28	29	31

In Sample Y above, the rule is to add 2, then add 3, then add 4, etc.,to each successive number in the series to get the next number. Therefore, the CORRECT choice is D.

1. 3 9 4 12 7 21
   A. 25
   B. 18
   C. 16
   D. 8   1.____

2. 5 3 6 3 9 5
   A. 20
   B. 18
   C. 10
   D. 3   2.____

3. 10 8 12 4 20 -12
   A. 52
   B. 48
   C. 0
   D. -26   3.____

4. 3 10 9 15 13 18
   A. 12
   B. 15
   C. 20
   D. 36   4.____

5. 1   1 3   9   13   65   A. 15   5.____
                                   B. 26
                                   C. 71
                                   D. 102

6. 2   6 5   15   13   39   A. 4   6.____
                                   B. 18
                                   C. 36
                                   D. 39

7. 48 8   40   10   30   15   A. 15   7.____
                                   B. 20
                                   C. 25
                                   D. 42

8. 20 5   30   10   50   25   A. 110   8.____
                                   B. 100
                                   C. 75
                                   D. 40

9. 4   24 12   60   20   80   A. 40   9.____
                                   B. 36
                                   C. 20
                                   D. 8

10. Below is a series of numbers. In this series, the numbers follow some definite order. Look   10.____
     at the numbers in the series and determine what the order is; then, from the suggested
     answers, consisting of two numbers each and lettered A, B, C, and D, choose the one
     that gives the next two numbers in the series.
     9 9 2 11 11 4 13

     A. 14 14   B. 13 6   C. 13 5   D. 14 6

11. In the letter series A, C, F, J, _____, the letter which logically belongs in the blank space   11.____
     is

     A. L   B. M   C. N   D. 0

Questions 12-16.

DIRECTIONS: Each series of numbers is made up according to a certain rule or order. Indi-
              cate the NEXT number in the series.

12. 7, 21, 42, 126, 252, _____   12.____

     A. 275   B. 294   C. 378   D. 756

13. 4, 10, 7, 13, 10, 16, _____   13.____

     A. 13   B. 12   C. 14   D. 18

14. 9, 27, 25, 75, 73, 219, _____   14.____

     A. 217   B. 216   C. 222   D. 637

15. 3, 9, 10, 30, 31, 93, _____   15._____

    A. 91   B. 92   C. 94   D. 83

16. 12, 6, 24, 12, 48, 24, _____   16._____

    A. 72   B. 96
    C. 144   D. none of the above

Questions 17-20.

DIRECTIONS: Each question or incomplete statement is followed by several suggested answers or completions. Select the one that BEST answers the question or completes the statement.

17. The number which logically belongs in the blank box is   17._____

6
12
4

3
18
1

9
7

    A. 6   B. 7   C. 8   D. 9

18. The number which logically belongs in the blank space is   18._____
3, 5, 9, 17, _____

    A. 25   B. 33   C. 39   D. 41

19. The number which logically belongs in the blank box is   19._____

3
6
2

4
12
3

2
6

    A. 11   B. 12   C. 15   D. 16

20. The number which logically belongs in the blank space is   20._____

    A. 11   B. 13   C. 16   D. 17

KEY (CORRECT ANSWERS)

1.	C		11.	D
2.	A		12.	D
3.	A		13.	A
4.	B		14.	A
5.	C		15.	C
6.	C		16.	B
7.	A		17.	A
8.	B		18.	B
9.	C		19.	B
10.	B		20.	D

—————

TEST 2

DIRECTIONS: The following consists of a series of numbers which follow in sequence according to a certain rule. Determine the rule and use it to select the next number from among the four choices given on the right side of each row.

1. 16 13 10 7

   A. 3
   B. 5
   C. 19
   D. None of these

1._____

2. 15 12 13 10 11 8 9

   A. 6
   B. 7
   C. 14
   D. None of these

2._____

3. 33 36 31 34 29 32

   A. 28
   B. 30
   C. 35
   D. None of these

3._____

4. 10 15 21 28 36

   A. 41
   B. 42
   C. 44
   D. None of these

4._____

5. 9 7.2 5.4 3.6 1.8

   A. 0
   B. .8
   C. .9
   D. None of these

5._____

6. 8 11 22 25 50 53 106

   A. 109
   B. 159
   C. 212
   D. None of these

6._____

7. 8 1/3 7 5 2/3 4 1/3

   A. 2
   B. 2 2/3
   C. 3
   D. None of these

7._____

8. 77 78 79 83 87 94 101

   A. 102
   B. 108
   C. 111
   D. None of these

8._____

9. 40 42 47 44 46 51 48

   A. 46
   B. 50
   C. 53
   D. None of these

9._____

10. 21   24   32   36   44   49   57   A. 60   10._____
                                             B. 63
                                           C. 65
                                         D. None of these

11. 4   11   14   20   22   27   A. 28   11._____
                                             B. 31
                                           C. 32
                                         D. None of these

12. 2 1/6 3 1/3   4 1/2   5 2/3   6 5/6   A. 7 1/2   12._____
                                           B. 8
                                         C. 9
                                         D. None of these

13. 9   14   21   25   32   35   42   A. 40   13._____
                                           B. 44
                                         C. 45
                                         D. None of these

14. 99   91   87   78   73   63   57   A. 46   14._____
                                           B. 49
                                         C. 68
                                         D. None of these

15. 40   35   30   24   18   13   A. 7   15._____
                                         B. 8
                                       C. 9
                                       D. None of these

KEY (CORRECT ANSWERS)

1.	D		6.	A
2.	A		7.	C
3.	D		8.	C
4.	D		9.	B
5.	A		10.	B

11.	A
12.	B
13.	B
14.	A
15.	B

TEST 3

DIRECTIONS: Each of the following series is made up according to some rule. Addition, subtraction, multiplication, division, or various combinations of these operations are used in forming each series. Discover the rule for each series and decide which of the four suggested answers is CORRECT as the next term. *PRINT THE LETTER OF THE CORRECT ANSWER IN THE SPACE AT THE RIGHT.*

Sample :   1   3   5   7
          A.   7   B . 8 C.   9 D.   10

The correct answer is C, since 9 is the next term in the series.

1. 12   0   10   0   8   0 _____   1.____
      A. 0   B. 6   C. 7   D. 10

2. 42   37   32   27 _____   2.____
      A. 22   B. 23   C. 24   D. 25

3. r^6 $6r$ r^5 $5r$ r^4 _____   3.____
      A. r^3 B. $3r$ C. $4r^3$ D. $4r$

4. 2   4   8   16   3   2 _____   4.____
      A. 46   B. 48   C. 54   D. 64

5. 8   11   14   17 _____   5.____
      A. 18   B. 19   C. 20   D. 21

6. 1   4   7   10   13 _____   6.____
      A. 17   B. 16   C. 15   D. 14

7. 4   5   7   8   10 _____   7.____
      A. 14   B. 13   C. 12   D. 11

8. 17   17   13   9   9 _____   8.____
      A. 4   B. 5   C. 6   D. 7

9. ab   4589   2ab   458   3ab _____   9.____
      A. 45   B. 58   C. 48   D. 4ab

10. $\frac{a+4}{2a}$ $\frac{a+10}{5a}$ $\frac{a+16}{8a}$ 10.____

      A. $\frac{a+18}{9a}$ B. $\frac{a+20}{11a}$ C. $\frac{a+22}{11a}$ D. $\frac{a+22}{12a}$

11. 64   32   16   8 _____   11.____

    A. 0   B. 2   C. 4   D. 6

12. 56342 xy^2 5634 $x2y^3$ 563 x^3y^4 _____   12.____

    A. x^4y^5 B. y^4y^5 C. 63   D. 56

13. 48.08   24.04   12.02 _____   13.____

    A. 6.06   B. 6.02   C. 6.01   D. 6.1

14. 2   6   10   11   15   19 _____   14.____

    A. 20   B. 21   C. 22   D. 23

15. $2y^3$-10 $6y^8$-16 $10y^{13}$-22 _____   15.____

    A. $16y^{18}$-28   B. $16y^{16}$-24   C. $14y^{16}$-24   D. $14y^{18}$-28

16. $4y^8$ $5y^7$ $4y^6$ $7y^5$ $4y^4$ _____   16.____

    A. $5y^7$ B. $9y^3$ C. $4y^2$ D. $5y^3$

17. 2   5   9   14   20 _____   17.____

    A. 27   B. 26   C. 25   D. 24

18. 3   2   4   3   5   4 _____   18.____

    A. 6   B. 5   C. 4   D. 3

19. 2   4   6   7   9   11 _____   19.____

    A. 15   B. 14   C. 12   D. 11

20. 3   8   13   18   23 _____   20.____

    A. 31   B. 29   C. 28   D. 27

21. 1   3   6   10   15 _____   21.____

    A. 17   B. 19   C. 20   D. 21

22. 3/5   1 1/5   1 4/5   2 2/5 _____   22.____

    A. 2 1/2   B. 2 4/5   C. 3   D. 3 1/5

23. 2   4   8   14   22 _____   23.____

    A. 30   B. 32   C. 34   D. 36

24. 4   5   10   11   22   23 _____   24.____

    A. 24   B. 44   C. 45   D. 46

25. 1   3   7   15 _____   25.____

    A. 31   B. 29   C. 27   D. 22

26. 24   23   22   20   19   18 _____   26._____

    A. 13   B. 14   C. 15   D. 16

27. 5/32   5/16   5/8   1 1/4   2 1/2 _____   27._____

    A. 5   B. 3 3/4   C. 3 1/2   D. 3 1/4

28. 5/108   5/36   5/12   5/4   3 3/4 _____   28._____

    A. 11 1/4   B. 7 1/4   C. 6 3/4   D. 6 1/4

29. 1   1   2   6   24 _____   29._____

    A. 124   B. 120   C. 96   D. 42

30. 1   4   9   16 _____   30._____

    A. 23   B. 24   C. 25   D. 27

KEY (CORRECT ANSWERS)

1.	B	16.	D
2.	A	17.	A
3.	D	18.	A
4.	D	19.	C
5.	D	20.	C
6.	B	21.	D
7.	D	22.	C
8.	B	23.	B
9.	A	24.	D
10.	C	25.	A
11.	C	26.	D
12.	D	27.	A
13.	C	28.	A
14.	A	29.	B
15.	D	30.	C

TEST 4

DIRECTIONS: Each question or incomplete statement is followed by several suggested answers or completions. Select the one that BEST answers the question or completes the statement. *PRINT THE LETTER OF THE CORRECT ANSWER IN THE SPACE AT THE RIGHT.*

1. 1, 2, 3, 4, _____
   A. 8   B. 7   C. 6   D. 5

   1._____

2. 1, 5, 9, 13, _____
   A. 15   B. 17   C. 22   D. 19

   2._____

3. A   B   D   E   G   H _____
   A. K   B. I   C. F   D. J

   3._____

4. C, E, G, K, M, _____
   A. V   B. S   C. Q   D. R

   4._____

5. A, D, G, J, _____
   A. L   B. M   C. N   D. K

   5._____

6. b, c, d, f, g, h, _____
   A. i   B. j   C. k   D. l

   6._____

7. f, e, d, c, _____
   A. 3, 4, 5, 6   B. 6, 5, 4, 3
   C. z, y, x. w   D. 2, 4, 6, 8

   7._____

8. A, 1, D, 4, J, 10, M, _____
   A. 13   B. 14   C. 16   D. 18

   8._____

9. 1, 3, 9, 27, _____
   A. 36   B. 69   C. 45   D. 81

   9._____

10. 1203004000500 _____
    A. 600   B. 0   C. 006   D. 00

    10._____

11. 1, 2, 4, 7, 11, _____
    A. 16   B. 14   C. 18   D. 15

    11._____

12. 4, 9, 16, _____
    A. 23   B. 25   C. 27   D. 24

    12._____

13. If A = B, then X = 101
    If A is greater than B, X = 102
    If A is less than B, X = 103
    If A = 0, X = 104.
    Now, if A - B = 3 and B is greater than O, then x =

    A. 101   B. 102   C. 103   D. 104

13.____

14. 2000, 1999, 1996, 1991, _____

    A. 1986   B. 1899   C. 1984   D. 1987

14.____

15. $a = b$, $b \neq c$
    Which is NOT true?

    A. $a + b \neq c$ B. $a - 1 = c$
    C. $b + 1 = c$ D. $c - 1 = a$

15.____

16. 1, 8, 22, 50, _____

    A. 64   B. 106   C. 134   D. 100

16.____

17. 3, 8, 15, 26, 39, _____

    A. 51   B. 45   C. 56   D. 47

17.____

18. XooXXoXo _____

    A. oo   B. oX   C. Xo   D. XX

18.____

19. XXoooo _____

    A. one o   B. 6 X's
    C. 5 X's   D. one o, three X's

19.____

20. 4, 6, 8, 10, 14, _____

    A. 18   B. 20   C. 24   D. 16

20.____

21. 2, 2, 4, 12, 48, _____

    A. 60   B. 96   C. 144   D. 240

21.____

22. XoooXXXXX

    A. 3 X's, 2 o's   B. 5 o's
    C. 7 X's   D. 7 o's

22.____

23. 2, 5, 13, 36, _____

    A. 72   B. 49   C. 68   D. 104

23.____

24. XooXXXoo _____

    A. oX   B. Xo   C. XX   D. oo

24.____

25. a   cd   ghi   mnop _____

    A. uvwx   B. vwxyz   C. wxyz   D. uvwxy

25.____

KEY (CORRECT ANSWERS)

1.	D		11.	A
2.	B		12.	B
3.	D		13.	B
4.	C		14.	C
5.	B		15.	B
6.	B		16.	B
7.	B		17.	C
8.	A		18.	B
9.	D		19.	B
10.	C		20.	D

21.	D
22.	D
23.	D
24.	D
25.	D

LETTER SERIES

COMMENTARY

Letter-series problems, also variously denoted as alphabetic series and/or progressions, constitute an important method for measuring quantitative ability on the part of senior and/or supervisory personnel as applicants for mid-level or senior-level positions.

Through this instrument, numerical reasoning - the usual technique for measuring mathematical ability - is substituted for by the comparatively abstract procedure of using letters instead of numbers -an admittedly more unusual and complex discipline.

Even more challenging than the number-series question, and of the highest order of difficulty, the letter-series question consists of a series of letters (instead of numbers), which is to be followed and carried forward (or backward) according to a definite order or sequence. Basically, the element of abstractness (i.e., letters instead of numbers) serves to compound this question.

A valuable, concrete suggestion to the examinee, as an aid in solving alphabetic-series problems, is to begin by writing out the alphabet (e.g., in columns of five letters) and keeping this visual aid immediately in front of him so that he may be enabled to solve the question more readily that way. Such a listing follows:

```
A    B    C    D    E
F    G    H    I    J
K    L    M    N    O
P    Q    R    S    T
U    V    W    X    Y
Z
```

SAMPLE QUESTIONS

DIRECTIONS: In each question in this test, there is, at the left, a series of several letters which follow some definite order, and, underneath, there are five sets of two letters each.

Look at the letters in the series at the left and find out what order they follow. Now decide what the next two letters in that series would be if the order were continued. Then find those two letters in one of the five sets of letters below and print in the space at the right the letter of the correct answer.

SAMPLE QUESTION 1 x c x d x e x
A. f x   B. f g   C. x f   D. e f   E. x g

Explanation
The order in this series is the letter x alternating with letters in a certain alphabetical order starting with c so that if the series were continued for two or more letters, it would read:

x c x d x e x f x

and f x are those two letters you would look for.

In the five sets of letters lettered A, B, C, D, and E, in the above question, the set f x is labeled A. Therefore, you should indicate A in the space at the right.

<u>SAMPLE QUESTION 2</u> u u t t s s r
A. r r   B. r q   C. q r   D. q q   E. r s

<u>Explanation</u>
The order in this series is pairs of letters starting with u u and going backward through the alphabet so that if the series were continued for two more letters, it would read:

u u t t s s r r q

and r q are those two letters you would look for.

In the five sets of letters lettered A, B, C, D, and E, in the above question, the set r q is labeled B. Therefore, you should indicate B in the space at the right.

EXAMINATION SECTION
TEST 1

DIRECTIONS: In each series below, determine what the order of the letters is and decide what the next two letters should be. From the suggested answers below, choose the one that gives the next two letters in the series and indicate the CORRECT answer in the space at the right. *PRINT THE LETTER OF THE CORRECT ANSWER IN THE SPACE AT THE RIGHT.*

1. A Z B Y C   1.____
    A. D W   B. W D   C. X D   D. D X

2. A C F J   2.____
    A. O U   B. O W   C. N U   D. N W

3. Z X V T   3.____
    A. S Q   B. S R   C. R Q   D. R P

4. M N O L K P Q   4.____
    A. J I   B. S T   C. J S   D. I T

5. Y Z A B W X C   5.____
    A. V D   B. D U   C. U D   D. D V

6. A B B C D D E F F   6.____
    A. G G   B. G H   C. H H   D. H I

7. Q A B Q B C Q C D   7.____
    A. E Q   B. D Q   C. Q E   D. Q D

8. L A M Z L B M Y L   8.____
    A. C X   B. C M   C. M C   D. M X

9. Y Z A W X B U   9.____
    A. V C   B. C D   C. C X   D. V D

10. N M Z M N Y N M X   10.____
    A. N M   B. N W   C. M N   D. M W

11. A Z W T B Q N K C   11.____
    A. I F   B. I E   C. H E   D. H F

12. Z Y Y X X X W W W W   12.____
    A. W V   B. V V   C. V U   D. U U

13. A D F I K   13.____
    A. N Q   B. N P   C. M Q   D. M P

14. ZVSOLH   14.____

    A. EA   B. CE   C. EC   D. EB

15. AABBBBAAABBBBBAAAA   15.____

    A. AA   B. AB   C. BA   D. BB

16. WTURSP   16.____

    A. QN   B. MN   C. OR   D. RN

17. EIGKIMK   17.____

    A. OK   B. NK   C. OM   D. NM

18. HABCHBCDH   18.____

    A. CD   B. DE   C. AC   D. CE

19. ACEEGIKKM   19.____

    A. QQ   B. OO   C. OQ   D. NQ

20. ZYXXXWVUUUT   20.____

    A. TS   B. SS   C. TR   D. SR

KEY (CORRECT ANSWERS)

1.	C	11.	C
2.	A	12.	B
3.	D	13.	B
4.	A	14.	A
5.	B	15.	D
6.	B	16.	A
7.	D	17.	C
8.	B	18.	A
9.	A	19.	C
10.	C	20.	D

TEST 2

DIRECTIONS: In each series below, determine what the order of the letters is and decide what the next letters should be. From the suggested answers below, choose the one that gives the letters in the series and indicate the CORRECT answer in the space at the right. *PRINT THE LETTER OF THE CORRECT ANSWER IN THE SPACE AT THE RIGHT.*

1. A B C C C D E F F F G H   1._____
   A. H H   B. H I   C. I J   D. I I

2. Z X X V T R R   2._____
   A. R P   B. P P   C. P M   D. P N

3. L A B B L B C C L   3._____
   A. D D   B. C D   C. D E   D. C E

4. Y U W W Y U T T Y   4._____
   A. U Q   B. Y U   C. Q Q   D. U U

5. B E D C F E D   5._____
   A. E G   B. G F   C. F G   D. G H

6. Z Z Y Y Y X X W W W V   6._____
   A. V V   B. U U   C. V U   D. U T

7. A D F I K N   7._____
   A. R T   B. P R   C. P S   D. Q S

8. W U T R Q   8._____
   A. P O   B. P N   C. O N   D. O M

9. B C C E F F   9._____
   A. H I   B. G H   C. H J   D. G G

10. A Z Y B C X   10._____
    A. W D   B. D V   C. D W   D. W V

11. P K A P K C P   11._____
    A. K D   B. K E   C. P E   D. D K

12. A B C Z A B C Y A   12._____
    A. C X   B. B X   C. B C   D. C B

13. L A B B C L B C C D   13._____
    A. D L   B. L C   C. L E   D. L D

14. M M A Z M M A Y M M

    A. M A   B. A B   C. M X   D. A X

14.____

15. Z Z Z Y X X X W V

    A. V V   B. V U   C. U U   D. U V

15.____

16. M N O P N O P M O P M N

    A. P M   B. O P   C. M O   D. P N

16.____

17. G H I I H I G G I G

    A. H I   B. I H   C. H H   D. H G

17.____

18. A E F B F E C E F

    A. G F   B. D E   C. G E   D. D F

18.____

19. J A J J B J J J C

    A. J J   B. J D   C. J E   D. D J

19.____

20. E H G J I L

    A. O N   B. K N   C. K M   D. O M

20.____

KEY (CORRECT ANSWERS)

1.	D	11.	B
2.	D	12.	C
3.	B	13.	B
4.	A	14.	D
5.	B	15.	A
6.	C	16.	A
7.	C	17.	C
8.	C	18.	D
9.	A	19.	A
10.	A	20.	B

TEST 3

DIRECTIONS: In each series below, determine what the order of the letters is and decide what the next letters should be. From the suggested answers below, choose the one that gives the letters in the series and indicate the CORRECT answer in the space at the right. *PRINT THE LETTER OF THE CORRECT ANSWER IN THE SPACE AT THE RIGHT.*

1. A B B A C C A D D   1._____
   A. E E A   B. A A E   C. A E E   D. E E E

2. A C E G I   2._____
   A. J K L   B. K N P   C. K M O   D. J L N

3. Z Z Y X X W V   3._____
   A. V U U   B. U U T   C. U T T   D. V U T

4. Z X Y W U V T   4._____
   A. R Q P   B. R S Q   C. S Q R   D. R P Q

5. C B B A D C C B E   5._____
   A. D C C   B. D D C   C. E D D   D. E D C

6. X Y Z Z V W X X T U   6._____
   A. V V R   B. U V S   C. U V R   D. V V S

7. M N L O K P J   7._____
   A. Q I R   B. I Q R   C. Q R I   D. I R Q

8. M Y Z K W X I   8._____
   A. J U V   B. J V U   C. U V G   D. U V H

9. D A B C H E F G   9._____
   A. H L K   B. L I J   C. L J K   D. H K J

10. A A D D D G G J J J   10._____
    A. M M O   B. M P P   C. M N N   D. M M P

11. L N N L L N N N L L L   11._____
    A. N N L   B. N L L   C. L L L   D. N N N

12. F G H H G H F F H   12._____
    A. H F G   B. F F G   C. H F F   D. F G G

13. Z A B Y X C D   13._____
    A. W U E   B. W V E   C. E W V   D. E V U

14. A M N B M M N C M M M N   14.____

    A. D M M   B. D M N   C. D N N   D. D N M

15. Y O Y O P Y O P Q Y   15.____

    A. O R Y   B. O P Q   C. P Q Y   D. O Q R

16. D C A B H G E F L   16.____

    A. K I J   B. K J I   C. I J K   D. I K J

17. A M N E N M I M N   17.____

    A. M M N   B. N M N   C. N N M   D. M N M

18. T Z X V T T Z X V V T T T   18.____

    A. Z Z X   B. Z X V   C. X Z Z   D. X V Z

19. A B Z B A Y A B X B   19.____

    A. W A B   B. A W B   C. A W A   D. W B A

20. R A S A C R A C E S A   20.____

    A. C G R   B. C O S   C. C E G   D. C E R

KEY (CORRECT ANSWERS)

1. C	11. D
2. C	12. D
3. D	13. B
4. B	14. A
5. B	15. B
6. A	16. A
7. A	17. D
8. C	18. B
9. B	19. C
10. D	20. C

TEST 4

DIRECTIONS: In each series below, determine what the order of the letters is and decide what the next two letters should be. From the suggested answers below, choose the one that gives the next two letters in the series and indicate the CORRECT answer in the space at the right. *PRINT THE LETTER OF THE CORRECT ANSWER IN THE SPACE AT THE RIGHT.*

1. D Z D Z Y D Z Y X D Z

    A. Y X W   B. Y D X   C. Y X D   D. D Y W   1.____

2. Y Z A W X B U V C

    A. D S T   B. S D E   C. D E S   D. S T D   2.____

3. F A L G A L L H A L L L

    A. I L L   B. I A L   C. L I L   D. L A I   3.____

4. A M N O C O N M E M N O G

    A. O M N   B. M O N   C. M N O   D. O N M   4.____

5. D C B A H G F E L K

    A. I J L   B. J I P   C. J I O   D. I J M   5.____

6. W X Y Z X Y Z W YZ X W Z

    A. Y X W   B. Y W X   C. W X Y   D. W Y X   6.____

7. B J K L B B J K L L B B B J

    A. K L L   B. K K L   C. L K B   D. L L B   7.____

8. R S C B A S R A B C R S C

    A. B A S   B. A B S   C. A S B   D. B S A   8.____

9. V V V T V V T T V T T T

    A. V V V   B. T T T   C. T T V   D. V V T   9.____

10. A Z X D V T G R P

    A. K N M   B. J O M   C. J N L   D. K O N   10.____

11. A E I B F J C G K D

    A. I M E   B. I L E   C. H M E   D. H L E   11.____

12. C C M N O P C C N O P Q C C O P Q R

    A. C C Q   B. C C P   C. C P Q   D. C Q R   12.____

13. L O M N J Q K P H

    A. S R I   B. R I S   C. S I R   D. R S I   13.____

14. YYYBBWWWDDUU   14.____

    A. FFS   B. UFF   C. FFF   D. UFS

15. PQRZZQRPYYRPQXXP   15.____

    A. QWW   B. QRW   C. RQW   D. RRW

16. KDEKDFKDGK   16.____

    A. DHK   B. HDK   C. DIK   D. IKD

17. MLAKJBIHC   17.____

    A. GFE   B. DEF   C. DFG   D. GFD

18. ZKZZLZKZZMZKZZ   18.____

    A. KNZ   B. NZZ   C. KZN   D. NZK

19. ARRBRCRRDRE   19.____

    A. RFR   B. FRR   C. RRF   D. FFR

20. CBAXFEDXIHGX   20.____

    A. JKL   B. LJX   C. LKJ   D. JKX

KEY (CORRECT ANSWERS)

1.	A	11.	D
2.	D	12.	B
3.	B	13.	C
4.	D	14.	B
5.	B	15.	B
6.	C	16.	A
7.	A	17.	D
8.	A	18.	D
9.	B	19.	C
10.	C	20.	C

TEST 5

DIRECTIONS: In each of the following questions, there is a series of letters and numbers which follow some definite order, and underneath there are four sets of two or three letters each. Look at the letters and numbers in the series and determine what the order is. Then, from the suggested answers below, select the set that gives the next set of letters in the series in their correct order. *PRINT THE LETTER OF THE CORRECT ANSWER N THE SPACE AT THE RIGHT.*

1. A Z 1 Y B 2 C X   1.____

    A. D 3   .B. 3 D   C. 3 W   D. W 3

2. Y 2 W 3 U 2 S 3   2.____

    A. Q 3   B. R 3   C. Q 2   D. R 2

3. Y Z A 9 W X B 8 U V   3.____

    A. 7 D   B. C D   C. W 7   D. C 7

4. I I Q A B 2 1 Q B C 3 1 Q C D 4   4.____

    A. 1 D E   B. 5 Q E   C. 5 Q 1   D. 1 Q D

5. N M 8 Z M N 5 Y N M 8 X   5.____

    A. M N 5   B. N M 5   C. M N 8   D. N M 8

6. A 1 D 9 G 2 J 8   6.____

    A. M 7   B. N 3   C. M 3   D. N 7

7. A A 8 9 B B 9 8 C C 8   7.____

    A. 8 D   B. 9 D   C. 9 E   D. 8 E

8. 4 4 H A B C 5 4 H D E F 6 4 H G   8.____

    A. H I 4   B. I 7 4   C. H 7 4   D. H I 7

9. Z 7 X X Y 7 7 X X X 7 7 7 X X   9.____

    A. W 7   B. 7 7   C. 7 W   D. W X

10. B D 1 2 B F 2 3 B H 3 4 B   10.____

    A. I 5 6   B. J 5 6   C. I 4 5   D. J 4 5

11. Y W 1 1 2 U S 1 1 3 Q 0 1 1 4   11.____

    A. M L S   B. N M 5   C. M K 1   D. N L 1

12. A C 6 B D 5 C E 6   12.____

    A. D F   B. D 5   C. F 5   D. F G

13. 2 P K A 2 P K B 2 P   13.____

    A. K 2   B. P K   C. P C   D. K C

14. MM33AMM44BM

    A. M5C   B. M55   C. 55C   D. 5CM

14.____

15. LALL9LAMM8LA

    A. N7L   B. NN7   C. NNL   D. NL7

15.____

16. ACD4EGH5I

    A. KL6   B. JL6   C. JK6   D. KM6

16.____

17. C1BBAF2EEDI3H

    A. GG4   B. HGL   C. G4L   D. HG4

17.____

18. 42MN24L042KP2

    A. 2JR   B. 4JQ   C. 4QJ   D. JQ2

18.____

19. 3Y3YA3YAB3YABC3

    A. YCD   B. YAD   C. YAB   D. YBC

19.____

20. 543DZ543DY54

    A. 3DX   B. 3EX   C. 3DE   D. 3ED

20.____

KEY (CORRECT ANSWERS)

1.	C	11.	C
2.	C	12.	A
3.	D	13.	D
4.	D	14.	B
5.	A	15.	B
6.	C	16.	A
7.	B	17.	B
8.	D	18.	B
9.	A	19.	C
10.	D	20.	A

NONVERBAL REASONING

DIRECTIONS: In each question, there are five drawings (A-E presented from left to right). One drawing does NOT belong with the other four. You are to decide which drawing does NOT belong and PRINT THE LETTER of that drawing on your answer sheet.

EXAMPLES

EXAMPLE A:
    C does NOT belong because the eye is incomplete.

EXAMPLE B:
    A does not belong because it is a hammer and the rest are objects relating to food.

EXAMPLE C:
    E does not belong because while there are 2 each of the straight stick figures and squares, there is only one cat made of circular strokes.

EXAMPLE D:
    C does not belong because it is thicker than the other pens, has a clip on its cap and it is a fountain pen while the rest are ballpoint pens.

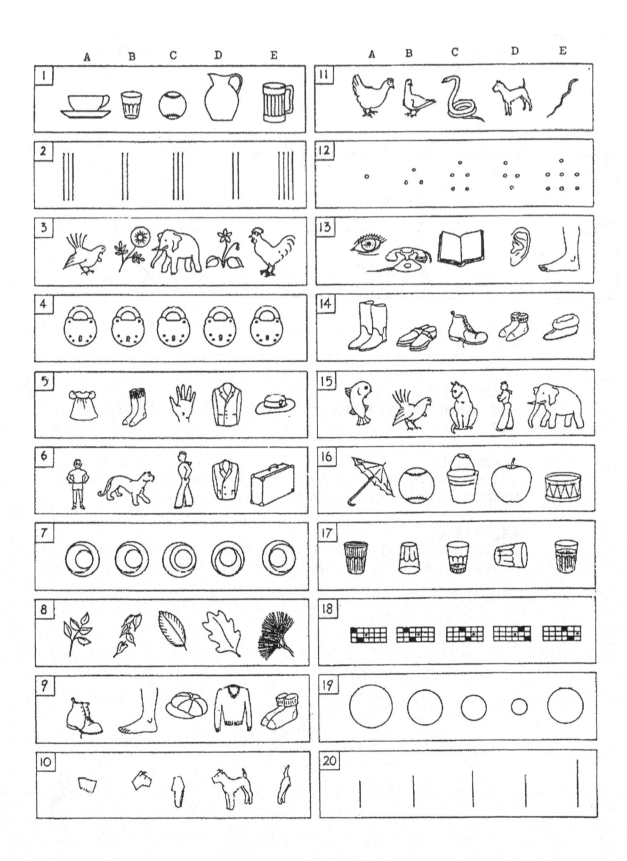

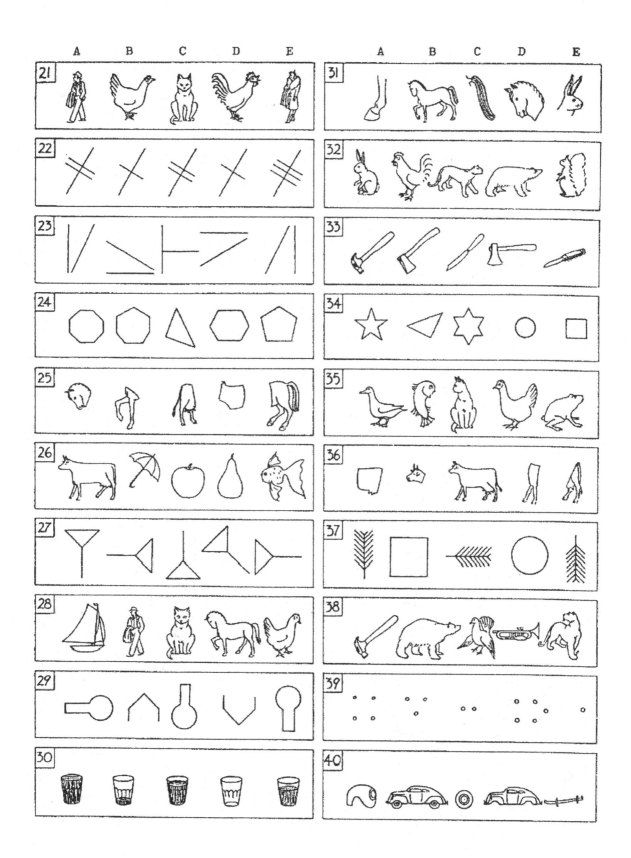

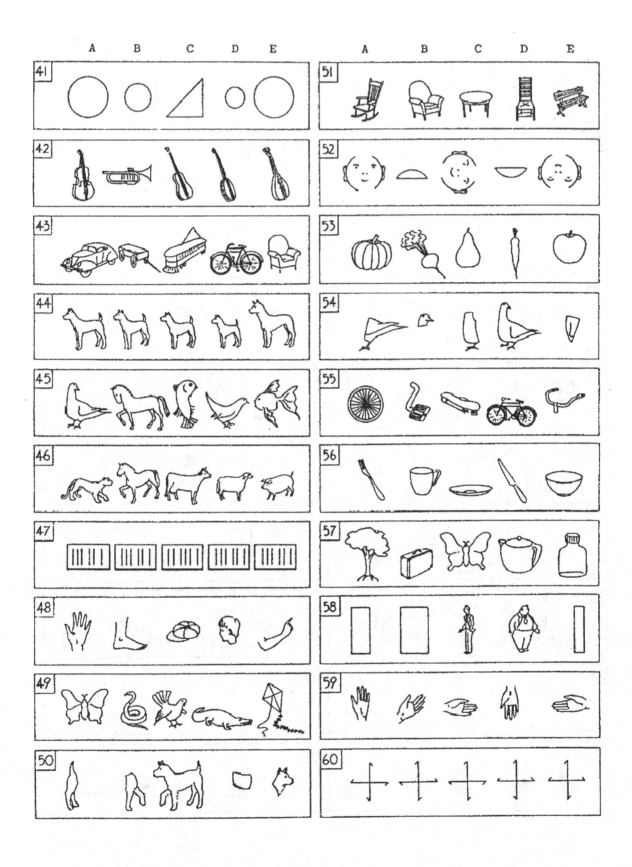

KEY (CORRECT ANSWERS)

1.	C	16.	D	31.	E	46.	A
2.	E	17.	D	32.	B	47.	C
3.	C	18.	D	33.	A	48.	C
4.	C	19.	E	34.	D	49.	E
5.	C	20.	D	35.	C	50.	C
6.	B	21.	C	36.	C	51.	C
7.	C	22.	E	37.	D	52.	C
8.	E	23.	C	38.	A	53.	A
9.	B	24.	C	39.	D	54.	D
10.	D	25.	C	40.	B	55.	D
11.	D	26.	B	41.	C	56.	C
12.	D	27.	D	42.	B	57.	A
13.	E	28.	A	43.	E	58.	A
14.	D	29.	A	44.	E	59.	B
15.	D	30.	D	45.	B	60.	D

———

VERBAL ANALOGIES

EXAMINATION SECTION
TEST 1

DIRECTIONS: In Questions 1 to 10, the first two *italicized* words have a relationship to each other. Determine that relationship, and then match the third *italicized* word with the one of the lettered choices with which it has the same relationship as the words of the first pair have to each other. *PRINT THE LETTER OF THE CORRECT ANSWER IN THE SPACE AT THE RIGHT.*

In order to help you understand the procedure, a sample question is given:

SAMPLE: *dog* is to *bark* as *cat* is to
A. animal   B. small   C. meow
D. pet   E. snarl

The relationship between *dog* and *bark* is that the sound which a dog normally emits is a bark. In the same way, the sound which a cat emits is a meow. Thus, C is the CORRECT answer.

1. *Fine* is to *speeding* as *jail* is to   1.____

    A.   bars   B.   prisoner   C.   warden
    D.   confinement   E.   steal

2. *Orchid* is to *rose* as *gold* is to   2.____

    A.   watch   B.   copper   C.   mine   D.   coin   E.   mint

3. *Pistol* is to *machine gun* as *button* is to   3.____

    A.   coat   B.   bullet   C.   zipper
    D.   tailor   E.   needle and thread

4. *Spontaneous* is to *unrehearsed* as *planned* is to   4.____

    A.   completed   B.   organized   C.   restricted
    D.   understood   E.   informal

5. *Friendly* is to *hostile* as *loyalty* is to   5.____

    A.   fealty   B.   evil   C.   devotion
    D.   warlike   E.   treachery

6. *Fear* is to *flight* as *bravery* is to   6.____

    A.   courage   B.   danger   C.   resistance
    D.   injury   E.   unyielding

7. *Economical* is to *stingy* as *sufficient* is to   7.____

    A.   abundant   B.   adequate   C.   expensive
    D.   needy   E.   greedy

8. *Astronomer* is to *observation* as *senator* is to

    A. caucus   B. election   C. convention
    D. legislation   E. patronage

8.____

9. *Hunger* is to *food* as *exhaustion* is to

    A. labor   B. play   C. illness
    D. debility   E. rest

9.____

10. *Entertainment* is to *boredom* as *efficiency* is to

    A. ignorance   B. government   C. waste
    D. expert   E. time and motion stud-
                     ies

10.____

KEY (CORRECT ANSWERS)

1.	E		6.	C
2.	B		7.	A
3.	C		8.	D
4.	B		9.	E
5.	E		10.	C

TEST 2

DIRECTIONS: In Questions 1 to 10, the first two *italicized* words have a relationship to each other. Determine that relationship, and then match the third *italicized* word with the one of the lettered choices with which it has the same relationship as the words of the first pair have to each other. *PRINT THE LETTER OF THE CORRECT ANSWER IN THE SPACE AT THE RIGHT.*

1. *Diamond* is to *glass* as *platinum* is to   1._____

   A. jewelry   B. metal   C. aluminum
   D. mine   E. white

2. *Water* is to *aqueduct* as *electricity* is to   2._____

   A. meter   B. battery   C. fuse   D. wire   E. solenoid

3. *Oratory* is to *filibuster* as *reign* is to   3._____

   A. tyrant   B. terror   C. government
   D. bluster   E. confusion

4. *Gravity* is to *gaiety* as *taunt* is to   4._____

   A. ridicule   B. console   C. avoid
   D. amuse   E. condone

5. *Electron* is to *atom* as *earth* is to   5._____

   A. sun   B. solar system   C. moon
   D. planet   E. center

6. *Flattery* is to *adulation* as *cruelty* is to   6._____

   A. pain   B. barbarity   C. censorious
   D. compassion   E. duality

7. *Rowboat* is to *oar* as *automobile* is to   7._____

   A. land   B. engine   C. driver
   D. passenger   E. piston

8. *Friction* is to *oil* as *war* is to   8._____

   A. conference   B. peace   C. munitions
   D. satellite   E. retaliation

9. *Disease* is to *infection* as *reaction* is to   9._____

   A. control   B. injury   C. relapse
   D. stipulation   E. sensation

10. *Persecution* is to *martyr* as *swindle* is to   10._____

    A. embezzler   B. refuge   C. confidence man
    D. bank   E. dupe

KEY (CORRECT ANSWERS)

1.	C	6.	B
2.	D	7.	B
3.	E	8.	A
4.	B	9.	E
5.	B	10.	E

———

TEST 3

In Questions 1 to 10, the first two *italicized* words have a relationship to each other. Determine that relationship, and then match the third *italicized* word with the one of the lettered choices with which it has the same relationship as the words of the first pair have to each other. *PRINT THE LETTER OF THE CORRECT ANSWER IN THE SPACE AT THE RIGHT.*

1. *Woman* is to *man* as *Mary* is to   1._____

    A. woman   B. child   C. female   D. John   E. male

2. *Land* is to *ocean* as *soldier* is to   2._____

    A. river   B. sailor   C. shore   D. uniform   E. sailing

3. *Sugar* is to *candy* as *flour* is to   3._____

    A. eat   B. cook   C. candy   D. bread   E. sweet

4. *Sorrow* is to *joy* as *laugh* is to   4._____

    A. amuse   B. tears   C. fun   D. weep   E. cry

5. *Heat* is to *fire* as *pain* is to   5._____

    A. injury   B. wind   C. weather   D. cool   E. summer

6. *Grass* is to *cattle* as *milk* is to   6._____

    A. growing   B. lawn   C. baby   D. green   E. sun

7. *Winter* is to *spring* as *autumn* is to   7._____

    A. summer   B. winter   C. warm   D. cold   E. flower

8. *Rising* is to *falling* as *smile* is to   8._____

    A. climbing   B. baking   C. scolding
    D. frown   E. laughing

9. *Day* is to *night* as *succeed* is to   9._____

    A. fail   B. sunshine   C. evening
    D. afternoon   E. morning

10. *Apple* is to *fruit* as *corn* is to   10._____

    A. orange   B. eat   C. grain   D. cereal   E. food

KEY (CORRECT ANSWERS)

1.	D	6.	C
2.	B	7.	B
3.	D	8.	D
4.	E	9.	A
5.	A	10.	C

———

TEST 4

DIRECTIONS: In Questions 1 to 10, the first two *italicized* words have a relationship to each other. Determine that relationship, and then match the third *italicized* word with the one of the lettered choices with which it has the same relationship as the words of the first pair have to each other. *PRINT THE LETTER OF THE CORRECT ANSWER IN THE SPACE AT THE RIGHT.*

1. *Robin* is to *feathers* as *cat* is to   1.____

    A. sing   B. fur   C. eat   D. bird   E. fly

2. *Late* is to *end* as *early* is to   2.____

    A. prompt   B. enter   C. begin   D. start   E. end

3. *Beginning* is to *end* as *horse* is to   3.____

    A. cart   B. automobile   C. wagon
    D. travel   E. ride

4. *Kitten* is to *cat* as *baby* is to   4.____

    A. rabbit   B. mother   C. dog   D. cow   E. lamb

5. *Little* is to *weak* as *big* is to   5.____

    A. boy   B. man   C. tall   D. baby   E. strong

6. *Arm* is to *hand* as *leg* is to   6.____

    A. knee   B. toe   C. elbow   D. foot   E. finger

7. *Alive* is to *dead* as *well* is to   7.____

    A. grow   B. sick   C. decay   D. sleep   E. play

8. *In* is to *out* as *bad* is to   8.____

    A. up   B. open   C. good   D. shut   E. on

9. *Dust* is to *dry* as *mud* is to   9.____

    A. wet   B. blow   C. splash   D. fly   E. settle

10. *Width* is to *wide* as *height* is to   10.____

    A. high   B. low   C. tall   D. brief   E. short

KEY (CORRECT ANSWERS)

1.	B		6.	D
2.	C		7.	B
3.	A		8.	C
4.	B		9.	A
5.	E		10.	C

———

TEST 5

DIRECTIONS: In Questions 1 to 10, the first two *italicized* words have a relationship to each other. Determine that relationship, and then match the third *italicized* word with the one of the lettered choices with which it has the same relationship as the words of the first pair have to each other. *PRINT THE LETTER OF THE COR-RECT ANSWER IN THE SPACE AT THE RIGHT.*

1. *Above* is to *below* as *before* is to   1.____

    A.   beyond   B.   behind   C.   beside   D.   between   E.   after

2. *Start* is to *stop* as *begin* is to   2.____

    A.   go   B.   run   C.   wait   D.   finish   E.   work

3. *Everything* is to *nothing* as *always* is to   3.____

    A.   forever   B.   usually   C.   never
    D.   sometimes   E.   something

4. *Search* is to *find* as *question* is to   4.____

    A.   answer   B.   reply   C.   study
    D.   problem   E.   explain

5. *Top* is to *spin* as *spear* is to   5.____

    A.   bottom   B.   roll   C.   throw   D.   sharp   E.   pin

6. *Scale* is to *weight* as *thermometer* is to   6.____

    A.   weather   B.   temperature   C.   pounds
    D.   spring   E.   chronometer

7. *Congress* is to *senator* as *convention* is to   7.____

    A.   election   B.   chairman   C.   delegate
    D.   nominee   E.   representative

8. *Dividend* is to *investor* as *wage* is to   8.____

    A.   employee   B.   salary   C.   consumer
    D.   price   E.   employer

9. *Terminate* is to *commence* as *adjourn* is to   9.____

    A.   enact   B.   convene   C.   conclude
    D.   veto   E.   prorogue

10. *Administrator* is to *policy* as *clerk* is to   10.____

    A.   subornation   B.   organization   C.   coordination
    D.   direction   E.   application

KEY (CORRECT ANSWERS)

1.	E	6.	B
2.	D	7.	C
3.	C	8.	A
4.	A	9.	B
5.	C	10.	E

EXAMINATION SECTION
TEST 1

DIRECTIONS: Below are 10 groups of statements and conclusions, numbered 1 through 10.
For each group of statements, select the one conclusion lettered A, B, C,
which is fully supported by and is based SOLELY on the statements. *PRINT
THE LETTER OF THE CORRECT ANSWER IN THE SPACE AT THE RIGHT.*

1. He is either approved or disapproved for this examination. But, he is not approved.   1._____
Therefore, he is

    A. qualified   B. disapproved   C. a taxpayer

2. In planning the itinerary for Mr. Kane, his secretary told him: Route 20 runs parallel to   2._____
Route 6. Route 6 runs parallel to Route 18.
Mr. Kane concluded that,
Therefore, Route

    A. 20 is north of Route 6
    B. 18 intersects Route 20
    C. 20 is parallel to Route 18

3. Either the valedictorian is more intelligent than the salutatorian, or as intelligent, or less   3._____
intelligent.
But the valedictorian is not more intelligent, nor is she less intelligent.
Therefore, the valedictorian is

    A. less intelligent than the salutatorian
    B. as intelligent as the salutatorian
    C. more intelligent than the salutatorian

4. If the date for the examination is changed, it will be held July 28, or it will be postponed   4._____
until October 15.
The date is not changed.
Therefore, the examination

    A. will probably be held July 28
    B. date is uncertain
    C. will be held July 28, or it will be postponed until October 15

5. Joan transcribes faster than Nancy.   5._____
Nancy transcribes faster than Anne.
Therefore,

    A. Nancy transcribes faster than Joan
    B. Joan transcribes faster than Anne
    C. Nancy has had longer experience than Anne in taking dictation

6. The files in Division D contain either pending matter, completed case records, or dead   6._____
material.
They do not contain pending matter.
Therefore, they contain

    A.   completed case records
    B.   completed case records and dead material
    C.   either completed case records or dead material

7.   Either stenographer B in pool C types faster than stenographer A in pool D, or she types   7._____
    at the same rate as stenographer A, or she types slower than stenographer A. But, she
    does not type faster than stenographer A, nor does she type slower than stenographer
    Therefore, stenographer

    A.   B does not type as fast as stenographer A
    B.   B is more efficient than stenographer A
    C.   A types as fast as stenographer B

8.   Miss Andre can be eligible for retirement when she has been in city service 35 years, or   8._____
    if she is 55 years of age. She is fifty-four years old and has been in city service 36 years.
    Therefore, she

    A.   is not eligible for retirement now
    B.   is eligible for retirement now
    C.   will be eligible for retirement only if she stays in city service for another year

9.   If K is L, O is P; if M is N, Q is R.   9._____
    Either K is L, or M is N.
    Therefore,

    A.   K is P or M is R
    B.   either O is P or Q is R
    C.   the conclusion is uncertain

10.   If the employee is in error, the supervisor's refusal to listen to his side is unreasonable. If   10._____
    he is not in error, the supervisor's refusal is unjust. But the employee is in error or he is
    not.
    Therefore, the supervisor's refusal

    A.   may be considered later
    B.   is either unreasonable or it is unjust
    C.   is justifiable

KEY (CORRECT ANSWERS)

1.	B	6.	C
2.	C	7.	C
3.	B	8.	B
4.	B	9.	B
5.	B	10.	B

TEST 2

Questions 1-5

DIRECTIONS: Below are 5 groups of statements and conclusions, numbered 1 through 5. For each group of statements, select the one conclusion lettered A, B, C, which is fully supported by and is based SOLELY on the statements. *PRINT THE LETTER OF THE CORRECT ANSWER IN THE SPACE AT THE RIGHT.*

1. Three desks are placed in a straight row just inside the door in our office. Desk 1 is farther from the door than Desk 2. Desk 3 is farther from the door than Desk 1. Which desk is in the middle position from the door? Desk

    A. 1   B. 2   C. 3

1.____

2. The problem is either correct or incorrect or is unsolvable.
The problem is not correct.
Therefore, the

    A.   problem is incorrect
    B.   problem is either incorrect or is unsolvable
    C.   conclusion is uncertain

2.____

3. Village E is situated between City F and Village G.
City F is situated between Village G and Town H.
Therefore, Village E is

    A.   not situated between Village G and Town H
    B.   situated between City F and Town H
    C.   situated nearer to City F than to Town H

3.____

4. Jurisdiction No. 1 is between Jurisdictions No. 2 and No. 3.
Jurisdiction No. 2 is between Jurisdictions No. 3 and No. 4.
Therefore, Jurisdiction No. 1 is

    A.   not between Jurisdictions No. 3 and No. 4
    B.   between Jurisdictions No. 2 and No. 4
    C.   nearer to Jurisdiction No. 2 than to No. 4

4.____

5. Five candidates (A, B, C, D, and E) are seated in the same room. D is between A and B, E is between A and D. C is the same distance from A and E, and D is the same distance from A and B.
Therefore,

    A.   E is nearer to B than to A
    B.   C is nearer to E than to D
    C.   B is nearer to E than to D

5.____

Questions 6-10.

DIRECTIONS: Each question or incomplete statement is followed by several suggested answers or completions. Select the one that BEST answers the question or completes the statement. *PRINT THE LETTER OF THE CORRECT ANSWER IN THE SPACE AT THE RIGHT.*

6. If John is older than Mary and Mary is younger than Jane, then   6.____

    A. twice Mary's age is less than the sum of the ages of John and Jane
    B. the sum of the ages of John and Mary exceeds the age of Jane
    C. the ages of John and Jane are equal
    D. three times Mary's age equals the sum of the ages of John and Jane

7. John is older than Mary, Henry is older than Mary.   7.____
It follows, therefore, that

    A. John and Henry are the same age
    B. the sum of the ages of John and Mary exceeds the age of Henry
    C. Mary's age is less than half of the sum of John's and Henry's ages
    D. none of the preceding three statements is true

8. The average of 9 numbers is 70.   8.____
It follows that

    A. the sum of the numbers is 630
    B. the median of the numbers is 70
    C. the median of the numbers cannot be 70
    D. no two of the numbers can be equal

9. John is twice as old as Mary.   9.____
The only statement about their ages which is NOT true is

    A. in five years, John will be twice as old as Mary
    B. in five years, the sum of their ages will be 10 more than the present sum of their ages
    C. Mary's present age is one-third of the sum of their present ages
    D. two years ago, the difference between their ages was the same as it will be two years hence

10. A is taller than B; C is 2 inches shorter than B.   10.____
The one statement of the following four statements which is NOT necessarily true is

    A. B is taller than C
    B. A is taller than C
    C. A is taller than C by more than 2 inches
    D. B's height is the average of the heights of A and C

KEY (CORRECT ANSWERS)

1.	A	6.	A
2.	B	7.	C
3.	C	8.	D
4.	C	9.	A
5.	B	10.	D

TEST 3

DIRECTIONS: Each question or incomplete statement is followed by several suggested answers or completions. Select the one that BEST answers the question or completes the statement. *PRINT THE LETTER OF THE CORRECT ANSWER IN THE SPACE AT THE RIGHT.*

1. A stenographer can BEST deal with the situation which arises when her pencil breaks during dictation by

    A. asking the person dictating to lend her one
    B. being equipped at every dictation with several pencils
    C. going back to her desk to secure another one
    D. making a call to the supply room for some pencils

1.____

2. Accuracy is of greater importance than speed in filing CHIEFLY because

    A. city offices have a tremendous amount of filing to do
    B. fast workers are usually inferior workers
    C. there is considerable difficulty in locating materials which have been filed incorrectly
    D. there are many varieties of filing systems which may be used

2.____

3. Many persons dictate so rapidly that they pay little attention to matters of punctuation and English, but they expect their stenographers to correct errors.
    This statement implies MOST clearly that stenographers should be

    A. able to write acceptable original reports when required
    B. good citizens as well as good stenographers
    C. efficient clerks as well as good stenographers
    D. efficient in language usage

3.____

4. A typed letter should resemble a picture properly framed.
    This statement MOST emphasizes

    A. accuracy   B. speed
    C. convenience   D. neatness

4.____

5. Of the following, the CHIEF advantage of the use of a mechanical check is that it

    A. guards against tearing in handling the check
    B. decreases the possibility of alteration in the amount of the check
    C. tends to prevent the mislaying and loss of checks
    D. facilitates keeping checks in proper order for mailing

5.____

6. Of the following, the CHIEF advantage of the use of a dictating machine is that the

    A. stenographer must be able to take rapid dictation
    B. person dictating tends to make few errors
    C. dictator may be dictating letters while the stenographer is busy at some other task
    D. usual noise in an office is lessened

6.____

7. The CHIEF value of indicating enclosures beneath the identification marks on the lower left side of a letter is that it   7.____

    A. acts as a check upon the contents before mailing and upon receiving a letter
    B. helps determine the weight for mailing
    C. is useful in checking the accuracy of typed matter
    D. requires an efficient mailing clerk

8. The one of the following which is NOT an advantage of the window envelope is that it   8.____

    A. saves time since the inside address serves also as an outside address
    B. gives protection to the address from wear and tear of the mails
    C. lessens the possibility of mistakes since the address is written only once
    D. tends to be much easier to seal than the plain envelope

9. A question as to proper syllabication of a word at the end of a line may BEST be settled by consulting   9.____

    A. the person who dictated the letter
    B. a shorthand manual
    C. a dictionary
    D. a file of letters

10. Mailing a letter which contains many erasures is undesirable CHIEFLY because   10.____

    A. paper should not be wasted
    B. some stenographers are able to carry on some of the correspondence in an office without consulting their superiors
    C. correspondence should be neat
    D. erasures indicate that the dictator was not certain of what he intended to say in the letter

---

KEY (CORRECT ANSWERS)

1.	B	6.	C
2.	C	7.	A
3.	D	8.	D
4.	D	9.	C
5.	B	10.	C

TEST 4

DIRECTIONS: Each question or incomplete statement is followed by several suggested answers or completions. Select the one that BEST answers the question or completes the statement. *PRINT THE LETTER OF THE CORRECT ANSWER IN THE SPACE AT THE RIGHT.*

1. A charter operates for a city in somewhat the same fashion as

    A.   the United States Supreme Court functions with regard to federal legislation
    B.   the United States Constitution operates for the entire country
    C.   the Governor functions for New York State
    D.   a lease for a landlord

1.____

2. All civil employees should be especially interested in the activities of the United States Supreme Court PRIMARILY because

    A.   its decisions provide certain kinds of important general rules
    B.   the Supreme Court consists of nine persons appointed by the President
    C.   the American Constitution is the finest document which man has ever produced
    D.   the President's plan for reorganization of the court may be revived

2.____

3. Of the following, it is most frequently argued that labor problems are of concern to the civil employee PRIMARILY because

    A.   the problems of labor are the same as the problems of government
    B.   newspapers carry considerable information about labor problems
    C.   the civil employee is a wage or salary earner
    D.   a government is of the people, for the people, and by the people

3.____

4. Warfare in any part of the world should be of interest to the civil employee PRIMARILY as a result of the fact that

    A.   strict American neutrality is secured by not permitting the sale of munitions to any country at war
    B.   war has not been declared though warfare is raging
    C.   the United States participates in the meetings of the UN
    D.   facilities for transportation and communication have produced a "smaller" world

4.____

5. Cities regulate certain aspects of housing CHIEFLY because

    A.   the city is the largest municipality in the country
    B.   zoning is the concern of all residents of the city
    C.   housing affects health
    D.   the state constitution makes regulation optional

5.____

6. In general, it is PROBABLY true that the functions which a city administers are those

    A.   most necessary to the preservation of the well-being of its residents
    B.   of little or no interest to private business
    C.   forbidden to the state
    D.   not capable of being financed by private business

6.____

7. There is no more convincing mark of a cultured speaker or writer than accuracy of state-   7.____
   ment.
   This statement stresses the importance of

   A. new ideas
   B. facts
   C. acquiring a pleasing speaking voice
   D. poise

8. When a department is called, the voice which answers the telephone is, to the person   8.____
   calling, the department itself.
   This statement implies *most clearly* that

   A. only one person should answer the telephone in each office
   B. a clerk with a pleasing, courteous telephone manner is an asset to an office
   C. an efficient clerk will terminate all telephone conversations as quickly as possible
   D. making personal telephone calls is looked upon with disfavor in some offices

9. Probably the CHIEF advantage of filling higher vacancies by promotion is that this proce-   9.____
   dure

   A. stimulates the worker to improve his work and general knowledge and technique
   B. provides an easy check on the work of the individual
   C. eliminates personnel problems in a department
   D. harmonizes the work of one department with that of all other departments

10. Greatest efficiency is reached when filing method and filing clerk are harmoniously   10.____
    adjusted to the needs of an office.
    This statement means *most nearly* that

    A. the filing method is more important than the clerk in securing the successful han-
       dling of valuable papers
    B. almost any clerk can do office filing well
    C. a good clerk using a good filing system assures good filing
    D. every office needs a filing system

KEY (CORRECT ANSWERS)

1.	B	6.	A
2.	A	7.	B
3.	C	8.	B
4.	D	9.	A
5.	C	10.	C

TEST 5

DIRECTIONS: Each question or incomplete statement is followed by several suggested answers or completions. Select the one that BEST answers the question or completes the statement. *PRINT THE LETTER OF THE CORRECT ANSWER IN THE SPACE AT THE RIGHT.*

1. Your superior, Mr. Hotchkiss, is in conference and has requested that he not be disturbed.
   The condition under which you would MOST probably disturb the conference is:

   A. A Mr. Smith, whom you have not seen before, says he has important business with Mr, Hotchkiss
   B. Mrs. Hotchkiss telephones, saying there has been a serious accident at home
   C. You do not know how a certain letter should be filed and wish to ask the advice of Mr. Hotchkiss
   D. A fellow clerk wishes to ask Mr. Hotchkiss whether a particular city department handles certain matters

   1._____

2. Your superior directs you to find certain papers. You know the purpose for which the papers are to be used. In the course of your search for the papers, you come across certain material which would be very useful for the purpose to be served by the papers. You should

   A. bring the papers to your superior and ask whether he wants the other materials
   B. go to your superior immediately and ask whether he wishes both the materials and the papers or only one of the two
   C. bring to your superior the other materials, together with the papers you were directed to find
   D. bring only the other materials to your superior and point out the manner in which these materials are of greater value than the papers

   2._____

3. If a fellow employee asks you a question to which you do not know the answer, you should say,

   A. "I don't know. What's the difference?"
   B. "The answer to that question forms no part of my duties here."
   C. "My dear sir, the thing for you to do is to look the matter up yourself because it is your responsibility, not mine."
   D. "I'm sorry. I don't know."

   3._____

4. In general, it is PROBABLY true that MOST people are

   A. so self-seeking that they pay no attention to the wants, needs, or behavior of others
   B. so changeable that one never knows what his fellow employee is likely to do next
   C. not worth the trouble to bother about
   D. quite ready to help others

   4._____

5. Of the following, the one which is NOT a reason for avoiding clerical errors is that

   A. time is lost
   B. money is wasted
   C. many clerks are very intelligent
   D. serious consequences may follow

   5._____

49

6. Of the following, the MAIN reason for keeping a careful record of incoming mail is that   6._____

    A. some people are less industrious than others
    B. this record helps to speed up outgoing mail
    C. this record is a kind of legal evidence
    D. this information may be useful in answering questions which may arise

7. Of the following, the MAIN reason for using a calculating machine is that   7._____

    A. a lesser knowledge of arithmetic is needed
    B. a more attractive product is obtained
    C. greater speed and accuracy are obtained
    D. it is not difficult to learn how to operate a calculating machine

8. Of the following, the MAIN reason for being polite over the telephone is that   8._____

    A. persons who are speaking over the telephone cannot see each other
    B. politeness makes for pleasant business relationships
    C. it is not at all difficult or costly to be courteous
    D. one's voice is of great importance because voice reflects mood

9. Because telephone directories contain printed pages, they are called books.   9._____
This statement assumes *most nearly* that

    A. some books do not contain printed pages
    B. not all telephone directories are books which contain printed pages
    C. material which contains printed pages is called a book
    D. all books which contain printed pages are called telephone directories

10. Mr. Cross must be using a budget because he has been able to reduce his unnecessary   10._____
expenses.
On the basis of only the material included in this statement, it may MOST accurately
be said that this statement assumes that

    A. all people who use budgets lower certain types of expenses
    B. some people who do not use budgets reduce unnecessary expenses
    C. some people who use budgets do not reduce unnecessary expenses
    D. all types of expenses are reduced by the use of a budget

---

KEY (CORRECT ANSWERS)

1.	B		6.	D
2.	C		7.	C
3.	D		8.	B
4.	D		9.	C
5.	C		10.	A

REASONING AND JUDGMENT

EXAMINATION SECTION
TEST 1

DIRECTIONS: Each question or incomplete statement is followed by several suggested answers or completions. Select the one that BEST answers the question or completes the statement. *PRINT THE LETTER OF THE CORRECT ANSWER IN THE SPACE AT THE RIGHT.*

1. Lapland consists of the most northern parts of Norway, Sweden, and Finland, and the Kola Peninsula in Russia. The inhabitants, called Lapps, are very hardy people who farm and fish for a livelihood. Their meat, milk, and furs come from the reindeer, which is their only domestic animal.
   There is no country named Lapland, so we cannot ask,

   A. "Who is president of Lapland?"
   B. "What kind of education is there in Lapland?"
   C. "What is the climate in Lapland?"
   D. "Are any of the Lapps wealthy?"

   1.____

2. Induction is a method of reasoning by which general laws are inferred from the observation of a large number of individual cases. The laws thus derived are based not upon logical necessity but upon consistency among observations.
   Since any new observation conceivably could fail to follow the inductive law which it would be predicted to follow, an inductive law is never

   A. sought in scientific research
   B. as useful as a deductive law
   C. used as a basis for action
   D. more than probably true

   2.____

3. A lion, finding a hare asleep, was about to devour it when he saw a deer passing. He left the hare and chased the deer, which was so swift that it escaped him. When the lion returned to eat the hare, he found that it had been awakened by the noise and had escaped.
   This story was told to make the point that men often lose moderate gains by trying for

   A. easier ones   B. larger ones
   C. sure profit   D. great losses

   3.____

4. In Norse mythology, no god was better loved than Balder, the god of light and peace. He was slain by the trickery of Loki, a jealous god.
   When the dark winter comes to the Norseland, the people say, "All nature grieves for Balder," and when the spring comes again, they say,

   A. "Summer is here again."
   B. "Balder has never lived."
   C. "Loki will never return to earth."
   D. "The spirit of Balder has returned."

   4.____

5. Living organisms are able to exist at great ocean depths in spite of the tremendous pressure of the water so long as their, body spaces are not filled with air or any other gas.
This is possible because the pressure is equally applied on all sides of the organism and
the same pressure is maintained inside and outside. Similarly, man does not feel the
effects of pressure in the atmosphere exerted on him at 14.7 pounds per square inch, but
he cannot withstand the great pressure of water below depths of 100 feet because his
body contains spaces filled with _____ pressure.

    A. water at low   B. air at the same
    C. water at high   D. air at low

5.____

6. The oak tree has long been a symbol of strength and bravery. Mindful of this symbolism,
the Romans, who were a hardy people, decorated their war heroes with crowns of
_____ leaves.

    A. maple   B. olive   C. laurel   D. oak

6.____

7. In aviation, the ceiling is the distance from the ground to the bottom of the clouds when
the sky is more than half-covered. When there is heavy fog on the ground, the ceiling is
said to be zero. When the sky is clear or there are only scattered clouds, the ceiling is
unlimited. An airplane pilot must know what the ceiling is before takeoff so that he can
determine the proper flight

    A. altitude   B. direction   C. instruments   D. speed

7.____

8. In THE RIGHTS OF MAN, Thomas Paine wrote, *"Every age and generation must be as
free to act for itself in all oases as the ages and generations which preceded it. The van-
ity and presumption of governing beyond the grave is the most ridiculous and insolent of ·
ail tyrannies. Man has no property in man; neither has any generation a property in the
generations which are to follow."*
According to this, citizens of the United States should respect the Constitution
because they believe it is right and not because it is

    A. debatable   B. old   C. English   D. misunderstood

8.____

9. Before newspapers were common, a man called a town crier was appointed to make
public announcements. The town crier was an important person in England and in the
British North American colonies, but he disappeared when newspapers became more
widely distributed. Nowadays we often hear news before we read it in the paper.
We hear it from an electronic town crier -

    A. the theater   B. a radio or a television set
    C. a town meeting   D. a phonograph

9.____

10. The opal is a gem that reflects a number of beautiful colors. For a long time, opals were
unpopular because of a superstition that it was bad luck to wear them unless they were
one's birthstone.
Few people believe this superstition anymore, and opals have become more

    A. transparent   B. colorful   C. popular   D. beautiful

10.____

11. Newton's third law of motion states that for every action there is an equal and opposite reaction. When a gun is fired, the force that pushes the bullet forward is equal to the force with which the gun recoils.
Space vehicles, having left the earth's atmosphere, can maneuver by firing small rockets in the direction

    A. of the earth
    B. in which they wish to go
    C. opposite to their destination
    D. at right angles to their destination

11._____

12. When the purchasing power of the dollar steadily declines over a period of time, we speak of *inflation*. The reverse situation, in which a dollar buys more than formerly, is called deflation.
Inflation and deflation, then, are defined by changes in the relation between

    A. borrowing and lending   B. money and goods
    C. supply and demand   D. decrease and increase

12._____

13. The seed gatherers were a group of Indians who lived in the arid region between the Rocky Mountains and the Sierra Nevada. They were called seed gatherers because of the way in which they got most of their food. Seeds and berries suitable to eat grew in different regions at different times of the year.
For this reason, the seed gatherers

    A. were skilled archers   B. changed homes often
    C. fished in the sea   D. made fancy baskets

13._____

14. The men of the Coast Guard rescue many people from disasters at sea. Their work is often dangerous because they sometimes have to go out on a rescue mission under very bad conditions.
The men have excellent equipment, and they are well-trained, but their duties involve great

    A. speed   B. preparation   C. risks   D. thrills

14._____

15. A crocodile can snap a wooden plank in two with its powerful jaws. But a man can hold the jaws of a crocodile together with very little effort.
The crocodile exerts the greatest amount of power when

    A. snapping at wood   B. opening its mouth
    C. C. lashing its tail   D. closing its jaws

15._____

16. All of Alaska is farther west than the westernmost part of the continental United States. Juneau, the capital of Alaska, is in the same time zone as California, although its longitude should place it in the Yukon time zone. Some of the Aleutian Islands, a part of Alaska, are on one side of the 180 meridian and some are on the other, but the date line does not follow the 180 meridian and does not cut the Aleutians.
The result is that although there are four time zones in the United States, they are all

    A. on the same side of the date line
    B. on standard time
    C. really west of Greenwich
    D. in the Western Hemisphere

16._____

17. In Greek mythology, a chimera was a fire-breathing female monster with the head of a lion, the body of a goat, and the tail of a dragon. Of course, there really was no such animal, but the idea was so fantastic that we use the name chimera now for any   17.____

    A. deliberate falsehood
    B. figment of the imagination
    C. strange animal
    D. hybrid animal

18. The German shepherd is intelligent, alert, loyal, highly trainable, and has a good disposition. It is frequently used as a guide dog for the blind.   18.____
It is sometimes called *German police dog* because so many of this breed have been trained for

    A. seeing eye dogs   B. police work
    C. army scouts   D. rescue work

19. Unless an adequate supply of protein is included in a person's diet, loss of weight and even death may result. The problem of determining the amount of protein needed is important in rationing food in war or in famine. The minimal requirement of protein to maintain the body in health is less when the protein consumed is animal protein than when it is vegetable protein.   19.____
In some parts of the world, protein deficiency is a problem because the diet of the people is almost completely made up of

    A. animal proteins   B. fish
    C. solids   D. cereals

20. Emerson said, *"Character is adroitness to keep the old and trodden 'round, and power and courage to make new roads to new and better goals."*   20.____
This means that the person of high character is both

    A. conformist and creator   B. friendly and aloof
    C. student and laborer   D. popular and unpopular

KEY (CORRECT ANSWERS)

1.	A		11.	C
2.	D		12.	B
3.	B		13.	B
4.	D		14.	C
5.	D		15.	D
6.	D		16.	A
7.	A		17.	B
8.	B		18.	B
9.	B		19.	D
10.	C		20.	A

TEST 2

DIRECTIONS: Each question or incomplete statement is followed by several suggested answers or completions. Select the one that BEST answers the question or completes the statement. *PRINT THE LETTER OF THE CORRECT ANSWER IN THE SPACE AT THE RIGHT.*

1. The small Boston terrier has a dark coat with white chest, neck, and feet. Many people are drawn to this dog because of its neat appearance and large brown eyes. The Boston terrier is a popular pet because it likes people and

    A. grows so large   B. bites postmen
    C. is hard to train   D. makes friends easily

1.____

2. The gradations of the moral faculties in the higher animals and man are so imperceptible that to deny to the first a certain sense of responsibility and consciousness would certainly be an exaggeration of the difference between animals and man.
When animals fight with one another, when they associate for a common purpose, when they warn one another of danger, when they come to the rescue of another, when they display pain and joy, they manifest impulses of the same kind as are considered among the

    A. most general in the animal kingdom
    B. animal instincts of man
    C. divine provisions for man
    D. moral attributes of man

2.____

3. In ancient times, a country guaranteed its treaty promises by giving hostages to the other party. The hostages were often important people in their own country. They were held as prisoners and could be killed if their country failed to keep its treaty promises.
Today, most countries rely on the good faith of other countries and on public opinion to ensure that they will keep their treaties, and the hostage system

    A. is strictly observed
    B. is no longer used
    C. protects treaty makers
    D. has grown in effectiveness

3.____

4. The Pekingese was held in great esteem by Chinese royalty. The dog was bred to accentuate marks that were related in various ways to the upper classes of society. A white spot on the forehead of a Pekingese was admired, for this mark was associated with the Buddha.
A mark round the dog's body resembling a sash was quite admirable, for during the time when the Pekingese breed was so much admired,

    A. sashes were used to hold the outer garments together
    B. only high-ranking officials could wear sashes
    C. it was difficult to breed a dog with a sash mark
    D. sash marks signified royal blood

4.____

5. A recent U.S. study showed that of 100 high school seniors who received national aca-   5._____
   demic scholarships, nine out of ten read at least one book a month, while of 100 high
   school seniors accepted by various colleges but not awarded scholarships, only six out
   of ten read at least one book a month.
   This shows that those who read more are MOST likely to

   A. waste time   B. achieve more
   C. become librarians   D. spend less money

6. Turbines in motor vehicles cannot be operated on gasoline containing lead. Diesel fuel,   6._____
   on which turbines can be operated, is available only on major turnpikes and on roads that
   trucks use.
   Thus, if regular cars are to utilize turbines,

   A. highways must be rerouted
   B. the turbines must be small
   C. diesel fuel distribution must be expanded
   D. filling stations must stop selling regular gasoline

7. A gun collector of my acquaintance owns an old rifle that sold for about $35 twenty years   7._____
   ago and would now bring a price of $400 to $450. But it isn't always easy to make money
   on antiques. Experts warn that people who have never dabbled in antiques should study
   the market carefully, choose a few specialties, read every available book in those fields,
   and consult reliable dealers before buying. They say that few pieces will be acquired
   cheaply by the

   A. inexperienced seller   B. gun collector
   C. novice collector   D. country tourist

8. Dinosaurs were the largest land animals ever known. They were sixty to ninety feet long.   8._____
   These figures are not guesses; they are based on measurements of bones that have
   been

   A. found   B. painted   C. reproduced   D. molded

9. Painting goes back at least as far as the time of cavemen. Wall paintings have been   9._____
   found inside some of their caves. It is believed that these pictures were not drawn primarily for decoration because most of them are

   A. pictures of animals rather than of people
   B. far back in the cave away from all light
   C. unrelated to the cavemen's lives
   D. intricate drawings that have beauty

10. The ermine, a native of northern countries, is a weasel with valuable fur. In the summer   10._____
    the fur is brown, but as the weather gets cooler, the fur gets lighter until it is pure white
    during the coldest part of the year. Since most people prefer the white ermine pelts, most
    ermine trapping is done

    A. with specialized traps   B. in early fall
    C. after the snow disappears   D. during the winter

11. The pilot of an airplane is dependent upon the plane's radio for communication from the   11.____
    ground concerning takeoff, landing, the movements of other planes, and the weather.
    The safety of the passengers in the plane is dependent upon this communication. In
    case the radio is out of order, a pilot may use other signals, such as lights, but the radio is
    very important.
    Even small planes are usually equipped with.

    A. radios   B. landing gear   C. horns   D. pilots

12. Although more men than women play golf, women have played the game for many years.   12.____
    Mary, Queen of Scots, who lived in the sixteenth century, may have been the first woman
    golfer. She used the term *cadet* (pupil) for the boy who carried her clubs around the
    course.
    This term is still used today, but the spelling has been changed to

    A. Scotsman   B. cadet   C. caddy   D. golfer

13. According to Emerson, *"A man is a center for nature, running out threads of relation*   13.____
    through everything, fluid and solid, material and elemental... How few materials are yet
    used by our arts! It would seem as if each waited like the enchanted princes in fairy tales,
    for a destined human deliverer. All that is yet inanimate will one day speak and reason.
    Unpublished nature will have its whole secret told."
    If Emerson were to come to life in the twentieth century, he would

    A. lose his faith in fairy tales
    B. not be surprised by man's advancement in outer space
    C. feel compelled to use more materials in his arts
    D. be frightened by this industrial age

14. At one time, California had to ship its products around Cape Horn, which is at the south-   14.____
    ern tip of South America, to get them to the eastern part of the United States. This route
    was long, but the land routes were worse because of the mountains, deserts, and plains.
    It is not surprising that California planned a big celebration in 1914 to emphasize the
    importance of the opening of

    A. the Panama Canal   B. eastern harbors
    C. European routes   D. Chinese trade

15. Gordius, mythical king of Phrygia, tied an intricate knot in the thong that held the pole of   15.____
    his chariot to the yoke. An oracle had declared that he who untied the knot should be
    master of Asia. Many tried and failed. Alexander the Great looked at the knot and quickly
    cut it with his sword. We use the expression *to cut the Gordian knot* to mean to

    A. do the impossible
    B. use your head instead of your hands
    C. solve a difficult problem by bold action
    D. become an oracle

16. Many millions of dollars worth of gold, silver, and jewels have gone down with ships in   16.____
    numerous ship disasters. These treasures lie at the bottom of almost every major body of
    water in the world.
    It is not surprising that divers spend a great deal of time and money looking for

    A. treasure islands   B. sunken treasure
    C. scientific data   D. new oceans

17. The following quotation is from Thomas Hobbes: *"Nature has made men so equal in the*   17.____
faculties of body and mind as that though there be found one man sometimes manifestly
stronger in body, or of quicker mind than another, yet when all is reckoned together, the
difference between man and man is not so considerable as that one man can thereupon
claim to himself any benefit to which another

    A. has already attained."
    B. is capable of attaining."
    C. may not reach as well as he."
    D. would deny him."

18. The Louvre in Paris has the restoration of a stone found in 1868 at Dhiban in what was   18.____
ancient Moab. The stone is believed to have been carved by a scribe about 800 B.C. and
is of interest to scholars of ancient languages. When the French tried to buy the stone,
the Arabs broke it into many pieces, hoping to get more money for it.
The French bought some of the larger pieces and were able to make the restoration of
the entire stone because a French embassy official at Constantinople (now Istanbul)
had

    A. made a paper cast of the stone
    B. hidden the original from the Turks
    C. had the writing deciphered
    D. handled the financial arrangements

19. There are many primitive countries in the world that have never taken a census, an offi-   19.____
cial count of the population. Population figures from these countries are

    A. accurate   B. too high   C. estimates   D. lost

20. The National Audubon Society reported that their 1962 census of bald eagles in the   20.____
United States, excluding Alaska, was 3807, as compared to 3642 in 1961. Of 118 dead
eagles reported to the society in 1962, 91 had been shot. There is great concern that the
bald eagle, which is the national bird, may completely disappear.
The Audubon Society urges a nationwide campaign to educate the public not to
_____ eagles.

    A. protect   B. feed   C. harm   D. count

KEY (CORRECT ANSWERS)

1.	D	11.	A
2.	D	12.	C
3.	B	13.	B
4.	B	14.	A
5.	B	15.	C
6.	C	16.	B
7.	C	17.	C
8.	A	18.	A
9.	B	19.	C
10.	D	20.	C

TEST 3

DIRECTIONS: Each question or incomplete statement is followed by several suggested answers or completions. Select the one that BEST answers the question or completes the statement. *PRINT THE LETTER OF THE CORRECT ANSWER IN THE SPACE AT THE RIGHT.*

1. A library may be very large, but if it is in disorder, it is not as useful as one that is small but

    A. disordered   B. closed to the public
    C. nearby   D. well arranged

    1.____

2. It is no great wonder if in the long process of time, while fortune takes her course hither and thither, numerous coincidences should spontaneously occur.
   If the number of subjects to be wrought upon be infinite, it is all the more easy for fortune, with such an abundance of material, to

    A. effect this similarity of results
    B. fill all men with wonder
    C. prevent spontaneous coincidences
    D. effect a man's success

    2.____

3. Clearinghouses are useful in reducing the volume of concrete interbank transactions. Each member bank sends to the clearinghouse a record of the money it has paid out on checks drawn on each other member.
   When the lists are compared, equal reciprocal debts are

    A. reduced   B. collected   C. recorded   D. canceled

    3.____

4. Many citizens of other nations deposit their money in banks in Switzerland. The Swiss banks carefully protect the identities of their depositors, a matter of some importance to certain depositors. An agent trying to determine if someone has money in a particular Swiss bank sometimes tries to make a deposit in the name of that person.
   Since the acceptance of such a deposit would imply that the account did exist, Swiss banks will not

    A. cash large checks for depositors
    B. accept deposits that have been mailed in
    C. allow foreigners to open checking accounts
    D. accept deposits from unidentified persons

    4.____

5. Very few states have done anything to ensure that untrained people are not allowed to carry guns. Safe gun loading can be taught, and if people had to pass a test before they could obtain a hunting license, the number of shooting accidents would probably

    A. pass laws   B. fail   C. increase   D. decrease

    5.____

6. In a Dutch auction, so called because it originated in the Netherlands, the auctioneer offers an object for sale at a price above its value. He gradually reduces the price until someone accepts it. In a regular auction, the auctioneer asks for an opening bid, which is always low. Then the auctioneer tries to get people to make higher bids and sells when no one will raise the bid.
   These two methods, though opposite in procedure, may both reach a sale at the highest price

    A. anyone is willing to pay   B. that is fair to the buyer
    C. that the object is worth   D. the seller can demand

    6.____

7. Optical glass is used in cameras, telescopes, eyeglasses, and many kinds of scientific equipment. The glass is almost flawless; it must be made with great care and only from the finest materials.
For these reasons, optical glass is

   A. expensive   B. scientific   C. brittle   D. unavailable

7.____

8. It was quite understandable that it was the policy of the old priest-nobles of Egypt and India to divert their peoples from becoming familiar with the seas and to represent the occupation of a seaman as incompatible with the purity of the highest caste.
The sea deserved to be hated by those who wished to maintain the old aristocracies, inasmuch as

   A. the sea has been the mightiest instrument in the leveling of mankind
   B. the life of a sailor was quite dangerous
   C. many of the sailors lost their lives while on voyages
   D. the priest-nobles were trying to further the spread of education

8.____

9. Six cities of ancient Palestine were set aside as places of refuge for people who had killed any person unawares. In these cities, the accused could receive a fair trial. If he was found guilty of intentional murder, he was returned for punishment to the place from which he had escaped.
But if the killing was found to be accidental or not willful, the accused was allowed to remain safely in

   A. his boyhood home   B. a country of exile
   C. the city of refuge   D. the original prison

9.____

10. The average density of a cubic foot of earth is about 5.5 times that of a cubic foot of water. This is determined by dividing the earth mass by its volume. However, rocks on the earth's surface have an average density of approximately 2.7.
Therefore, in order to offset the lighter weight of the surface materials, the interior of the earth MUST have a density

   A. of 5.5   B. greater than 5.5
   C. less than 5.5   D. less than 2.7

10.____

11. Our opinions and actions are influenced to a great extent by words - the words we read and the words we hear. Yet we do not carefully attend to the subtle implications, good or bad, conveyed by these words through association.
Some words are slippery: they gloss over the actual attributes of the thing to which they refer. For example, the supporters of a favored point of view are *progressive* while those who hold an opinion less to our liking are *radical*.
The words that are chosen imply

   A. only one interpretation   B. precisely what they state
   C. no subtle connotation   D. more than they state

11.____

12. When the Mormons who settled in the Valley of the Great Salt Lake applied for statehood   12.____
in 1849, they wanted the name of the state to be Deseret. Deseret is the Mormon word
for honeybee, which the Mormons had taken as a symbol of the work they all had to do to
make the desert productive. They were refused statehood and remained the Territory of
Utah until 1896, when Utah became the forty-fifth state. The state seal has a beehive on
it, and the official motto of the state is *Industry.* These are tributes to Utah's

    A. acceptance as a state   B. principal occupation
    C. Ute Indians   D. early Mormon settlers

13. Pythagoras, an ancient Greek, discovered the true nature of the harmonic series by   13.____
observing the vibration of a single taut string stretched over a resonator. When a mov-
able bridge was placed at the string's midpoint, the string vibrated in two segments at
twice the speed at which it vibrated without a bridge. When moved to a third of the
string's length, the string would vibrate in three segments at three times the speed. This
phenomenon was repeated with each successive position of the bridge. Thus, Pythagoras was able to express the pitch relationships of the harmonic series in terms of

    A. mathematical ratios   B. string lengths
    C. musical notation   D. chemical formulas

14. Not only were the Romans undemocratic, but at no period of its history did Rome love   14.____
equality. In the Republic, rank was determined by wealth. The census was the basis of
the social system. Every citizen had to declare his fortune before a magistrate, and his
grade was then assigned him.
Poverty and wealth established the

    A. legal differences between men
    B. democratic system of the Republic
    C. need for a strong judicial system
    D. social equality among men

15. A surveyor's chain has 100 links, each 792 inches long. The chain is a unit of measure-   15.____
ment that for most purposes would be very awkward, but it is particularly useful in surveying land because ten square chains made on acre. The original measuring
instrument was actually made of chains. A surveyor's chain has 100 links, each 792
inches long. The chain is a unit of measurement that for most purposes would be very
awkward, but it is particularly useful in surveying land because ten square chains made
on acre.
The original measuring instrument was actually made of chains.

    A. numerical   B. accurate   C. awkward   D. easy

16. Millions of people in the world spend as much as one-third of their days by hauling water.   16.____
Their diets are determined by a water shortage that restricts the variety of their agricultural products.
If the scientists of the United States can increase the water supply of arid regions by
removing the salt from sea-water, they will gain

    A. new travel opportunities abroad   B. new export articles
    C. the gratitude of millions   D. great profits from friends

17. *"A friend stands at the door,*
    In either tight-closed hand
    Hiding rich gifts, three hundred
    And three score."
    These lines are from a poem titled   17.____

    A. EASTER MORNING   B. CHRISTMAS EVE
    C. NEW YEAR'S EVE   D. THANKSGIVING DAY

18. Our repugnance to death increases in proportion to our consciousness of having lived in   18.____
    vain - to the

    A. usefulness of our lives
    B. keenness of our disappointments
    C. intensity of our physical suffering
    D. greatness of our vanity

19. The ripeness or unripeness of the occasion must ever be well weighed; and generally it   19.____
    is good to commit the beginnings of all great actions to Argus with his hundred eyes, and
    the ends to Briareus with his hundred hands; first to watch, and then to

    A. consider   B. decide   C. begin   D. speed

20. Benjamin Franklin said, *"We may perhaps learn to deprive large masses of their Gravity,*   20.____
    and give them absolute Levity for the sake of easy Transport. Agriculture may diminish
    its Labour and double its Produce; all Diseases may by sure means be prevented or
    cured, not excepting even that of old Age, and our Lives lengthened at pleasure even
    beyond the antediluvian Standard. O that moral science were in as fair a way of

    A. Acceptance   B. Cure   C. Religion   D. Study

KEY (CORRECT ANSWERS)

1.	D	11.	D
2.	A	12.	D
3.	D	13.	A
4.	D	14.	A
5.	D	15.	D
6.	A	16.	C
7.	A	17.	C
8.	C	18.	B
9.	C	19.	D
10.	B	20.	D

EXAMINATION SECTION
TEST 1

DIRECTIONS: Each question or incomplete statement is followed by several suggested answers or completions. Select the one that BEST answers the question or completes the statement. *PRINT THE CORRECT ANSWER IN THE SPACE AT THE RIGHT.*

1. The OPPOSITE of defeat is

    A. glory   B. honor   C. victory
    D. success   E. hope

1.____

2. If 3 pencils cost 10 cents, how many pencils can be bought for 50 cents?

2.____

3. A dog does NOT always have

    A. eyes   B. bones   C. a nose
    D. a collar   E. lungs

3.____

4. The OPPOSITE of strange is

    A. peculiar   B. familiar   C. unusual
    D. quaint   E. extraordinary

4.____

5. A lion MOST resembles a

    A. dog   B. goat   C. cat   D. cow   E. horse

5.____

6. Sound is related to quiet in the same way that sunlight is to

    A. darkness   B. evaporation   C. bright
    D. a cellar   E. noise

6.____

7. A party consisted of a man and his wife, his three sons and their wives, and two children in each son's family. How many were there in the party?

7.____

8. A man ALWAYS has

    A. children   B. nerves   C. teeth
    D. home   E. wife

8.____

9. The OPPOSITE of stingy is

    A. wealthy   B. extravagant   C. poor
    D. economical E. generous

9.____

10. Lead is cheaper than silver because it is

    A. duller   B. more plentiful   C. softer
    D. uglier   E. less useful

10.____

Questions 11-13.

DIRECTIONS: Answer Questions 11 through 13 by choosing the CORRECT proverb meaning given below.

A. Eat heartily at a good feast.
B. Only exceptional misfortunes harm all concerned.
C. Don't invite trouble by stirring it up.
D. Strong winds blow harder than weak ones.
E. Too much of anything is no better than a sufficiency.
F. Tired dogs need lots of sleep.

11. Which statement above explains the proverb, *Let sleeping dogs lie?*   11._____

12. Which statement above explains the proverb, *Enough is as good as a feast?*   12._____

13. Which statement above explains the proverb, *It's an ill wind that blows nobody good?*   13._____

14. A radio is related to a telephone as _____ is to a railroad train.   14._____

    A. a highway   B. an airplane   C. gasoline
    D. speed   E. noise

15. If a boy can run at the rate of 8 feet in 1/3 of a second, how far can he run in 10 seconds?   15._____

16. A debate ALWAYS involves   16._____

    A. an audience   B. judges   C. a prize
    D. a controversy   E. an auditorium

17. Of the five words below, four are alike in a certain way. Which one is NOT like these four?   17._____

    A. Walk   B. Run   C. Kneel   D. Skip   E. Jump

18. The OPPOSITE of frequently is   18._____

    A. seldom   B. occasionally   C. never
    D. sometimes   E. often

19. A thermometer is related to temperature as a speedometer is to   19._____

    A. fast   B. automobile   C. velocity
    D. time   E. heat

20. Which word makes the TRUEST sentence? Women are _____ shorter than their husbands.   20._____

    A. always   B. usually   C. much
    D. rarely   E. never

21. 1 6 2 7 3 8 4 9 5 10 7 11   21._____
One number is wrong in the above series.
What should that number be?

22. All children in this class are good students.   22._____
John is not a good student.
John is a member of this class.
If the first two statements are true, the third is

    A. true   B. false   C. not certain

23. A boat race ALWAYS has 23.____

    A. oars   B. spectators   C. victory
    D. contestants   E. sails

24. 4 2 3 1 5 6 8 7 3 4 6 6 4 3 2 5 1 8 6 7 9   24.____
Which number in this row appears a second time nearest the beginning?

25. The sun is related to the earth as the earth is to   25.____

    A. clouds   B. rotation   C. the universe
    D. the moon   E. circumference

KEY (CORRECT ANSWERS)

1. C		11. C	
2. 15		12. E	
3. D		13. B	
4. B		14. B	
5. C		15. 240	
6. A		16. D	
7. 14		17. C	
8. B		18. A	
9. E		19. C	
10. B		20. B	

21. 6
22. B
23. D
24. 3
25. D

TEST 2

1. Which word makes the TRUEST sentence?
   A youth is _____ wiser than his father.

   A. never   B. rarely   C. much
   D. usually   E. always

1.____

2. The OPPOSITE of graceful is

   A. weak   B. ugly   C. slow
   D. awkward   E. uncanny

2.____

3. A grandmother is always _____ than her granddaughter.

   A. smarter   B. more quiet   C. older
   D. smaller   E. slower

3.____

Questions 4-6.

DIRECTIONS: Answer Questions 4 through 6 by choosing the CORRECT proverb meaning given below.

   A. Even the darkest situations have their bright aspects.
   B. The final result is more important than the intermediate steps.
   C. Handsome persons always do pleasing things.
   D. All comes out well in the end.
   E. Persons whose actions please us seem good-looking.
   F. Clouds shimmer as if they were made of silver.

4. Which statement above explains the proverb, *All's well that ends well?*

4.____

5. Which statement above explains the proverb, *Every cloud has a silver lining?*

5.____

6. Which statement above explains the proverb, *Handsome is that handsome does?*

6.____

7. If the settlement of a difference between two parties is made by a third party, it is called a(n)

   A. compromise   B. truce   C. promise
   D. injunction   E. arbitration

7.____

8. Oil is to toil as _____ is to hate.

   A. love   B. work   C. boil   D. ate   E. hat

8.____

9. Of the five words below, four are alike in a certain way.
   Which one is NOT like these four?

   A. Push   B. Hold   C. Lift   D. Drag   E. Pull

9.____

10. If 10 boxes full of apples weigh 300 pounds and each box when empty weighs 3 pounds, how many pounds do all the apples weigh?

10._____

11. The OPPOSITE of sorrow is

11._____

    A. fun   B. success   C. hope
    D. prosperity   E. joy

12. A B C D E F G H I J K L M N O P Q R S T U V W X Y Z
If all the odd-numbered letters in the alphabet were crossed out, what would be the twelfth letter NOT crossed out?

12._____

13. What letter in the word *unfortunately* is the same number in the word (counting from the beginning) as it is in the alphabet?

13._____

14. Such traits as honesty, sincerity, and loyalty constitute one's

14._____

    A. personality   B. reputation   C. wisdom
    D. character   E. success

15. If 3 1/3 yards of cloth cost 25 cents, what will 10 yards cost?

15._____

16. same means small little the as
If the above words were arranged to make a good sentence, with what letter would the second word of the sentence begin? (Make it like a printed capital.)

16._____

17. George is younger than Frank.
James is younger than George.
Frank is older than James.
If the first two statements are true, the third is

17._____

    A. true   B. false   C. not certain

18. Suppose that the first and second letters in the word *abolitionist* were interchanged, also the third and fourth letters, the fifth and sixth, etc.
Print the letter that would be the tenth letter counting to the right.

18._____

19. 0 1 3 6 10 15 21 29 36
One number is wrong in the above series.
What should that number be?

19._____

20. If 3 1/2 yards of cloth cost 70 cents, what will 4 1/2 yards cost?

20._____

21. A person who never pretends to be anything other than what he is, is said to be

21._____

    A. loyal   B. hypocritical   C. sincere
    D. meek   E. courageous

22. Which of these words is related to many as exceptional is to ordinary?

22._____

    A. None   B. Each   C. More   D. Much   E. Few

23. The OPPOSITE of cowardly is

23._____

    A. brave   B. strong   C. treacherous
    D. loyal   E. friendly

24. Which one of the five words below is MOST unlike the other four? 24.____

    A. Fast   B. Agile   C. Quick   D. Run   E. Speedy

25. Some of Brown's friends are Catholics. 25.____
Some of Brown's friends are lawyers.
Some of Brown's friends are Catholic lawyers.
If the first two statements are true, the third is

    A. true   B. false   C. not certain

KEY (CORRECT ANSWERS)

1.	B	11.	E
2.	D	12.	X
3.	C	13.	L
4.	B	14.	D
5.	A	15.	75
6.	E	16.	M
7.	E	17.	A
8.	D	18.	N
9.	B	19.	28
10.	270	20.	90

21.	C
22.	E
23.	A
24.	D
25.	C

TEST 3

DIRECTIONS: Each question or incomplete statement is followed by several suggested answers or completions. Select the one that BEST answers the question or completes the statement. *PRINT THE CORRECT ANSWER IN THE SPACE AT THE RIGHT.*

1. How many of the following words can be made from the letters in the word *strangle,* using any letter any number of times: greatest, tangle, garage, stresses, related, grease, nearest, reeling?

    1.____

2. To insist that trees can talk to one another is

    A. absurd   B. misleading   C. improbable
    D. unfair   E. wicked

    2.____

3. Of the things following, four are alike in a certain way.
    Which one is NOT like these four?

    A. Snow   B. Soot   C. Cotton   D. Ivory   E. Milk

    3.____

4. A square is related to a circle in the same way in which a pyramid is related to

    A. a solid   B. Egypt   C. height
    D. a cone   E. a circumference

    4.____

5. If the following words were seen on a wall by looking in a mirror on the opposite wall, which word would appear exactly the same as if seen directly?

    A. Meet   B. Rotor   C. Mama   D. Deed   E. Toot

    5.____

6. If a strip of cloth 32 inches long will shrink to 28 inches when washed, how many inches long will a 24-inch strip of the same cloth be after shrinking?

    6.____

7. Which of the following is a trait of character?

    A. Ability   B. Reputation   C. Hate
    D. Stinginess   E. Nervousness

    7.____

8. Find the two letters in the word *coming* which have just as many letters between them in the word as in the alphabet. Print the one of these letters that comes FIRST in the alphabet.

    8.____

9. Modern is to ancient as _____ is to yesterday.

    A. tomorrow   B. time   C. up-to-date
    D. history   E. today

    9.____

10. 1 2 4 8 16 32 64 96
    One number is wrong in the above series.
    What should that number be?

    10.____

11. If George can ride a bicycle 40 feet while Frank runs 30 feet, how far can George ride while Frank runs 45 feet?

    11.____

12. L U L R V E L U R E U L U U L V E L L U V L U R U L O E V L U E   12.____
Count each L in this series that is followed by a U next to it if the U is not followed by an R next to it.
Tell how many L's you count.

13. A man who is in favor of marked change is said to be   13.____

    A.   democratic   B.   conservative   C.   radical
    D.   anarchistic   E.   republican

14. Print the letter which is the fourth letter to the left of the letter midway between N and R in   14.____
the alphabet.

Questions 15-17.

DIRECTIONS: Questions 15 through 17 are to be answered on the basis of the following figure.

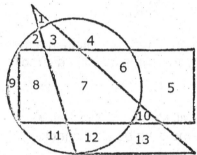

15. What number is in the space which is in the rectangle but not in the triangle or in the cir-   15.____
cle?

16. What number is in the same geometrical figure or figures (and no other) as the number   16.____
3?

17. How many spaces are there that are in any one but only one geometrical figure?   17.____

18. A line is related to a surface as a point is to a   18.____

    A.   circle   B.   line   C.   solid
    D.   dot   E.   intersection

19. One cannot become a good lawyer without diligent study.   19.____
George studies law diligently.
George will become a good lawyer.
If the first two statements are true, the third is

    A.   true   B.   false   C.   not certain

20. honesty traits Generosity character of desirable and are   20.____
If the above words are arranged to make the BEST sentence, with what letter will the
last word of the sentence end? (Print the letter as a capital.)

21. A man who carefully considers all available information before making a decision is said   21.____
to be

    A. influential   B. prejudiced   C. decisive
    D. hypocritical   E. impartial

22. A hotel serves a mixture of 2 parts cream and 3 parts milk.   22.____
How many pints of milk will it take to make 25 pints of the mixture?

23. _____ is related to stars as physiology is to blood.   23.____

    A. Telescope   B. Darkness   C. Astronomy
    D. Light waves   E. Chemistry

24. A statement based upon a supposition is said to be   24.____

    A. erroneous   B. ambiguous   C. distorted
    D. hypothetical   E. doubtful

25. If a wire 40 inches long is to be cut so that one piece is 2/3 as long as the other piece,   25.____
how many inches long must the shorter piece be?

KEY (CORRECT ANSWERS)

1.	6	11.	60
2.	A	12.	4
3.	B	13.	C
4.	D	14.	L
5.	E	15.	5
6.	21	16.	12
7.	D	17.	7
8.	G	18.	B
9.	E	19.	C
10.	128	20.	R

21.	E
22.	15
23.	C
24.	D
25.	16

EXAMINATION SECTION
TEST 1

DIRECTIONS: Select the word or phrase which has the same meaning, or most nearly the same meaning, as the CAPITALIZED word. *PRINT THE LETTER OF THE CORRECT ANSWER IN THE SPACE AT THE RIGHT.*

1. A CAR is to   1.____

    A. start fires with   B. eat on   C. take pictures with
    D. ride in   E. draw with

2. INK is used to   2.____

    A. walk on   B. write with   C. cut with
    D. serve with   E. stand on

3. POOR means having very little   3.____

    A. money   B. hair   C. sun   D. time   E. snow

4. COMBAT   4.____

    A. point   B. report   C. fight   D. start   E. admit

5. A MISTAKE is something done   5.____

    A. first   B. wrong   C. next   D. often   E. alone

6. HOWL   6.____

    A. roar   B. design   C. propose   D. depart   E. succeed

7. PHONY   7.____

    A. tough   B. neutral   C. vivid   D. fake   E. hasty

8. ADVICE   8.____

    A. record   B. visit   C. bridge   D. opinion   E. minute

9. BURLAP   9.____

    A. tunnel   B. medicine   C. soil   D. engine   E. fabric

10. A SEAMSTRESS is a woman who   10.____

    A. writes   B. sews   C. sings   D. paints   E. bakes

11. APPROACH means to come   11.____

    A. through   B. with   C. into   D. between   E. near

12. ABANDON   12.____

    A. look over   B. hold on   C. lift up   D. fall down   E. give up

13. BARELY   13.____

    A. generally   B. scarcely   C. completely
    D. especially   E. gradually

14. SNEER   14._____

    A. listen with interest   B. practice with care   C. look with scorn
    D. lift with ease   E. dance with joy

15. ELIGIBLE   15._____

    A. lonesome B. careless   C. qualified   D. inferior   E. profound

16. EXCLUDE   16._____

    A. educate B. excite   C. eliminate   D. encourage E. ensure

17. JUVENILE   17._____

    A. haunted B. youthful   C. intimate   D. favorable   E. unable

18. JOLT   18._____

    A. justify   B. join   C. judge   D. jar   E. journey

19. GRATIFY   19._____

    A. heat   B. shout   C. hope   D. charge   E. please

20. RAFTER   20._____

    A. angel   B. canal   C. beam   D. lamb   E. trunk

21. LANK   21._____

    A. slender   B. grateful   C. musical   D. lively   E. rare

22. CONSOLE   22._____

    A. compare   B. conclude   C. comfort   D. command   E. collect

23. MANIPULATE   23._____

    A. reserve   B. devote   C. handle   D. inquire   E. introduce

24. CONCRETE   24._____

    A. clean   B. mean   C. low   D. nice   E. real

25. DESTITUTE   25._____

    A. respectful B. divine   C. urgent   D. slippery   E. needy

26. BASTION   26._____

    A. fortification   B. qualification   C. appropriation
    D. legislation   E. illustration

27. FOREGO   27._____

    A. represent   B. sacrifice   C. justify
    D. determine   E. display

28. MACKINTOSH   28._____

     A. raincoat   B. tractor   C. honeybee
     D. cartoon   E. saucepan

29. TRAJECTORY   29._____

     A. curved path   B. ill health   C. bold type
     D. glorious spirit   E. strong back

30. A TRIPHTHONG is a combination of three   30._____

     A. fossils   B. cables   C. diagrams
     D. vowels   E. atoms

31. WHIST   31._____

     A. captain   B. game   C. soul   D. finger   E. rock

32. FETID   32._____

     A. exhausted   B. stinking   C. pathetic
     D. meager   E. insane

33. BEZANT   33._____

     A. hotel   B. coin   C. mill   D. harbor   E. desk

34. SCINTILLATE   34._____

     A. develop   B. whistle   C. ruin   D. breathe   E. flash

35. GLIB   35._____

     A. unaware   B. fluent   C. reluctant
     D. philosophical   E. inquisitive

36. DINT   36._____

     A. supply   B. wish   C. force   D. price   E. demand

37. SARCOPHAGUS   37._____

     A. coffin   B. insect   C. interview
     D. wharf   E. mushroom

38. DIABOLO   38._____

     A. bed   B. dance   C. game   D. mark   E. record

39. LEMPIRA   39._____

     A. chair   B. money   C. salt   D. earth   E. music

40. PYROPE   40._____

     A. reptile   B. heather   C. slogan   D. mantle   E. garnet

KEY (CORRECT ANSWERS)

1.	D	11.	E	21.	A	31.	B
2.	B	12.	E	22.	C	32.	B
3.	A	13.	B	23.	C	33.	B
4.	C	14.	C	24.	E	34.	E
5.	B	15.	C	25.	E	35.	B
6.	A	16.	C	26.	A	36.	C
7.	D	17.	B	27.	B	37.	A
8.	D	18.	D	28.	A	38.	C
9.	E	19.	E	29.	A	39.	B
10.	B	20.	C	30.	D	40.	E

EXAMINATION SECTION
TEST 1

DIRECTIONS: Each question or incomplete statement is followed by several suggested answers or completions. Select the one that BEST answers the question or completes the statement. *PRINT THE LETTER OF THE CORRECT ANSWER IN THE SPACE AT THE RIGHT.*

Questions 1-25.

DIRECTIONS: Select the word with the MOST appropriate meaning for the italicized word in each of Questions 1 through 25.

1. The directions were *explicit*.

    A. petulant   B. satiric   C. awkward
    D. unequivocal   E. foreign

1.____

2. The teacher explained *mutability*.

    A. change   B. harmony   C. annihilation
    D. ethics   E. candor

2.____

3. He was a *secular* man.

    A. holy   B. evil   C. worldly
    D. superior   E. small

3.____

4. They submitted a list of their *progeny*.

    A. experiments   B. books   C. holdings
    D. theories   E. offspring

4.____

5. She admired his *sententious* replies.

    A. simple   B. pithy   C. coherent
    D. lucid   E. inane

5.____

6. He believed in the ancient *dogma*.

    A. priest   B. prophet   C. seer
    D. doctrine   E. ruler

6.____

7. They studied a Grecian *archetype*.

    A. model   B. urn   C. epic   D. ode   E. play

7.____

8. The *insurrection* was described on the front page.

    A. surgery   B. pageant   C. ceremony
    D. game   E. revolt

8.____

9. He was known for his *procrastination*.

    A. justification   B. learning   C. delay
    D. ambition   E. background

9.____

10. The doctor analyzed the *toxic* ingredients   10.____

    A. poisonous   B. anemic   C. trivial
    D. obscure   E. distinct

11. It was a *portentous* occurrence.   11.____

    A. pleasant   B. decisive   C. ominous
    D. monetary   E. hearty

12. His *espousal* of the plan was applauded.   12.____

    A. explanation   B. rejection   C. ridicule
    D. adoption   E. revision

13. Her condition was *lachrymose*.   13.____

    A. improved   B. tearful   C. hopeful
    D. precocious   E. tenuous

14. It was a *precarious* situation.   14.____

    A. uncomplicated   B. peaceful   C. precise
    D. uncertain   E. precipitous

15. He was lost in a *reverie*.   15.____

    A. chancery   B. dream   C. forest
    D. cavern   E. tarn

16. The hero was a young *gallant*.   16.____

    A. suitor   B. fool   C. gull
    D. lawyer   E. executive

17. Their practices were *nefarious*.   17.____

    A. unprofitable   B. ignorant   C. multifarious
    D. wicked   E. wishful

18. He insisted upon the *proviso*.   18.____

    A. stipulation   B. pronunciation   C. examination
    D. supply   E. equipment

19. The spirit came from the *nether* regions.   19.____

    A. frozen   B. lower   C. lost
    D. bright   E. mysterious

20. His actions were *malevolent*.   20.____

    A. unassuming   B. silent   C. evil
    D. peaceful   E. constructive

21. He had a *florid* complexion.   21.____

    A. sanguine   B. pallid   C. fair
    D. sickly   E. normal

22. The lawyer explained the legal *parlance*.   22.____

    A. action   B. maneuver   C. situation
    D. language   E. procedure

23. They were present at the *interment*.   23.____

    A. concert   B. trial   C. embarkation
    D. burial   E. performance

24. He made a *moot* point.   24.____

    A. definite   B. sensible   C. debatable
    D. strong   E. correct

25. They carefully examined the *cryptic* message.   25.____

    A. occult   B. legible   C. valid
    D. familiar   E. warning

Questions 26-40.

DIRECTIONS: Indicate the number of syllables in each of the following words.

26. vicissitude   26.____

27. blown   27.____

28. maintenance   28.____

29. symbolization   29.____

30. athletics   30.____

31. actually   31.____

32. friend   32.____

33. perseverance   33.____

34. physiology   34.____

35. pronunciation   35.____

36. vacuum   36.____

37. sophomore   37.____

38. opportunity   38.____

39. hungry   39.____

40. temperament   40.____

Questions 41-60.

DIRECTIONS: Indicate the one misspelled word in each of the following Questions 41 through 60 by indicating the letter of the misspelled word in the space at the right.

#	A.	B.	C.	D.	E.	
41.	holiday	noticeable	fourty	miiniature	yeast	41.____
42.	grievance	murmur	occurance	business	captain	42.____
43.	succeed	vegatable	pleasant	picnicking	shepherd	43.____
44.	psychology	plebian	exercise	fiery	concise	44.____
45.	ninety	optimistic	professor	repitition	siege	45.____
46.	tarriff	absence	grammar	license	balloon	46.____
47.	dissipation	ecstasy	prarie	narriage	consistent	47.____
48.	supersede	twelfth	vacillate	playright	expense	48.____
49.	fundamental	government	accomodate	cafeteria	surely	49.____
50.	cemetary	indispensable	dormitory	environment	divine	50.____
51.	irritible	permissible	irresistible	rhythmical	source	51.____
52.	interprete	opinion	guard	familiar	possible	52.____
53.	conscience	existence	loneliness	leisure	exhileration	53.____
54.	villian	weird	seize	tragedy	crystal	54.____
55.	develop	bachelor	dilemna	operate	synonym	55.____
56.	university	connoiseur	aisle	transferred	division	56.____
57.	zoology	conscious	aptitude	restaurant	sacriligious	57.____
58.	tendency	vital	analyze	consistant	proceed	58.____

| 59. | A. proceedure | B. surround | C. disastrous | 59._____ |
| | D. beginning | E. arrival | | |

| 60. | A. encrease | B. pursuing | C. necessary | 60._____ |
| | D. tyranny | E. strength | | |

Questions 61-80.

DIRECTIONS: Indicate the part of speech for each italicized word in the following sentences by selecting the letter of the part of speech from the key above each set of questions.
   A. Noun
   B. Pronoun
   C. Verb
   D. Adjective
   E. Adverb

61. You are entirely *wrong*.   61._____

62. On *Sunday,* we will attend church.   62._____

63. *That* is the main problem.   63._____

64. He was invited to the party, *Saturday*.   64._____

65. I shall introduce a *technical* term.   65._____

66. It was a *novel* turn of events.   66._____

67. He wanted *that* gift for himself.   67._____

68. A few definitions will help *us* to understand.   68._____

69. He let them reach their own *conclusions*.   69._____

70. I must ask *you* to remain silent.   70._____

   A. Preposition
   B. Conjunction
   C. Pronoun
   D. Adverb
   E. Adjective

71. *This* is a stupid answer.   71._____

72. He solved the mystery *without* the police.   72._____

73. She felt *secure* in his protection.   73._____

74. He believed in the *scientific* method.   74._____

75. Do not destroy their *traditional* beliefs.   75._____

76. They chartered the bus, *but* they did not go.   76._____

77. The young men are *quiet* with fear.   77.____

78. She talked *cheerfully* to the visitors.   78.____

79. The candidate was *certain* of victory.   79.____

80. I hope you will take *that* with you.   80.____

Questions 81-100.

DIRECTIONS: Indicate the use of each italicized word in the following sentences by choosing the letter of the CORRECT usage from the key above each set of questions.
      A.   Subject of Verb
      B.   Predicate Nominative or Subjective Complement
      C.   Predicate Adjective
      D.   Direct Object of Verb
      E.   Indirect Object of Verb

81. They made *him* president of the club.   81.____

82. There was nothing *odd* about the situation.   82.____

83. Give them *time* enough for thought.   83.____

84. He supervised the *work* himself.   84.____

85. Will you do *me* a favor?   85.____

86. The salad dressing tasted *good*.   86.____

87. In the crash, the *body* was thrown forward.   87.____

88. On a bench in the park was a single *man*.   88.____

89. There were two *men* who carried the trunk.   89.____

90. I am older than *you*.   90.____

      A.   Object of Preposition
      B.   Subject of Infinitive
      C.   Direct Object of Verb
      D.   Indirect Object of Verb
      E.   Predicate Nominative or Subjective Complement

91. Let *them* suffer the consequences.   91.____

92. Offer *them* the key to the apartment.   92.____

93. He heard the *bell* ring.   93.____

94. Let *us* try another solution.   94.____

95. No one except *John* had volunteered.   95.____

96. Show *us* one example of your style.   96._____

97. Will you send *her* the flowers?   97._____

98. I want *you* to take her home.   98._____

99. He told his *father* that he would obey.   99._____

100. Do not write on the second *page.*   100._____

Questions 101-115.

DIRECTIONS: Indicate the kind of verbal italicized in the following sentences by choosing the appropriate letter from the key below.
   A. Gerund
   B. Participle
   C. Infinitive

101. The manuscript, *corrected* and typed, was on the desk,   101._____

102. He heard the bullet *ricochet.*   102._____

103. *Finding* the answer is a difficult task.   103._____

104. The animal, *hidden* from view, was trembling.   104._____

105. *Pretending* to be asleep, he listened attentively.   105._____

106. The professor, a *qualified* lecturer, entered the room.   106._____

107. They enjoyed *camping* at the lake.   107._____

108. Let them *come* to me.   108._____

109. He was annoyed by the *buzzing* sound.   109._____

110. It was a *stimulating* performance.   110._____

111. He had an accident while *returning* to the city.   111._____

112. *Encouraged* to study, the class opened the books.   112._____

113. He heard the gun *explode.*   113._____

114. They called him the *forgotten* man.   114._____

115. *Realizing* his mistake, he apologized.   115._____

Questions 116-130.

DIRECTIONS: Indicate the CORRECT punctuation for the following sentences by choosing the letter of the correct punctuation from the key below where brackets appear.

A. Comma
B. Semicolon
C. Colon
D. Dash
E. No punctuation

116. He explained [ ] that he could not attend.

116._____

117. The executive [ ] prepared for the interview and entered the room.

117._____

118. She admitted [ ] that the suggestion was wrong.

118._____

119. He did not object [ ] to dealing with them.

119._____

120. The chairman disagreed [ ] the members did not.

120._____

121. You must report to duty on November 10 [ ] 1988.

121._____

122. The father [ ] and two sons went fishing.

122._____

123. Act on the following problems [ ] administration, supervision, and policy.

123._____

124. This is excellent [ ] it has insight.

124._____

125. "I will take the car [ ]" he said.

125._____

126. I will do it [ ] however, you must help me.

126._____

127. When the show ended [ ] he returned home.

127._____

128. Stop [ ] making all of that noise.

128._____

129. Be firm [ ] exercise your authority.

129._____

130. The first example is poor [ ] the second is good.

130._____

Questions 131-150.

DIRECTIONS: Place a C in the space at the right if the sentence is correctly punctuated and a W in the space at the right if the sentence is incorrectly punctuated.

131. Its later than you think.

131._____

132. While I was eating the toast burned.

132._____

133. The fire started at ten oclock in the morning.

133._____

134. She asked, "Did you say, 'I will go?"

134._____

135. Richards handling of the question warranted praise.

135._____

136. July 4 is a holiday.   136._____

137. Oh perhaps you are right.   137._____

138. Will you answer the door, John?   138._____

139. While he was bathing the dog came in.   139._____

140. He was a calm gentle person.   140._____

141. He wore a new bow tie.   141._____

142. The shout "Block that kick" echoed upon the field.   142._____

143. Ladies and gentlemen take your seats.   143._____

144. However you must do your work.   144._____

145. My brothers are: John, Bill, and Charles.   145._____

146. While I was painting the neighbor opened the door.   146._____

147. One should fight for honor: not fame.   147._____

148. "Will you sing" he asked?   148._____

149. He played tennis, and then bowled.   149._____

150. On Monday April 5, we leave for Europe.   150._____

KEY (CORRECT ANSWERS)

1.	D	31.	4	61.	D	91.	C	121.	A
2.	A	32.	1	62.	A	92.	D	122.	E
3.	C	33.	4	63.	B	93.	C	123.	C
4.	E	34.	5	64.	A	94.	C	124.	D
5.	B	35.	5	65.	D	95.	A	125.	A
6.	D	36.	2	66.	D	96.	C	126.	B
7.	A	37.	3	67.	D	97.	C	127.	A
8.	E	38.	5	68.	B	98.	C	128.	E
9.	C	39.	2	69.	A	99.	C	129.	B
10.	A	40.	3	70.	B	100.	A	130.	B
11.	C	41.	C	71.	C	101.	B	131.	W
12.	D	42.	C	72.	A	102.	B	132.	W
13.	B	43.	B	73.	D	103.	A	133.	C
14.	D	44.	B	74.	E	104.	B	134.	W
15.	B	45.	D	75.	E	105.	A	135.	W
16.	A	46.	A	76.	B	106.	B	136.	C
17.	D	47.	C	77.	E	107.	A	137.	W
18.	A	48.	D	78.	D	108.	C	138.	C
19.	B	49.	C	79.	E	109.	B	139.	W
20.	C	50.	A	80.	C	110.	B	140.	W
21.	A	51.	A	81.	D	111.	A	141.	C
22.	D	52.	A	82.	C	112.	B	142.	W
23.	D	53.	E	83.	D	113.	C	143.	W
24.	C	54.	A	84.	D	114.	B	144.	W
25.	A	55.	C	85.	E	115.	A	145.	W
26.	3	56.	B	86.	C	116.	E	146.	W
27.	1	57.	E	87.	A	117.	E	147.	W
28.	3	58.	D	88.	B	118.	E	148.	W
29.	5	59.	A	89.	A	119.	E	149.	W
30.	3	60.	A	90.	C	120.	B	150.	W

EXAMINATION SECTION
TEST 1

DIRECTIONS: Each question or incomplete statement is followed by several suggested answers or completions. Select the one that BEST answers the question or completes the statement. *PRINT THE LETTER OF THE CORRECT ANSWER IN THE SPACE AT THE RIGHT.*

Questions 1-16.

DIRECTIONS: Each sentence below has one or two blanks, each blank indicating that something has been omitted. Beneath the sentence are five words or sets of words labeled A through E. Choose the word or set of words that, when inserted in the sentence, BEST fits the meaning of the sentence as a whole.

Example:
Medieval kingdoms did not become constitutional republics overnight; on the contrary, the change was _____.

   A. unpopular   B. unexpected
   C. advantageous   D. sufficient
   E. gradual

The CORRECT answer is E.

1. The audience responded enthusiastically to Wynton Marsalis' performance of Duke Ellington's music; some of the pieces were interrupted by _____.   1.____

   A. melodies   B. interpretations   C. insinuations
   D. assertions   E. applause

2. People often learn more effectively when studying in groups, and many report that they enjoy these cooperative ventures more than _____ sessions.   2.____

   A. temporary   B. solitary   C. collective
   D. unscheduled   E. curtailed

3. Although Russians rank this poet among their _____ authors, his works have not been _____ in translation.   3.____

   A. strangest;understood   B. greatest; appreciated
   C. wittiest; neglected   D. dullest; enjoyed
   E. firmest; altered

4. The annual summer _____ of the ice sheet covering that part of the sea provides _____ for marine creatures because it releases into the water the algae community that had been trapped in the ice.   4.____

   A. drifting; warmth   B. growth; fodder
   C. thinning; light   D. shifting; space
   E. melting; food

5. Lead in paint and in gasoline has been found to be such an environmental hazard that its use is now _____.   5.____

    A. condoned   B. insufficient   C. restricted
    D. rampant   E. unmonitored

6. Astronomy is no longer _____ the shortcomings of human vision; it now benefits from instruments that can *see* throughout a much broader spectrum.   6.____

    A. independent of   B. ambivalent toward
    C. limited by   D. knowledgeable about
    E. fixated on

7. The introductory essay was a(n) _____ effort in that each of the three editors wrote the portion concerning her own field of expertise.   7.____

    A. collaborative   B. disagreeable   C. indisputable
    D. enduring   E. unrealistic

8. Texas author Larry McMurtry suggests that those who _____ the moral character of cowboys have been seduced by the idea that a rugged, _____ way of life is less corrupting than the life cities have to offer.   8.____

    A. understand;reprobate   B. slander;unfettered
    C. ignore; sinister   D. romanticize;political
    E. idealize;rural

9. Margaret Mead studied ways that some non-Western societies deal effectively with certain human experiences and suggested that such strategies might offer remedies for _____ in American responses to similar events.   9.____

    A. ideals   B. assumptions
    C. idiosyncrasies   D. shortcomings
    E. improvisations

10. Goya's success as a painter for the Spanish court was _____, for the royal family continued to give him its patronage while he produced art that was widely interpreted as an indictment of monarchical rule.   10.____

    A. paradoxical   B. quixotic   C. auspicious
    D. exemplary   E. unfulfilled

11. A short-term pessimist but a long-term optimist, she predicts _____ transition from an epoch of competition to one of _____.   11.____

    A. an instantaneous; leisure
    B. a retrograde; affluence
    C. an insidious; terror
    D. a turbulent; fraternity
    E. a beneficent; militarism

12. The _____ the conflict unleashed in the nation's people have made it impossible for them, even decades later, to discuss the subject with _____.   12.____

    A. passions; equanimity   B. fears; trepidation
    C. hatreds; anger   D. visions; honor
    E. emotions; hesitation

13. The _____ of the service sector in our country disturbs many who believe that service   13._____
    industries are of less _____ than manufacturing in promoting economic well-being.

    A. productivity; versatility
    B. balance; volatility
    C. burgeoning; value
    D. contribution; interest
    E. decline; significance

14. The award-winning design of this solar-heated house has an _____ value over and   14._____
    above the _____ value it possesses due to the rise in the price of fossil fuels.

    A. accessible; unwarranted   B. ostentatious; superficial
    C. ephemeral; ecological   D. ornamental; artistic
    E. aesthetic; pragmatic

15. Giant pandas tend to move _____; they have little need for speed.   15._____

    A. implacably   B. spontaneously   C. dexterously
    D. deliberately   E. resoundingly

16. Helga gave orders in such a _____ way that it was clear she expected people to obey   16._____
    her immediately.

    A. peremptory   B. timorous   C. garrulous
    D. facetious   E. redundant

Questions 17-22.

DIRECTIONS: Questions 17 through 22 are to be answered on the basis of the following pas-
              sage, which is adapted from a survey of two hundred years of Hispanic theater
              in the Southwest.

        The majority of the plays produced in the Hispanic theater in the southwestern United
    States during the early decades of the twentieth century were examples of the plays typi-
    cally produced in the major cities of Mexico and Spain. Playwrights and impresarios did not
    hesitate to deal with controversial material. Many of their plays dealt with the his torical and
(5) current circumstances ofHispanic people in the Southwest, but always with seriousness
    and propriety.

        Also produced, however, were *revistas*. The *revista* was a genre that specialized in
    piquant political satire and commentary: it was a forum for articulating grievances, for pok-
    ing fun at the governments of both Mexico and the United States, for satirically considering
(10) the Mexican Revolution, and for contrasting Mexican American culture with Mexican cul-
    ture. This social and political commentary was carried out despite the fact that both audi-
    ences and performers were mostly immigrants who felt themselves liable to deportation or
    repatriation.
    It should be emphasized that, from the beginning of the Hispanic theater in the Southwest,
(15) the relationship of performers and theaters with the community was close. The Hispanic
    theater served to reinforce the sense of community by bringing all Spanish speakers
    together in a cultural act: the preservation and support of the language and art of Mexican
    people and other Hispanic people in the face of the threat of domination from Anglo-Ameri-
    can culture. Theater, more than any other art form, became essential to promoting ethnic

(20) and national identification and to solidifying the colony of expatriates. Thus, in addition to its artistic functions within the expatriate Mexican community, theater took on specific social functions that were not widely assumed by theaters in Mexico and Spain.

      The professional theater houses became temples of culture where the Hispanic community as a whole, regardless of social class, religion, or region of origin, could gather and, in the

(25) words of a theater critic writing in 1930, *keep the lamp of our culture lighted.* In 1916 a drama critic for San Antonio's LA PRENSA underlined the social and nationalistic functions of the theater: *Attending the artistic performances at the Teatro Juarez can be considered a patriotic deed which assists in cultural solidarity in support of a modest group of Mexican actors who are fighting for their livelihood in a foreign land and who introduce us to the*

(30) *most precious jewels of contemporary theater in our native tongue that is, the sweet and sonorous language of Cervantes.* Thus the Hispanic theater became an institution in the Southwest for the preservation of the Hispanic culture and the Spanish language in a foreign environment and for resistance to the influence of the dominant Anglo-American soci-

(34) ety.

17.   The passage is PRIMARILY concerned with the   17._____

     A.   differences among various kinds of plays produced in the Southwest
     B.   social and political function of the Hispanic theater in the Southwest
     C.   relationship between Mexican theater and the theater of the Southwest
     D.   celebration of theater as an important art form
     E.   political views of Hispanic actors and playwrights

18.   The author gives the MOST emphasis to which of the following aspects of the Hispanic   18._____
theater?
The

     A.   theater's superiority to other art forms
     B.   importance of satirical plays
     C.   theater's difference from theater in Mexico and Spain
     D.   economic situation of actors and producers
     E.   theater's role in building a sense of community

19.   Which of the following BEST describes the author's attitude toward those who partici-   19._____
pated in performances of *revistas?*

     A.   Criticism of their lack of seriousness
     B.   Mild criticism of their attitude toward government
     C.   Admiration for the understatement of their political commentary
     D.   Admiration for the subtlety of their art
     E.   Respect for their determination

20.   By quoting LA PRENSA's drama critic (lines 27-32), the author of the passage PRIMA-   20._____
RILY intends to

     A.   demonstrate the financial plight of expatriate actors
     B.   show appreciation for great artistic performances
     C.   praise the translation done for the Hispanic theater
     D.   draw attention to the influence of Cervantes
     E.   emphasize the role of theater in establishing cultural unity

21. Which of the following can be inferred from the remarks of LA PRENSA's drama critic about the performances at the Teatro Juarez (lines 27-32)?
The

    A. actors were not willing to boast about their talents
    B. critic recently had seen a play that dealt with matters of wealth and poverty
    C. language used in the productions did not meet the critic's approval
    D. actors were in a precarious economic situation
    E. performance was taking place during a time of intense military conflict

21.____

22. In the final statement in the passage, the author suggests that

    A. only professional theatrical institutions can preserve Hispanic culture
    B. only the theater can preserve culture in a foreign environment
    C. Hispanic people used the theater as an instrument of economic opportunity
    D. preserving Hispanic culture was important in a non-Hispanic political environment
    E. theater was the least understood of all southwestern art forms

22.____

Questions 23-29.

DIRECTIONS: Questions 23 through 29 are to be answered on the basis of the following passages, which discuss the relationship between people and technology in modern society.

Passage 1

    Anti-technologists treat technology as something that has escaped from human control. In the face of today's excruciatingly complex problems, it is understandable that many people agree with them. When people engage in technological activities, these activities appear to have consequences, not only physical but also intellectual, psychological, and
(5) cultural. Thus, anti-technologists argue, technology is deterministic. It causes other things to happen. Someone invents the automobile, for example, and it changes the way people think as well as the way they act. It changes their living patterns, their values, and their expectations in ways that were not anticipated when the automobile was first introduced. Some of the changes appear to be not only unanticipated but undesired. Nobody wanted
(10) traffic jams, accidents, and pollution. Therefore, technological advance seems to be independent of human direction. But sober thought reveals that technology is not an independent force, much less a thing, but merely one of the types of activities in which people engage.
    The anti-technologists discount completely the integrity and intelligence of the ordinary
(15) person. Indeed, pity and disdain for the individual citizen are essential aspects of anti-technology. One of its dogmas is that technological society forces people to consume things that they do not really desire. How can we respond to this falsehood? One might observe that the consumers who buy cars and electric can openers could, if they chose, buy oboes and oil paints, sailboats and hiking boots, chess sets and recordings of Mozart. Or, could
(20) they not help purchase a kidney machine that would save their neighbor's life? If people are vulgar, foolish, and selfish in their choice of purchases, is it not the worst sort of excuse to blame this on technological society? Indeed, wouldn't
people prefer being called vulgar to being told that they have no will with which to make choices of their own?

Passage 2

A happy technologist once asserted that everyone lampoons modern technology but
(25) no one is prepared to give up his or her refrigerator. In the United States there is a general
perception that life-style, or the way in which one lives, is a matter of individual choice, at
least for a vast majority. Disregarding economic means for a moment, people think that one
can choose to lead either a bohemian life-style or a conventional one. But is one truly free
to choose to have a refrigerator or not? Is it a simple matter of life-style choice or do other
(30) institutional arrangements of society impinge with demands of their own?

A refrigerator (including freezer) performs several functions. It stores food (a necessity)
and cools drinks or produces ice for cooling drinks (a comfort or luxury). The latter category
is not an essential function. The desirability of cold beer, for example, is culturally or
socially induced; other cultures find warm beer more desirable, so people in those societies
(35) do not need a refrigerator to perform this particular function. Consider another society in
which it is possible for people to purchase their perishable food on a daily basis in markets
or small shops, easily accessible and within walking distance of their homes. This option is
not available to many people in the United States. The supermarket as a social institution,
not within walking distance of most people, has its own imperatives. One buys for a week of
(40) eating, not for a day, so storage in a refrigerator becomes essential to living. It is a necessity induced by a life-style over which individuals have little control. To chide individuals for
recalcitrance or perversity for their unwillingness to give up their refrigerators is to misjudge
profoundly the nature of contemporary technology and its induced social change. It is irrel-
evant to the argument whether or not a supermarket/refrigerator society has advantages
(45) over the other.
The only question is, do individuals have autonomy to choose freely one or the other?

23. In Passage 1, the author's attitude toward anti-technologists is BEST described as   23.____

    A. sympathetic   B. indifferent   C. amused
    D. fearful   E. critical

24. In line 11, *sober* MOST NEARLY means   24.____

    A. plain and uncomplicated   B. not intoxicated
    C. sensible   D. unimaginative
    E. alert

25. The author uses the word *dogmas* (line 16) to refer to what he considers to be   25.____

    A. religious truths   B. logical premises
    C. prophetic ideas   D. unassailable doctrines
    E. groundless assumptions

26. The author of Passage 2 argues that in much of the United States a refrigerator is an   26.____

    A. appliance that has both essential and culturally determined functions
    B. example of modern technology that allows individuals to pursue different life-styles
    C. invention that only recently has become affordable
    D. entity that is independent of a social institution such as the supermarket
    E. illustration of the mindless materialism of modern society

27. What would be the likely response of the author of Passage 2 to the discussion of cars in lines 8-13 of Passage 1?   27.____

    A. Consumers have a wide variety of cars from which to choose.
    B. Consumers in some areas must rely on cars for transportation.
    C. Consumers tend to perceive cars as a means of recreation.
    D. Cars are not as essential as refrigerators or medical equipment in most societies.
    E. Cars as possessions are overvalued in modern society.

28. Which BEST describes an assumption about people held by the authors of Passages 1 and 2?   28.____

    A. People themselves are to blame for problems in modern society.
    B. People should not be judged too hastily about the choices they make.
    C. The author of Passage 1 views people as reasonable, whereas the author of Passage 2 views them as unreasonable.
    D. The author of Passage 1 views people as altruistic, whereas the author of Passage 2 views them as selfish.
    E. The author of Passage 1 views all people as essentially honest, whereas the author of Passage 2 thinks that only a few are.

29. The author of Passage 1 and the author of Passage 2 DISAGREE most strongly about the   29.____

    A. value of particular products of modern technology
    B. seriousness of problems associated with modern technology
    C. availability of consumer goods in a modern technological society
    D. control that people have over the uses and effects of technology
    E. type of life-style enjoyed by the majority of people in a modern technological society

Questions 30-41.

DIRECTIONS: Each question below consists of a related pair of words or phrases, followed by five pairs of words or phrases labeled A through E. Select the pair that BEST expresses a relationship similar to that expressed in the original pair.

    Example: CRUMB : BREAD
        A. ounce : unit   B. splinter : wood
        C. water : bucket   D. twine : rope
        E. cream : butter

    The CORRECT answer is B.

30. WRITE : SCRIBBLE   30.____

    A. hear : mumble   B. draw : doodle
    C. study : concentrate   D. plan : design
    E. read : learn

31. MICROSCOPE : SMALL   31.____

    A. kilometer : metric   B. thermometer : hot
    C. telescope : distant   D. stethoscope : loud
    E. calculator : fast

32. CALLIGRAPHER : PAPER   32.____

    A. plumber : wrench   B. potter : kiln
    C. prospector : ore   D. painter : canvas
    E. printer : ink

33. WHIFF : NOSE   33.____

    A. applause : hands   B. lick : cat
    C. pout : lips   D. spark : fire
    E. glimpse : eyes

34. MANUAL : INSTRUCTIONS   34.____

    A. timetable : railroads   B. food : utensils
    C. bibliography : sources   D. magazine : subscriptions
    E. radio : listeners

35. ITINERARY : TRIP   35.____

    A. schedule : table   B. agenda : meeting
    C. amendment : document   D. diary : experience
    E. memorandum : record

36. ACROBAT : TRAPEZE   36.____

    A. boxer : ring   B. actor : role
    C. swimmer : lap   D. animal : cage
    E. vaulter : pole

37. MISNOMER : NAME   37.____

    A. error : mishap   B. variability : change
    C. exception : rule   D. misconception : idea
    E. misdeed : apology

38. RECONCILE : HARMONY   38.____

    A. cure : health   B. disturb : tranquility
    C. perform : entertainment   D. forecast : weather
    E. respect : admiration

39. PARABLE : ILLUSTRATIVE   39.____

    A. newspaper : daily   B. joke : amusing
    C. cliche : creative   D. lecture : spoken
    E. film : exposed

40. RAMBLE : DIGRESSIVE   40.____

    A. warn : protected   B. prattle : foolish
    C. praise : incorrect   D. whisper : audible
    E. babble : intelligible

41. LURK : FURTIVE   41.____

    A. threaten : menacing
    B. accuse : guilty
    C. misrepresent : understated
    D. respect : contemptuous
    E. spy : informative

Questions 42-52.

DIRECTIONS: Questions 42 through 52 are to be answered on the basis of the following pas-
             sage. Scientists are often considered to be objective, but we are reminded in
             this passage that scientists are just as much products of their own cultural
             prejudices as are other people. For example, despite the efforts of early anato-
             mists to represent the body accurately, early anatomical reproductions
             reflected the stereotypes of the eighteenth and nineteenth centuries: that
             physical and intellectual strength defined masculinity and motherhood defined
             femininity.

          In 1734 anatomist Bernard Albinus produced an illustration of the male human skele-
      ton that would serve as the model for anatomical illustration for more than 75 years. Albinus
      consciously sought to capture the details not of a particular body but of a universal and
      ideal type. Though Albinus' fame rested on his reputation for accuracy, at every step along
(5)   the way he sacrificed objectivity to the ideal. Having made precise measurements of his
      subject and transferred them exactly to paper, Albinus then eliminated anatomical details
      from his drawing that would have destroyed its symmetry.

          Having produced the perfect drawing of the male, Albinus lamented, *we lack a female
      skeleton.* And numerous drawings of female skeletons were made in subsequent years.
(10) But, although these drawings purported to represent <u>the</u> female skeleton, they differed
      greatly from one another.
          Marie Thiroux d' Arconville's rendering of a distinctively female skeleton, published in
      1759, captured the imagination of physicians for more than half a century. This illustration
      one of the very few drawn by a woman anatomist-might also be called the most *sexist* por-
(15) trayal of a female skeleton. Thiroux d'Arconville exaggerated, almost to the point of carica-
      ture, those parts of the body that were emerging as sites of political debate: the skull as a
      mark of intelligence and the pelvis as a measure of womanliness. She depicted the female
      skull (incorrectly) as smaller in proportion to the body than the man's. She also focused
      attention on the pelvis by exaggerating the narrowness of the ribs so that the pelvis
(20) appeared excessively large. It would seem that either Thiroux d'Arconville intended to
      emphasize narrow ribs and wide hips as a mark of femininity or she chose for her model a
      woman who had worn a corset throughout her life. As early as 1741, anatomist J.B. Win-
      slow had noted that regular use of the corset deforms the ribs.

          In 1796 the German anatomist Samuel Thomas von Soemmerring produced a rival
(25) female skeleton. He had spent years perfecting the illustration; when it was finished, he
      considered it to be of such *completeness and exactitude* that it made a perfect mate for
      the great Albinus male. As a model he selected the skeleton of a twenty-year-old woman
      who had borne a child. For proportions, he checked his drawing against classical statues of
      Venus. Von Soemmerring intended his skeleton to represent not an individual woman but
(30) (as a later commentator put it) *the most beautiful woman* as was imagined to exist in life.

Although Thiroux d'Arconville and von Soemmerring drew their female skeletons from nature and considered their work *exact,* great debate erupted over the precise features of the female skeleton. In contrast to Thiroux d'Arconville, von Soemmerring portrayed the skull of the female (correctly) as larger in proportion to the body than that of the male. He (35) drew the ribs smaller in proportion to the hips than the man's, but not remarkably so.

Despite (or perhaps because of) its exaggerations, the Thiroux d'Arconville skeleton became the favored drawing. Von Soemmerring's skeleton, by contrast, was attacked for its *inaccuracies.* Edinburgh physician John Barclay criticized von Soemmerring in particular for showing the incorrect proportion of the ribs to the hips; he argued that the female rib (40) cage is much smaller than that shown by von Soemmerring because women's restricted life-style required that they breathe less vigorously. Barclay concluded that von Soemmerring was an artist, but no anatomist.

Rejecting Thiroux d'Arconville's insistence that the female skull was smaller in proportion to the body than the male skull, von Soemmerring pointed out that women's skulls are (45) actually heavier than men's, relative to total body weight (1:6 for women, 1:8 to 1:10 for men).

Von Soemmerring's view was castigated, for it seemed to counter the idea that men were the more intelligent and creative of the species. In subsequent years, however, anatomists had to concede the truth of von Soemmerring's depiction of the female skull. Yet they (50) did not conclude that women's large skulls were loaded with heavy, high-powered brains. Rather than a mark of intelligence, women's large skulls were dismissed as a sign of incomplete development. John Barclay, for example, used the proportionally larger size of the female skull to support his theory that physiologically women resemble children, (54) whose skulls are also large relative to their body size.

42. The PRIMARY focus of the passage is on   42._____

    A. the effects of Albinus' pioneering work in human anatomy
    B. the influence of social ideas on scientific thinking
    C. conflicting definitions of the ideal male skeleton
    D. the changes in cultural values brought about by the study of anatomy
    E. how similar the male and female skeletons really are

43. According to the passage, Albinus misrepresented certain bone structures in order to   43._____

    A. enhance individual variations in the models he used
    B. make structural details more readily visible
    C. make the skeleton conform to his idea of aesthetic perfection
    D. surpass all previous anatomists in exactness
    E. emphasize differences between male and female skeletons

44. In line 10, *the* is underlined in order to indicate that   44._____

    A. artistic tastes were changing rapidly during this period
    B. the author is referring to a particular and very important drawing of a woman
    C. there was a great deal of similarity among the drawings mentioned
    D. the drawings were exact representations of the particular models used
    E. each artist intended the drawing to represent an ideal, universal woman

45. The passage supports which of the following statements about Thiroux d'Arconville's drawing?
    It.

    A. reflected physicians' superior knowledge of anatomy
    B. set a new standard for precision of detail
    C. was more reliable than drawings by male artists
    D. conformed to prevailing views about femininity
    E. was free of the inaccuracies of the classical era

45.____

46. The author MOST likely gives a description of von Soemmerring's human model (lines 33-35) in order to suggest that

    A. motherhood and youth were thought to be characteristics of the ideal woman
    B. Winslow's idea that corsets could be harmful was probably based on inadequate evidence
    C. no ordinary woman's skeleton could measure up to the classical idea of beauty
    D. von Soemmerring's powers of observation were superior to those of his critics
    E. von Soemmerring's ideas about skull size were affected by the youthfulness of his model

46.____

47. In line 32, *erupted* MOST NEARLY means

    A. ejected
    B. overflowed
    C. increased
    D. broke out
    E. became uncontrollable

47.____

48. The author uses the parenthetical phrase *or perhaps because of* in line 36 in order to suggest that

    A. Thiroux d'Arconville's contemporaries tended to share her prejudices
    B. exaggerated drawings are often more useful for conveying fine details
    C. artistic tastes of the eighteenth century regarded exaggeration as beautiful
    D. the author is uncertain about the causes of the drawing's popularity
    E. Thiroux d' Arconville was never fully understood by either the artists or the scientists of her day

48.____

49. The passage implies that von Soemmerring's chief reason for drawing the female skull proportionally larger than the male skull was his wish to

    A. reflect actual physical evidence
    B. correct the distortions in Albinus' work
    C. disprove Barclay's ideas
    D. suggest that women were more intelligent than men
    E. create an aesthetically pleasing work of art

49.____

50. The discussion in lines 39-42 about the size of the female rib cage CHIEFLY serves to

    A. show that scientists were concerned with both aesthetics and facts
    B. lead the reader to realize that neither Thiroux d' Arconville's nor von Soemmerring's drawings were entirely accurate

50.____

C. indicate the bias held by most scientists of the period by citing a representative view
D. contrast with the remarks about female beauty made by the *later commentator* (line 30)
E. present evidence in support of von Soemmerring's position in the debate

51. Barclay's appraisal of von Soemmerring (lines 40-43) was intended to   51.____

A. praise his skill as a draftsman
B. emphasize the beauty of his drawing
C. criticize the excessive embellishment of his drawing
D. cast doubt on the scientific accuracy of his drawing
E. suggest that creativity is an important factor in science

52. In line 49, *concede* MOST NEARLY means   52.____

A. acknowledge   B. compromise
C. renounce   D. disclose
E. surrender

Questions 53-60

DIRECTIONS: Questions 53 through 60 are to be answered on the basis of the following passage, which is adapted from an American writer's memoir of his childhood.

My father taught me skills and manners: he taught me to shoot, to drive fast, to read respectfully, to handle a boat, and to distinguish between good jazz music and bad. His codes were not novel, but they were rigid. A gentleman was a stickler for precision; life was no more than an inventory of small choices that together formed a man's character, entire.

(5)   He looked, and spoke, straight at you. He could stare down anyone. To me everything about him seemed outsized. Doing a school report on the Easter Islanders I found in an encyclopedia pictures of their huge sculptures, and there he was, massive head and nose, nothing subtle or delicate. He was in fact (and how diminishing those words, *in fact,* look to me now) an inch or two above six feet, full-bodied, a man who lumbered from here
(10) to there with deliberation. When I was a child I noticed that people were respectful of the cubic feet my father occupied; later I understood that I had confused respect with resentment.
I remember his shoes, so meticulously selected and cared for and used, thin-soled, with cracked uppers, older than I was or could ever be, shining dully and from the depths.
(15) Just a pair of shoes?
No: I knew before I knew any other complicated thing that for my father there was nothing he possessed that was *just* something. His pocket watch was not *just* a timepiece, it was a miraculous instrument. It struck the hour unassertively, musically, like a silver tine touched to a crystal glass, no hurry, you might like to know it's noon.

(20)   He despised black leather, said black shoes reminded him of black attache cases, of bankers, lawyers, look-before-you-leapers anxious not to offend their clients. He owned nothing black except his umbrella. His umbrella doubled as a shooting stick, and one afternoon at a soccer game he was sitting on it when a man asked him what he would do if it rained, sit wet or stand dry? I laughed. My father laughed also, but tightly, and he did

(25) not reply; nor did he ever again use this quixotic contraption. He took things, *things,* seriously.

When I was a boy, he introduced me, with ceremony, to a couple of family treasures: my great-grandfather's medical degree from Leyden and, set in blue-velvet cavities in a worn leather case, my grandfather's surgical instruments. These totems are gone now,
(30) lost during one or another last-minute, dark-of-night escape from a housewhere the rent was seven months overdue. Recently I bought a set of compasses and dividers solely because, snugged in their own blue-velvet nests, they returned me to evenings when I sat beside my father and he showed me the probes and scalpels. I would examine a piece, then return it to its place, and promise never to touch it without supervision. I was warned
(35) that microbes deadly beyond imagining still lurked on the blades, but there was no need to scare me away from them: I had never seen things so mysterious, cold, or menacing.

53. The passage portrays the father as a man who is PRIMARILY   53.____

    A. exuberant
    B. malicious
    C. long-winded
    D. complex and preoccupied with appearances
    E. generous and thoughtful toward others

54. The list of skills in the first sentence indicates the father's   54.____

    A. self-discipline   B. lack of subtlety
    C. impatience   D. practicality
    E. versatility

55. The author mentions the Easter Island statues (lines 5-9) in order to emphasize his father's apparent   55.____

    A. indifference   B. energy
    C. massiveness   D. good looks
    E. stodginess

56. Black leather (lines 20-23) represents which of the following for the father?   56.____

    A. Reckless pursuit of goals
    B. Extraordinary self-discipline
    C. Unabashed greed
    D. Excessive caution
    E. Admirably good manners

57. The incident at the soccer game (lines 23-25) shows that the father   57.____

    A. was too depressed to be able to enjoy jokes
    B. was unreasonably fearful of strangers
    C. was extremely sensitive to the judgment of others
    D. was able to compromise when necessary
    E. had an unpredictable and violent temper

58. The passage does all of the following to establish the father's character EXCEPT   58.____

    A. describe him physically
    B. quote his words directly

C.   recount the son's youthful attitude toward him
D.   show him interacting with others
E.   comment on his likes and dislikes

59.   The writer emphasizes an aspect of his father's character that is in ironic contrast to his   59.____
outsized and obtrusive appearance, which had *nothing subtle or delicate* (line 13) about
it.
This trait of his personality would be

A.   crude sense of humor
B.   animosity towards bankers and lawyers
C.   attention to detail exemplified by his meticulously selected shoes and his musically
     precise pocket watch
D.   the respect he inspired becuase of his formidable size
E.   a sentimental attachment to family heirlooms

60.   The style and tone of this passage may be described as being predominantly   60.____

A.   humorous and sarcastic
B.   poetic and metaphorical
C.   descriptive, reminiscent and nostalgic
D.   factual and pedantic
E.   sharply satiric

———

KEY (CORRECT ANSWERS)

1. E	11. D	21. D	31. C	41. A	51. D
2. B	12. A	22. D	32. D	42. B	52. A
3. B	13. C	23. E	33. E	43. C	53. D
4. E	14. E	24. C	34. C	44. E	54. E
5. C	15. D	25. E	35. B	45. D	55. C
6. C	16. A	26. A	36. E	46. A	56. D
7. A	17. B	27. B	37. D	47. D	57. C
8. E	18. E	28. B	38. A	48. A	58. B
9. D	19. E	29. D	39. B	49. A	59. C
10. A	20. E	30. B	40. B	50. C	60. C

EXAMINATION SECTION
TEST 1

DIRECTIONS: In the space provided at the right, write the letter of the word or expression that most nearly expresses the meaning of the word printed in italics.

1. *Calligraphy*

   A. weaving   B. handwriting
   C. drafting   D. mapmaking

   1._____

2. *Synchronize*

   A. happen at the same time
   B. follow immediately in time
   C. alternate between events
   D. postpone to a future time

   2._____

3. *Semblance*

   A. surface   B. diplomacy
   C. replacement   D. appearance

   3._____

4. *Circuitous*

   A. winding   B. mutual
   C. exciting   D. rugged

   4._____

5. *Curtail*

   A. threaten   B. strengthen
   C. lessen   D. hasten

   5._____

6. *Noxious*

   A. spicy   B. smelly
   C. foreign   D. harmful

   6._____

7. *Drivel*

   A. fatigue   B. scarcity
   C. nonsense   D. waste

   7._____

8. *Assuage*

   A. soothe   B. cleanse
   C. enjoy   D. reward

   8._____

9. *Intrepid*

   A. exhausted   B. fearless
   C. anxious   D. youthful

   9._____

10. *Treacherous*

    A. ignorant   B. envious
    C. disloyal   D. cowardly

    10._____

11. The court jester served the role of *buffoon*   11._____

    A. horseman   B. servant
    C. philosopher   D. clown

12. The guest of honor began to speak *nonchalantly* to the audience.   12._____

    A. casually   B. nervously
    C. seriously   D. quietly

13. The governor gave the reporter a *terse* answer to the complex question.   13._____

    A. rambling   B. inadequate
    C. brief   D. ridiculous

14. The servants were told to *adorn* the statues.   14._____

    A. decorate   B. remove
    C. wash   D. destroy

15. Any further discussion of the problem would be *redundant*.   15._____

    A. unprofitable   B. repetitive
    C. confusing   D. misleading

16. The challenge to society is to prevent a criminal from operating with *impunity*.   16._____

    A. threats of violence
    B. lack of detection
    C. guarantees of success
    D. freedom from punishment

17. The politician's *candor* surprised his listeners.   17._____

    A. honesty   B. comments
    C. viewpoint   D. examples

18. The horror film was filled with zombies and *cadavers*.   18._____

    A. ghosts   B. skeletons
    C. monsters   D. corpses

19. Leslie worked *diligently* on her school project.   19._____

    A. skillfully   B. resentfully
    C. industriously   D. hurriedly

20. The supervisor could not *coerce* the employee to take early retirement.   20._____

    A. request   B. force
    C. permit   D. advise

21. *Stow*   21._____

    A. pack   B. report
    C. interest   D. beg

22. *Irrepressible*   22._____

    A. unrestrainable   B. impatient
    C. unknowable   D. impractical

23. *Grimace*   23.____

    A. important development   B. point of view
    C. expression of disgust   D. act of spite

24. *Promenade*   24.____

    A. limp   B. walk
    C. jog   D. race

25. *Indicative*   25.____

    A. defensive   B. attractive
    C. disruptive   D. suggestive

26. *Medley*   26.____

    A. game   B. entertainment
    C. discussion   D. mixture

27. *Jaunty*   27.____

    A. mighty   B. dirty
    C. lively   D. petty

28. *Undue*   28.____

    A. genuine   B. wavy
    C. faultless   D. inappropriate

29. *Visage*   29.____

    A. appearance   B. vividness
    C. prospect   D. valor

30. *Avid*   30.____

    A. eager   B. easy
    C. dry   D. flat

31. That *bestial* act marked him for life.   31.____

    A. unkind   B. insensitive
    C. brutal   D. spiteful

32. The professor was regarded as an *erudite* teacher.   32.____

    A. rigid   B. scholarly
    C. demanding   D. reasonable

33. We could see the *knolls* from our window.   33.____

    A. rounded hills   B. groups of trees
    C. high waves   D. marshes

34. As the nurse prepared the shot, I *winced* in anticipation.   34.____

    A. moaned aloud   B. stared ahead
    C. lay still   D. shrank back

35. The president said that he would not *countenance* such policies.

    A. order   B. implement
    C. approve   D. introduce

35.____

36. The lawyer proved that the witness was a *prevaricator*.

    A. murderer   B. liar
    C. thief   D. fraud

36.____

37. The explorers followed the *tributary* to its origin.

    A. stream   B. lake
    C. trail   D. valley

37.____

38. She always comes to school *impeccably* groomed.

    A. carelessly   B. conservatively
    C. stylishly   D. flawlessly

38.____

39. Mrs. Royce *discreetly* answered all the questions asked about her neighbor.

    A. precisely   B. tactfully
    C. honestly   D. positively

39.____

40. The actor's *feigned* southern accent was praised by the critics.

    A. pretended   B. acquired
    C. unusual   D. low-pitched

40.____

KEY (CORRECT ANSWERS)

1. B	11. D	21. A	31. C
2. A	12. A	22. A	32. B
3. D	13. C	23. C	33. A
4. A	14. A	24. B	34. D
5. C	15. B	25. D	35. C
6. D	16. D	26. D	36. B
7. C	17. A	27. C	37. A
8. A	18. D	28. D	38. D
9. B	19. C	29. A	39. B
10. C	20. B	30. A	40. A

TEST 2

DIRECTIONS: In the space provided at the right, write the letter of the word or expression that most nearly expresses the meaning of the word printed in italics.

1. *Abduct*

   A. ruin
   C. fight

   B. aid
   D. kidnap

   1._____

2. *Demerit*

   A. outcome
   C. prize

   B. fault
   D. notice

   2._____

3. *Mutinous*

   A. silent
   C. rebellious

   B. oceangoing
   D. miserable

   3._____

4. *Negligent*

   A. lax
   C. cowardly

   B. desperate
   D. ambitious

   4._____

5. *Contest*

   A. disturb
   C. detain

   B. dispute
   D. distrust

   5._____

6. *Query*

   A. wait
   C. show

   B. lose
   D. ask

   6._____

7. *Insidious*

   A. treacherous
   C. internal

   B. excitable
   D. distracting

   7._____

8. *Palpitate*

   A. mash
   C. throb

   B. stifle
   D. pace

   8._____

9. *Animosity*

   A. hatred
   C. silliness

   B. interest
   D. amusement

   9._____

10. *Egotism*

    A. sociability
    C. self-confidence

    B. aggressiveness
    D. conceit

    10._____

11. Bob's account of the accident *incriminated* others.

    A. annoyed
    C. ignored

    B. involved
    D. helped

    11._____

12. When Jack left his position as chief of staff, he was completely *demoralized.* 12.____

    A. satisfied   B. frenzied
    C. liberated   D. disheartened

13. The architect designed a modern *edifice* of wood and red glass. 13.____

    A. framework   B. platform
    C. structure   D. false front

14. The speaker kept the meeting interesting with her *facetious* remarks. 14.____

    A. amusing   B. informal
    C. personal   D. factual

15. The new ruling set a *precedent* for all similar cases that would be tried in court. 15.____

    A. direction   B. standard
    C. regulation   D. test

16. The botanist wanted a picture of the tree because it was so *gnarled.* 16.____

    A. old   B. unusual
    C. fruitful   D. deformed

17. Harriet's *ostentatious* display of wealth is upsetting to her friends. 17.____

    A. frequent   B. thoughtless
    C. showy   D. unnatural

18. The answer was too *oblique* to receive full credit. 18.____

    A. indirect   B. repetitive
    C. disorganized   D. brief

19. The magician did the sleight-of-hand trick with remarkable *dexterity.* 19.____

    A. swiftness   B. assurance
    C. charisma   D. skill

20. The principal had no *qualms* about suspending the three boys for fighting. 20.____

    A. comments   B. misgivings
    C. arguments   D. regrets

21. *Resurrection* 21.____

    A. reassurance   B. encouragement
    C. fascination   D. revival

22. *Recede* 22.____

    A. take over   B. show off
    C. hold out   D. move back

23. *Fissure* 23.____

    A. opening   B. path
    C. mountain   D. landslide

24. *Delectable*   24.____

   A. carefree   B. elaborate
   C. delightful   D. deliberate

25. *Oblivious*   25.____

   A. understated   B. unmindful
   C. untrue   D. unappetizing

26. *Inevitable*   26.____

   A. unable   B. forceful
   C. certain   D. plain

27. *Paradox*   27.____

   A. incomplete response   B. sharp comment
   C. obvious truth   D. seeming contradiction

28. *Cataclysm*   28.____

   A. disaster   B. deception
   C. denial   D. debate

29. *Sanction*   29.____

   A. stop   B. expel
   C. approve   D. refund

30. *Assiduously*   30.____

   A. decidedly   B. diligently
   C. randomly   D. correctly

31. The judge ordered that *restitution* be provided for the robbery victims.   31.____

   A. apologies   B. recognition
   C. publicity   D. compensation

32. The trumpets announced the *imminent* arrival of the dignitary.   32.____

   A. approaching   B. delayed
   C. unexpected   D. distant

33. The shopper was *indignant* at the treatment given him by the clerk.   33.____

   A. embarrassed   B. pleased
   C. angry   D. surprised

34. The cook in the old diner had a *slatternly* appearance.   34.____

   A. dreary   B. sloppy
   C. homey   D. strange

35. The *nebulous* argument that he presented failed to explain the main issue.   35.____

   A. careful   B. complex
   C. vague   D. idealistic

36. The prisoner longed for the life of a *vagabond*.

    A. wanderer   B. millionaire
    C. celebrity   D. journalist

36.____

37. The entire neighborhood came out to see the *celestial* display.

    A. artistic   B. fantastic
    C. unusual   D. heavenly

37.____

38. Because the shopkeeper was upset, we were unable to *glean* the details of the robbery.

    A. connect   B. gather
    C. tell   D. comprehend

38.____

39. The problem rests not with her beliefs but with her excessive desire to *propagate* them.

    A. spread   B. live up to
    C. protect   D. justify

39.____

40. The young athlete tried to *emulate* his high school coach.

    A. obey   B. assist
    C. imitate   D. deceive

40.____

KEY (CORRECT ANSWERS)

1.	D	11.	B	21.	D	31.	D
2.	B	12.	D	22.	D	32.	A
3.	C	13.	C	23.	A	33.	C
4.	A	14.	A	24.	C	34.	B
5.	B	15.	B	25.	B	35.	C
6.	D	16.	D	26.	C	36.	A
7.	A	17.	C	27.	D	37.	D
8.	C	18.	A	28.	A	38.	B
9.	A	19.	D	29.	C	39.	A
10.	D	20.	B	30.	B	40.	C

TEST 3

DIRECTIONS: In the space provided at the right, write the letter of the word or expression that most nearly expresses the meaning of the word printed in italics.

1. *Intuition*   1.____

   A. payment   B. faith
   C. introduction   D. insight

2. *Compel*   2.____

   A. lengthen   B. help
   C. force   D. distract

3. *Vent*   3.____

   A. discharge   B. omit
   C. entertain   D. worship

4. *Cohort*   4.____

   A. commander   B. companion
   C. candidate   D. craftsman

5. *Ordeal*   5.____

   A. alternate route   B. logical sequence
   C. important duty   D. severe trial

6. *Fabrication*   6.____

   A. addition   B. remedy
   C. analysis   D. creation

7. *Unwitting*   7.____

   A. ordinary   B. unaware
   C. unnecessary   D. unadvisable

8. *Zealot*   8.____

   A. sharp tool   B. worthy cause
   C. eager person   D. extinct animal

9. *Indulge*   9.____

   A. spoil   B. surprise
   C. direct   D. compare

10. *Hamper*   10.____

    A. offer   B. confuse
    C. order   D. restrict

11. The first settlers in America faced a cold winter in the *vast* wilderness.   11.____

    A. unknown   B. untamed
    C. enormous   D. empty

12. Her very presence at the party *nettled* the other guests. 12.____

    A. embarrassed   B. irritated
    C. puzzled   D. quieted

13. The attorney was eager to *disclose* her evidence. 13.____

    A. examine   B. reorganize
    C. report   D. reveal

14. When the brakes failed, the bus nearly went off the road into a *chasm*. 14.____

    A. gorge   B. field
    C. river   D. wall

15. I avoid that restaurant because of its *insipid* food. 15.____

    A. spicy   B. tasteless
    C. overcooked   D. expensive

16. A *malicious* person is usually unpopular. 16.____

    A. conceited   B. selfish
    C. spiteful   D. stingy

17. He was able to *elude* the soldiers for only a short time. 17.____

    A. escape   B. train
    C. aid   D. restrain

18. The man *denounced* his neighbor because of her political activities. 18.____

    A. avoided   B. ridiculed
    C. spied on   D. condemned

19. The grapegrowers in California employ many *transient* workers. 19.____

    A. immigrant   B. youthful
    C. temporary   D. experienced

20. The money has been *allocated* for new school buses. 20.____

    A. set aside   B. raised
    C. spent   D. borrowed

21. *Larceny* 21.____

    A. criminal   B. burning
    C. name-calling   D. theft

22. *Simulate* 22.____

    A. delay   B. supply
    C. pretend   D. deny

23. *Lucid* 23.____

    A. clear   B. colorful
    C. lawful   D. old

24. *Remorse*   24.____

    A. anger   B. regret
    C. apology   D. coldness

25. *Laden*   25.____

    A. optimistic   B. refined
    C. burdened   D. worried

26. *Turbulence*   26.____

    A. control   B. interruption
    C. renewal   D. disorder

27. *Incessantly*   27.____

    A. instantly   B. brilliantly
    C. respectfully   D. continually

28. *Chronic*   28.____

    A. diseased   B. constant
    C. aged   D. unsafe

29. *Tepid*   29.____

    A. lukewarm   B. eager
    C. tearful   D. sharp

30. *Consensus*   30.____

    A. survey   B. contract
    C. association   D. agreement

31. Have you ever heard the saying, "To be *wary* is to be wise"?   31.____

    A. Thrifty   B. Healthy
    C. Careful   D. Industrious

32. Sherlock Holmes was noted for his superb power of *deduction*.   32.____

    A. imagination   B. reasoning
    C. extrasensory perception   D. concentration

33. The manager encouraged the staff to try to add to the store's *clientele*.   33.____

    A. good will   B. profits
    C. customers   D. variety of merchandise

34. The student was *disconcerted* when she saw her test score.   34.____

    A. upset   B. assured
    C. pleased   D. surprised

35. An automobile can be a *lethal* machine.   35.____

    A. expensive   B. deadly
    C. essential   D. magnificent

36. The general promised to *annihilate* the enemy's troops. 36.____

   A. pursue
   C. capture
   B. destroy
   D. surround

37. She is the owner of a *lucrative* construction company. 37.____

   A. small
   C. local
   B. reliable
   D. profitable

38. After Joan had completed her investigation, she realized that her *premise* was incorrect. 38.____

   A. assumption
   C. methodology
   B. conclusion
   D. information

39. During the campaign, the politicians often engaged in *acrimonious* debate. 39.____

   A. meaningless
   C. bitter
   B. brilliant
   D. loud

40. There is no value in this *sordid* film. 40.____

   A. boring
   C. experimental
   B. vile
   D. inferior

KEY (CORRECT ANSWERS)

1.	D	11.	C	21.	D	31.	C
2.	C	12.	B	22.	C	32.	B
3.	A	13.	D	23.	A	33.	C
4.	B	14.	A	24.	B	34.	A
5.	D	15.	B	25.	C	35.	B
6.	D	16.	C	26.	D	36.	B
7.	B	17.	A	27.	D	37.	D
8.	C	18.	D	28.	B	38.	A
9.	A	19.	C	29.	A	39.	C
10.	D	20.	A	30.	D	40.	B

TEST 4

DIRECTIONS: In the space provided at the right, write the letter of the word or expression that most nearly expresses the meaning of the word printed in italics.

1. *Defame*

   A. slander
   C. outwit

   B. depress
   D. arouse

   1.____

2. *Retaliation*

   A. recommendation
   C. revenge

   B. list
   D. victory

   2.____

3. *Zeal*

   A. boredom
   C. compassion

   B. enthusiasm
   D. trust

   3.____

4. *Unilateral*

   A. one-wheeled
   C. similar

   B. unanticipated
   D. one-sided

   4.____

5. *Gratuity*

   A. tip for service
   C. medal for achievement

   B. tool for printing
   D. thank you note

   5.____

6. *Bewitch*

   A. repel
   C. satisfy

   B. fascinate
   D. fear

   6.____

7. *Desist*

   A. cause
   C. help

   B. change
   D. stop

   7.____

8. *Bigotry*

   A. invention
   C. intolerance

   B. obstruction
   D. belief

   8.____

9. *Somber*

   A. gloomy
   C. lively

   B. gentle
   D. careful

   9.____

10. *Redemption*

    A. power
    C. religion

    B. sale
    D. deliverance

    10.____

11. The *eccentric* old lady loved her cats, her hats, and her tumble-down house.

    A. moody
    C. strange

    B. lovable
    D. friendly

    11.____

12. The author was totally displeased with the *abridged* version of his novel.   12._____

    A. televised   B. shortened
    C. translated   D. censored

13. He made the statement *assertively.*   13._____

    A. reluctantly   B. hastily
    C. positively   D. honestly

14. Because of his *inertia,* he seldom achieves his goal.   14._____

    A. temper   B. laziness
    C. stupidity   D. carelessness

15. The executive believes that people must be *ruthless* in order to succeed in business.   15._____

    A. powerful   B. dishonest
    C. reckless   D. merciless

16. The actress was described as having *mediocre* talent.   16._____

    A. ordinary   B. uncommon
    C. excellent   D. inferior

17. The *gaudy* dress is trimmed with pearls.   17._____

    A. elegant   B. worn out
    C. pretty   D. flashy

18. The class *extolled* the virtues of their teacher.   18._____

    A. listed   B. praised
    C. apologized for   D. explained

19. The child was both *gregarious* and hardworking in school.   19._____

    A. comfortable   B. prompt
    C. sociable   D. happy

20. Many *credulous* people are influenced by television advertisements to buy certain products.   20._____

    A. believing   B. uneducated
    C. clever   D. logical

21. *Tantalize*   21._____

    A. encourage   B. tease
    C. satisfy   D. quarrel

22. *Proximity*   22._____

    A. falseness   B. correctness
    C. favor   D. nearness

23. *Perceptible*   23._____

    A. capable   B. likeable
    C. observable   D. returnable

24. *Philanthropy*   24.____

    A. love of money   B. love of humanity
    C. love of stamps   D. love of words

25. *Havoc*   25.____

    A. respect   B. danger
    C. destruction   D. complications

26. *Consolidate*   26.____

    A. unite   B. sympathize
    C. void   D. profit

27. *Discrepancy*   27.____

    A. reduction   B. restraint
    C. looseness   D. difference

28. *Advocate* (verb)   28.____

    A. recommend   B. supply
    C. remove   D. vote

29. *Sedate*   29.____

    A. seated   B. composed
    C. bored   D. informal

30. *Superficial*   30.____

    A. buried   B. overhead
    C. external   D. important

31. Canoeing through the rapids is a *grueling* experience.   31.____

    A. exciting   B. uncomfortable
    C. rewarding   D. exhausting

32. He was *cognizant* of his responsibilities.   32.____

    A. aware   B. afraid
    C. weary   D. relieved

33. With Joe's *tenacity*, he is bound to succeed.   33.____

    A. intelligence   B. luck
    C. talent   D. persistence

34. When will the sales campaign be *initiated*?   34.____

    A. Approved   B. Planned
    C. Started   D. Tested

35. Joan's *vitality* is envied by many people.   35.____

    A. beauty   B. energy
    C. ability   D. popularity

36. In view of the circumstances, Jane's comment seemed *callous*.   36.____

    A. insensitive   B. misleading
    C. kind   D. true

37. Reading the letter left him in a *pensive* mood.   37.____

    A. calm   B. thoughtful
    C. happy   D. romantic

38. He answered the question *impetuously*.   38.____

    A. foolishly   B. hastily
    C. quietly   D. honestly

39. His *inane* suggestion fell on deaf ears.   39.____

    A. silly   B. detailed
    C. unusual   D. selfish

40. After being lost in the woods, Tom was *ravenous*.   40.____

    A. extremely tired   B. extremely thirsty
    C. extremely hungry   D. extremely angry

KEY (CORRECT ANSWERS)

1. A	11. C	21. B	31. D
2. C	12. B	22. D	32. A
3. B	13. C	23. C	33. D
4. D	14. B	24. B	34. C
5. A	15. D	25. C	35. B
6. B	16. A	26. A	36. A
7. D	17. D	27. D	37. B
8. C	18. B	28. A	38. B
9. A	19. C	29. B	39. A
10. D	20. A	30. C	40. C

TESTS IN SENTENCE COMPLETION / 1 BLANK
EXAMINATION SECTION
TEST 1

DIRECTIONS: Each question in this section consists of a sentence in which one word is missing; a blank line indicates where the word has been removed from the sentence. Beneath each sentence are five words, *one* of which is the missing word. You are to select the letter of the missing word by deciding which one of the five words BEST fits in with the meaning of the sentence. *PRINT THE LETTER OF THE CORRECT ANSWER IN THE SPACE AT THE RIGHT.*

1. A man who cannot win honor in his own _____ will have a very small chance of winning it from posterity.

    A. right   B. field   C. country   D. way   E. age

1.____

2. The latent period for the contractile response to direct stimulation of the muscle has quite another and shorte value, encompassing only a utilization period. Hence it is that the term *latent period* must be _____ carefully each time that it is used.

    A. checked   B. timed   C. introduced
    D. defined   E. selected

2.____

3. Many television watchers enjoy stories which contain violence. Consequently those television producers who are dominated by rating systems aim to _____ the popular taste.

    A. raise   B. control   C. gratify   D. ignore   E. lower

3.____

4. No other man loses so much, so _____, so absolutely, as the beaten candidate for high public office.

    A. bewilderingly   B. predictably   C. disgracefully
    D. publicly   E. cheerfully

4.____

5. Mathematics is the product of thought operating by means of _____ for the purpose of expressing general laws.

    A. reasoning   B. symbols   C. words
    D. examples   E. science

5.____

6. Deductive reasoning is that form of reasoning in which the conclusion must necessarily follow if we accept the premise as true. In deduction, it is _____ the premise to be true and the conclusion false.

    A. impossible   B. inevitable   C. reasonable
    D. surprising   E. unlikely

6.____

7. Because in the administration it hath respect not to the group but to the _____, our form of government is called a democracy.

    A. courts   B. people   C. majority
    D. individual   E. law

7.____

8. Before criticizing the work of an artist one needs to _____ the artist's purpose.   8.____

    A. understand   B. reveal   C. defend
    D. correct   E. change

9. Their work was commemorative in character and consisted largely of _____ erected   9.____
upon the occasion of victories.

    A. towers   B. tombs   C. monuments
    D. castles   E. fortresses

10. Every good story is carefully contrived: the elements of the story are _____ to fit with   10.____
one another in order to
make an effect on the reader.

    A. read   B. learned   C. emphasized
    D. reduced   E. planned

KEY (CORRECT ANSWERS)

1.	E	6.	A
2.	D	7.	D
3.	C	8.	A
4.	D	9.	C
5.	B	10.	E

TEST 2

DIRECTIONS: Each question in this section consists of a sentence in which one word is missing; a blank line indicates where the word has been removed from the sentence. Beneath each sentence are five words, *one* of which is the missing word. You are to select the letter of the missing word by deciding which one of the five words BEST fits in with the meaning of the sentence. *PRINT THE LETTER OF THE CORRECT ANSWER IN THE SPACE AT THE RIGHT.*

1. One of the most prevalent erroneous contentions is that Argentina is a country of _____   1.____
agricultural resources and needs only the arrival of ambitious settlers.

   A. modernized   B. flourishing   C. undeveloped
   D. waning   E. limited

2. The last official statistics for the town indicated the presence of 24,212 Italians, 6,450   2.____
Magyars, and 2,315 Germans, which ensures to the _____ a numerical preponderance.

   A. Germans   B. figures   C. town   D. Magyars   E. Italians

3. Precision of wording is necessary in good writing; by choosing words that exactly convey   3.____
the desired meaning, one can avoid _____.

   A. duplicity   B. incongruity   C. complexity
   D. ambiguity   E. implications

4. Various civilians of the liberal school in the British Parliament remonstrated that there   4.____
were no grounds for _____ of French aggression, since the Emperor showed less disposition to augment the navy than had Louis Philippe.

   A. suppression   B. retaliation   C. apprehension
   D. concealment   E. commencement

5. _____ is as clear and definite as any of our urges; we wonder what is in a sealed letter   5.____
or what is being said in a telephone booth.

   A. Envy   B. Curiosity   C. Knowledge
   D. Communication   E. Ambition

6. It is a rarely philosophic soul who can make a _____ the other alternative forever into   6.____
the limbo of forgotten things.

   A. mistake   B. wish   C. change   D. choice   E. plan

7. A creditor is worse than a master. A master owns only your person, but a creditor owns   7.____
your _____ as well.

   A. aspirations   B. potentialities   C. ideas
   D. dignity   E. wealth

8. People _____ small faults, in order to insinuate that they have no great ones.   8.____

   A. create   B. display   C. confess   D. seek   E. reject

9. Andrew Jackson believed that wars were inevitable, and to him the length and irregularity of our coast presented a _____ that called for a more than merely passive navy.

    A. defense   B. barrier   C. provocation
    D. vulnerability   E. dispute

9.____

10. The progressive yearly _____ of the land, caused by the depositing of mud from the river, makes it possible to estimate the age of excavated remains by noting the depth at which they are found below the present level of the valley.

    A. erosion   B. elevation   C. improvement
    D. irrigation   E. displacement

10.____

KEY (CORRECT ANSWERS)

1.	C	6.	D
2.	E	7.	D
3.	D	8.	C
4.	C	9.	D
5.	B	10.	B

TEST 3

DIRECTIONS: Each question in this section consists of a sentence in which one word is missing; a blank line indicates where the word has been removed from the sentence. Beneath each sentence are five words, *one* of which is the missing word. You are to select the letter of the missing word by deciding which one of the five words BEST fits in with the meaning of the sentence. *PRINT THE LETTER OF THE CORRECT ANSWER IN THE SPACE AT THE RIGHT.*

1. The judge exercised commendable _____ dismissing the charge against the prisoner. In spite of the clamor that surrounded the trial, and the heinousness of the offense, the judge could not be swayed to overlook the lack of facts in the case.

   A. avidity
   D. balance
   B. meticulousness
   E. querulousness
   C. clemency

   1.____

2. The pianist played the concerto _____, displaying such facility and skill as has rarely been matched in this old auditorium.

   A. strenuous
   D. casually
   B. spiritedly
   E. deftly
   C. passionately

   2.____

3. The Tanglewood Symphony Orchestra holds its outdoor concerts far from city turmoil in a _____, bucolic setting.

   A. spectacular
   D. chaotic
   B. atavistic
   E. catholic
   C. serene

   3.____

4. Honest satire gives true joy to the thinking man. Thus, the satirist is most _____ when he points out the hypocrisy in human actions.

   A. elated
   D. repressed
   B. humiliated
   E. disdainful
   C. ungainly

   4.____

5. She was a(n) _____ preferred the company of her books to the pleasures of cafe society.

   A. philanthropist
   D. extrovert
   B. stoic
   E. introvert
   C. exhibitionist

   5.____

6. So many people are so convinced that people are driven by _____ motives that they cannot believe that anybody is unselfish!

   A. interior
   D. selfish
   B. ulterior
   E. destructive
   C. unworth

   6.____

7. These _____ results were brought about by a chain of fortuitous events.

   A. unfortunate
   D. haphazard
   B. odd
   E. propitious
   C. harmful

   7.____

8. The bank teller's _____ of the funds was discovered the following month when the auditors examined the books.

   A. embezzlement
   D. assignment
   B. burglary
   E. theft
   C. borrowing

   8.____

9. The monks gathered in the _____ for their evening meal.   9._____

    A. lounge   B. auditorium   C. refectory
    D. rectory   E. solarium

10. Local officials usually have the responsibility in each area of determining when the need   10._____
is sufficiently great to _____ withdrawals from the community water supply.

    A. encourage   B. justify   C. discontinue
    D. advocate   E. forbid

————

KEY (CORRECT ANSWERS)

1.	D	6.	B
2.	E	7.	D
3.	C	8.	A
4.	A	9.	C
5.	E	10.	B

————

TEST 4

DIRECTIONS: Each question in this section consists of a sentence in which one word is missing; a blank line indicates where the word has been removed from the sentence. Beneath each sentence are five words, *one* of which is the missing word. You are to select the letter of the missing word by deciding which one of the five words BEST fits in with the meaning of the sentence. *PRINT THE LETTER OF THE CORRECT ANSWER IN THE SPACE AT THE RIGHT*

1. The life of the mining camps as portrayed by Bret Harte–boisterous, material, brawling–was in direct _____ to the contemporary Eastern world of conventional morals and staid deportment depicted by other men of letters.   1._____

   A. model   B. parallel   C. antithesis
   D. relationship   E. response

2. The agreements were to remain in force for three years and were subject to automatic _____ unless terminated by the parties concerned on one month's notice.   2._____

   A. renewal   B. abrogation   C. amendment
   D. confiscation   E. option

3. In a democracy, people are recognized for what they do rather than for their _____.   3._____

   A. alacrity   B. ability   C. reputation
   D. skill   E. pedigree

4. Although he had often loudly proclaimed his _____ concerning world affairs, he actually read widely and was usually the best informed person in his circle.   4._____

   A. weariness   B. complacency   C. condolence
   D. indifference   E. worry

5. This student holds the _____ record of being the sole failure in his class.   5._____

   A. flagrant   B. unhappy   C. egregious
   D. dubious   E. unusual

6. She became enamored _____ acrobat when she witnessed his act.   6._____

   A. of   B. with   C. for   D. by   E. about

7. This will _____ all previous wills.   7._____

   A. abrogates   B. denies   C. supersedes
   D. prevents   E. continues

8. In the recent terrible Chicago _____, over ninety children were found dead as a result of the fire.   8._____

   A. hurricane   B. destruction   C. panic
   D. holocaust   E. accident

9. I can ascribe no better reason why he shunned society than that he was a _____.   9._____

   A. mentor   B. Centaur   C. aristocrat
   D. misanthrope   E. failure

125

10. One who attempts to learn all the known facts before he comes to a conclusion may most   10.____
    aptly be described as a _____.

    A. realist   B. philosopher   C. cynic
    D. pessimist   E. skeptic

_____

KEY (CORRECT ANSWERS)

1.	C	6.	A
2.	A	7.	C
3.	E	8.	D
4.	D	9.	D
5.	D	10.	E

_____

TEST 5

DIRECTIONS: Each question in this section consists of a sentence in which one word is missing; a blank line indicates where the word has been removed from the sentence. Beneath each sentence are five words, *one* of which is the missing word. You are to select the letter of the missing word by deciding which one of the five words BEST fits in with the meaning of the sentence. *PRINT THE LETTER OF THE CORRECT ANSWER IN THE SPACE AT THE RIGHT.*

1. The prime minister, fleeing from the rebels who had seized the government, sought _____ in the church.

    1._____

    A. revenge   B. mercy   C. relief
    D. salvation   E. sanctuary

2. It does not take us long to conclude that it is foolish to fight the _____, and that it is far wiser to accept it.

    2._____

    A. inevitable   B. inconsequential   C. impossible
    D. choice   E. invasion

3. _____ is usually defined as an excessively high rate of interest.

    3._____

    A. Injustice   B. Perjury   C. Exorbitant
    D. Embezzlement   E. Usury

4. "I ask you, gentlemen of the jury, to find this man guilty since I have _____ the charges brought about him."

    4._____

    A. documented   B. questioned   C. revised
    D. selected   E. confused

5. Although the critic was a close friend of the producer, he told him that he could not _____ his play.

    5._____

    A. condemn   B. prefer   C. congratulate
    D. endorse   E. revile

6. Knowledge of human nature and motivation is an important _____ in all areas of endeavor.

    6._____

    A. object   B. incentive   C. opportunity
    D. asset   E. goal

7. Numbered among the audience were kings, princes, dukes, and even a maharajah, all attempting to _____ another in the glitter of their habiliments and the number of their escorts.

    7._____

    A. supersede   B. outdo   C. guide
    D. vanquish   E. equal

8. There seems to be a widespread feeling that peoples who are located below us in respect to latitude are _____ also in respect to intellect and ability.

    8._____

    A. superior   B. melodramatic   C. inferior
    D. ulterior   E. contemptible

9. This should be considered a(n) _____ rather than the usual occurrence.   9.____

    A. coincidence   B. specialty   C. development
    D. outgrowth   E. mirage

10. Those who were considered states' rights adherents in the early part of our history,   10.____
espoused the diminution of the powers of the national government because they had
always been _____ of these powers.

    A. solicitous   B. advocates   C. apprehensive
    D. mindful   E. respectful

KEY (CORRECT ANSWERS)

1.	E		6.	D
2.	A		7.	B
3.	E		8.	C
4.	A		9.	A
5.	D		10.	C

TEST 6

DIRECTIONS: Each question in this section consists of a sentence in which one word is missing; a blank line indicates where the word has been removed from the sentence. Beneath each sentence are five words, *one* of which is the missing word. You are to select the letter of the missing word by deciding which one of the five words BEST fits in with the meaning of the sentence. *PRINT THE LETTER OF THE CORRECT ANSWER IN THE SPACE AT THE RIGHT.*

1. We can see in retrospect that the high hopes for lasting peace conceived at Versailles in 1919 were _____.

   A. ingenuous   B. transient   C. nostalgic
   D. ingenious   E. specious

   1.____

2. One of the constructive effects of Nazism was the passage by the U.N. of a resolution to combat _____.

   A. armaments   B. nationalism   C. colonialism
   D. genocide   E. geriatrics

   2.____

3. In our prisons, the role of _____ often gains for certain inmates a powerful position among their fellow prisoners.

   A. informer   B. clerk   C. warden   D. trusty   E. turnkey

   3.____

4. It is the _____ liar, experienced in the ways of the world, who finally trips upon some incongruous detail.

   A. consummate   B. incorrigible   C. congenital
   D. lagrant   E. contemptible

   4.____

5. Anyone who is called a misogynist can hardly be expected to look upon women with _____ contemptuous eyes.

   A. more than   B. nothing less than   C. decidedly
   D. other than   E. always

   5.____

6. Demagogues such as Hitler and Mussolini aroused the masses by appealing to their _____ rather than to their intellect.

   A. emotions   B. reason   C. nationalism
   D. conquests   E. duty

   6.____

7. He was in great demand as an entertainer for his _____ abilities: he could sing, dance, tell a joke, or relate a story with equally great skill and facility.

   A. versatile   B. logical   C. culinary
   D. histrionic   E. creative

   7.____

8. The wise politician is aware that, next to knowing when to seize an opportunity, it is also important to know when to _____ an advantage.

   A. develop   B. seek   C. revise
   D. proclaim   E. forego

   8.____

9. Books on psychology inform us that the best way to break a bad habit is to _____ a new habit in its place.   9.____

   A. expel
   D. curtail
   B. substitute
   E. supplant
   C. conceal

10. The author who uses one word where another uses a whole paragraph, should be considered a _____ writer.   10.____

   A. successful
   D. prolix
   B. grandiloquent
   E. succinct
   C. experienced

————

KEY (CORRECT ANSWERS)

1.	A	6.	A
2.	D	7.	A
3.	A	8.	E
4.	A	9.	B
5.	D	10.	E

————

SENTENCE COMPLETION
EXAMINATION SECTION
TEST 1

DIRECTIONS: Each question in this part consists of a sentence in which one word is missing; a blank line indicates where the word has been removed from the sentence. Beneath each sentence are five words, one of which is the missing word. You are to select the number of the missing word by deciding which one of the five words BEST fits in with the meaning of the sentence. *PRINT THE LETTER OF THE CORRECT ANSWER IN THE SPACE AT THE RIGHT.*

1. Although they had little interest in the game they were playing, rather than be _____, they played it through to the end.

    A. inactive   B. inimical   C. busy
    D. complacent   E. vapid

    1.____

2. That he was unworried and at peace with the world could be, perhaps, observed from his _____ brow.

    A. unwrinkled   B. wrinkled   C. furrowed
    D. twisted   E. askew

    2.____

3. Among the hundreds of workers in the assembly plant of the factory, one was _____ because of his skill and speed.

    A. steadfast   B. condemned   C. consistent
    D. outstanding   E. eager

    3.____

4. The story of the invention of many of our best known machines is a consistent one: they are the result of a long series of experiments by many people; thus, the Wright Brothers in 1903 _____ the airplane rather than invented it.

    A. popularized   B. regulated   C. perfected
    D. contrived   E. developed

    4.____

5. As soon as the former political exile returned to his native country, he looked up old supporters, particularly those whom he knew to be _____ and whose help he might need.

    A. potent   B. pusillanimous   C. attentive
    D. free   E. retired

    5.____

6. A recent study of the New Deal shows that no other man than the President could have brought together so many _____ interests and combined them into so effective a political organization.

    A. secret   B. interior   C. predatory
    D. harmonious   E. conflicting

    6.____

7. A study of tides presents an interesting _____ in that, while the forces that set them in motion are universal in application, presumably affecting all parts of our world without distinction, the action of tides in particular areas is completely local in nature.

    A. phenomenon   B. maneuver   C. paradox
    D. quality   E. spontaneity

    7.____

8. Many of the facts that are found in the ancient archives constitute _____ that help shed light upon human activities in the past.

   8._____

   A. facts
   D. sources
   B. reminders
   E. indications
   C. particles

9. It is a regrettable fact that in a caste society which deems manual toil a mark of _____, rarely does the laborer improve his social position or gain political power.

   9._____

   A. inferiority
   D. hardship
   B. consolation
   E. brilliance
   C. fortitude

10. As a generalization, one can correctly say that crises in history are caused by the re-opening of questions which have been safely _____ for long periods of time.

   10._____

   A. debated
   D. settled
   B. joined
   E. unanswered
   C. recondite

KEY (CORRECT ANSWERS)

1. A
2. A
3. D
4. C
5. A

6. E
7. C
8. D
9. A
10. A

TEST 2

DIRECTIONS: Each question in this part consists of a sentence in which one word is missing; a blank line indicates where the word has been removed from the sentence. Beneath each sentence are five words, one of which is the missing word. You are to select the number of the missing word by deciding which one of the five words BEST fits in with the meaning of the sentence. *PRINT THE LETTER OF THE CORRECT ANSWER IN THE SPACE AT THE RIGHT.*

1. We can see in retrospect that the high hopes for lasting peace conceived at Versailles in 1919 were _____.

   A. ingenuous
   D. ingenious
   B. transient
   E. species
   C. nostalgic

   1._____

2. One of the constructive effects of Nazism was the passage by the U.N. of a resolution to combat _____.

   A. armaments
   D. genocide
   B. nationalism
   E. geriatrics
   C. colonialism

   2._____

3. In our prisons, the role of _____ often gains for certain inmates a powerful position among their fellow prisoners.

   A. informer
   D. trusty
   B. clerk
   E. turnkey
   C. warden

   3._____

4. It is the _____ liar, experienced in the ways of the world, who finally trips upon some incongruous detail.

   A. consummate
   D. flagrant
   B. incorrigible
   E. contemptible
   C. congenital

   4._____

5. Anyone who is called a misogynist can hardly be expected to look upon women with _____ contemptuous eyes.

   A. more than
   D. other than
   B. nothing less than
   E. always
   C. decidedly

   5._____

6. Demagogues such as Hitler and Mussolini aroused the masses by appealing to their _____ rather than to their intellect.

   A. emotions
   D. conquests
   B. reason
   E. duty
   C. nationalism

   6._____

7. He was in great demand as an entertainer for his _____ abilities: he could sing, dance, tell a joke, or relate a story with equally great skill and facility.

   A. versatile
   D. histrionic
   B. logical
   E. creative
   C. culinary

   7._____

8. The wise politician is aware that, next to knowing when to seize an opportunity, it is also important to know when to _____ an advantage.

   A. develop   B. seek   C. revise   D. proclaim   E. forego

   8._____

9. Books on psychology inform us that the best way to break a bad habit is to _____ a new habit in its place.   9._____

    A. expel   B. substitute   C. conceal
    D. curtail   E. supplant

10. The author who uses one word where another uses a whole paragraph, should be considered a _____ writer.   10._____

    A. successful   B. grandiloquent   C. succinct
    D. prolix   E. experienced

KEYS (CORRECT ANSWERS)

1. A
2. D
3. A
4. A
5. D

6. A
7. A
8. E
9. B
10. C

TEST 3

DIRECTIONS: Each question in this part consists of a sentence in which one word is missing; a blank line indicates where the word has been removed from the sentence. Beneath each sentence are five words, one of which is the missing word. You are to select the number of the missing word by deciding which one of the five words BEST fits in with the meaning of the sentence. *PRINT THE LETTER OF THE CORRECT ANSWER IN THE SPACE AT THE RIGHT.*

1. The prime minister, fleeing from the rebels who had seized the government, sought _____ in the church.

   A. revenge
   D. salvation
   B. mercy
   E. sanctuary
   C. relief

   1._____

2. It does not take us long to conclude that it is foolish to fight the _____, and that it is far wiser to accept it.

   A. inevitable
   D. choice
   B. inconsequential
   E. invasion
   C. impossible

   2._____

3. _____ is usually defined as an excessively high rate of interest.

   A. Injustice
   D. Embezzlement
   B. Perjury
   E. Usury
   C. Exorbitant

   3._____

4. "I ask you, gentlemen of the jury, to find this man guilty since I have _____ the charges brought against him."

   A. documented
   D. selected
   B. questioned
   E. confused
   C. revised

   4._____

5. Although the critic was a close friend of the producer, he told him that he could not _____ his play.

   A. condemn
   D. endorse
   B. prefer
   E. revile
   C. congratulate

   5._____

6. Knowledge of human nature and motivation is an important _____ in all areas of endeavor.

   A. object
   D. asset
   B. incentive
   E. goal
   C. opportunity

   6._____

7. Numbered among the audience were kings, princes, dukes, and even a maharajah, all attempting to _____ one another in the glitter of their habiliments and the number of their escorts.

   A. supersede
   D. vanquish
   B. outdo
   E. equal
   C. guide

   7._____

8. There seems to be a widespread feeling that peoples who are located below us in respect to latitude are _____ also in respect to intellect and ability.

   A. superior
   D. ulterior
   B. melodramatic
   E. contemptible
   C. inferior

   8._____

9. This should be considered a(n) _____ rather than the usual occurrence.   9.____

    A. coincidence   B. specialty   C. development
    D. outgrowth   E. mirage

10. Those who were considered states' rights aherents in the early part of our history   10.____
espoused the diminution of the powers of the national government because they had
always been _____ of these powers.

    A. solicitous   B. advocates   C. apprehensive
    D. mindful   E. respectful

KEYS (CORRECT ANSWERS)

1. E
2. A
3. E
4. A
5. D

6. D
7. B
8. C
9. A
10. C

TEST 4

DIRECTIONS: Each question in this part consists of a sentence in which one word is missing; a blank line indicates where the word has been removed from the sentence. Beneath each sentence are five words, one of which is the missing word. You are to select the number of the missing word by deciding which one of the five words BEST fits in with the meaning of the sentence. *PRINT THE LETTER OF THE CORRECT ANSWER IN THE SPACE AT THE RIGHT.*

1. The life of the mining camps as portrayed by Bret Harte - boisterous, material, brawling - was in direct _____ to the contemporary Eastern world of conventional morals and staid deportment depicted by other men of letters.
   A. model
   B. parallel
   C. antithesis
   D. relationship
   E. response

   1.____

2. The agreements were to remain in force for three years and were subject to automatic _____ unless terminated by the parties concerned on one month's notice.
   A. renewal
   B. abrogation
   C. amendment
   D. confiscation
   E. option

   2.____

3. In a democracy, people are recognized for what they do rather than for their _____.
   A. alacrity
   B. ability
   C. reputation
   D. skill
   E. pedigree

   3.____

4. Although he had often loudly proclaimed his _____ concerning world affairs, he actually read widely and was usually the best informed person in his circle.
   A. weariness
   B. complacency
   C. condolence
   D. indifference
   E. worry

   4.____

5. This student holds the _____ record of being the sole failure in his class.
   A. flagrant
   B. unhappy
   C. egregious
   D. dubious
   E. unusual

   5.____

6. She became enamored _____ the acrobat when she witnessed his act.
   A. of   B. with   C. for   D. by   E. about

   6.____

7. This will _____ all previous wills.
   A. abrogates
   B. denies
   C. supersedes
   D. prevents
   E. continues

   7.____

8. In the recent terrible Chicago _____, over ninety children were found dead as a result of the fire.
   A. hurricane
   B. destruction
   C. panic
   D. holocaust
   E. accident

   8.____

9. I can ascribe no better reason why he shunned society than that he was a _____.
   A. mentor
   B. Centaur
   C. aristocrat
   D. misanthrope
   E. failure

   9.____

10. One who attempts to learn all the known facts before he comes to a conclusion may most 10.____
    aptly be described as a

    A. realist   B. philosopher   C. cynic
    D. pessimist   E. skeptic

KEY (CORRECT ANSWERS)

    1. C
    2. A
    3. E
    4. D
    5. D

    6. A
    7. C
    8. D
    9. D
  10. E

TEST 5

DIRECTIONS: Each question in this part consists of a sentence in which one word is missing; a blank line indicates where the word has been removed from the sentence. Beneath each sentence are five words, one of which is the missing word. You are to select the number of the missing word by deciding which one of the five words BEST fits in with the meaning of the sentence. *PRINT THE LETTER OF THE CORRECT ANSWER IN THE SPACE AT THE RIGHT.*

1. The judge exercised commendable _____ in dismissing the charge against the prisoner. In spite of the clamor that surrounded the trial, and the heinousness of the offense, the judge could not be swayed to overlook the lack of facts in the case.

    A. avidity   B. meticulousness   C. clemency
    D. balance   E. querulousness

    1.____

2. The pianist played the concerto _____, displaying such facility and skill as has rarely been matched in this old auditorium.

    A. strenuously   B. deftly   C. passionately
    D. casually   E. spiritedly

    2.____

3. The Tanglewood Symphony Orchestra holds its outdoor concerts far from city turmoil in a _____, bucolic setting.

    A. spectacular   B. atavistic   C. serene
    D. chaotic   E. catholic

    3.____

4. Honest satire gives true joy to the thinking man. Thus, the satirist is most _____ when he points out the hypocrisy in human actions.

    A. elated   B. humiliated   C. ungainly
    D. repressed   E. disdainful

    4.____

5. She was a(n) _____ who preferred the company of her books to the pleasures of cafe society.

    A. philanthropist   B. stoic   C. exhibitionist
    D. extrovert   E. introvert

    5.____

6. So many people are so convinced that people are driven by _____ motives that they cannot believe that anybody is unselfish!

    A. interior   B. ulterior   C. unworthy
    D. selfish   E. destructive

    6.____

7. These _____ results were brought about by a chain of fortuitous events.

    A. unfortunate   B. odd   C. harmful
    D. haphazard   E. propitious

    7.____

8. The bank teller's _____ of the funds was discovered the following month when the auditors examined the books.

    A. embezzlement   B. burglary   C. borrowing
    D. assignment   E. theft

    8.____

9. The monks gathered in the _____ for their evening meal.   9._____

    A. lounge   B. auditorium   C. refectory
    D. rectory   E. solarium

10. Local officials usually have the responsibility in each area of determining when the need   10._____
    is sufficiently great to _____ withdrawals from the community water supply.

    A. encourage   B. justify   C. discontinue
    D. advocate   E. forbid

KEY (CORRECT ANSWERS)

  1. D
  2. B
  3. C
  4. A
  5. E

  6. B
  7. D
  8. A
  9. C
10. B

WRITTEN ENGLISH EXPRESSION

EXAMINATION SECTION
TEST 1

DIRECTIONS: In each of the sentences below, four portions are underlined and lettered. Read each sentence and decide whether any of the UNDERLINED parts contains an error in spelling, punctuation, or capitalization, or employs grammatical usage which would be inappropriate for carefully written English. If so, note the letter printed under the unacceptable form and indicate this choice in the space at the right. If all four of the underlined portions are acceptable as they stand, select the answer E.
(No sentence contains more than ONE unacceptable form.)

1. The revised procedure was quite different than the one which was employed
                  A   B   C   D
up to that time. No error
                  E

1. _____

2. Blinded by the storm that surrounded him, his plane kept going in circles.
   A   B   C   D
No error
   E

2. _____

3. They should give the book to whoever they think deserves it . No error
          A   B   C   D   E

3. _____

4. The government will not consent to your firm sending that package as
          A   B   C
second class matter. No error
     D   E

4. _____

5. She would have avoided all the trouble that followed if she would have waited
        A   B   C
ten minutes longer . No error
            D   E

5. _____

6. His poetry, when it was carefully examined, showed characteristics not unlike
   A   B   C
Wordsworth . No error
     D   E

6. _____

7. <u>In my opinion,</u> based upon long years of research, <u>I think</u> the plan offered by my
     A   B

    opponent is <u>unsound,</u> because it is not <u>founded</u> on true facts. <u>No error</u>
                C   D   E

7._____

8. The soldiers of <u>Washington's</u> army at Valley Forge <u>were</u> men ragged in
                A   B

    <u>appearance</u> but <u>who were</u> noble in character. <u>No error</u>
       C   D   E

8._____

9. Rabbits <u>have a distrust</u> of man <u>due to</u> the fact <u>that</u> they are <u>so often</u> shot.
               A   B   C   D

    <u>No error</u>
      E

9._____

10. <u>This</u> is the man <u>who</u> I believe <u>is</u> best <u>qualified</u> for the position. <u>No error</u>
     A   B   C   D   E

10._____

11. Her voice was <u>not only</u> <u>good,</u> but <u>she</u> also very clearly <u>enunciated.</u>
                 A   B   C   D

    <u>No error</u>
      E

11._____

12. <u>Today he</u> is wearing a <u>different</u> suit <u>than</u> the <u>one</u> he wore yesterday. <u>No error</u>
      A   B   C   D   E

12._____

13. Our work <u>is</u> to improve the club; if anybody <u>must</u> resign, let it <u>not</u> be you or
          A   B   C

    <u>I</u> . <u>No error</u>
    D   E

13._____

14. There was so much talking in back of me as I could not enjoy the music.   14._____
                                    A   B   C   D

    No error
    E

15. Being that he is that kind of boy , he cannot be blamed for the mistake. No error   15._____
         A   B   C   D   E

16.   The king, having read the speech, he and the queen departed . No error   16._____
              A   B   C   D   E

17. I am   so tired I can't scarcely stand. No error   17._____
       A   B   C   D   E

18. We are mailing bills to our customers in Canada , and, being eager to clear our   18._____
              A   B   C

    books before the new season opens, it is to be hoped they will send their remittances
                                                  D

    promptly. No error
               E

19. I   reluctantly   acquiesced   to the proposal . No error   19._____
     A   B   C   D   E

20. It   had lain   out in the rain all night . No error   20._____
     A   B   C   D   E

21. If he would have gone there, he would have seen a marvelous sight. No error   21._____
           A   B   C   D   E

22. The climate of Asia Minor is somewhat like Utah . No error   22._____
                 A   B   C   D   E

143

23. If _everybody_ _did_ _unto others_ as they _would wish_ others to do unto them,
     A   B   C   D

this world would be a paradise. _No error_
                             E

23._____

24. _This_ was the jockey _whom_ I saw _was_ most likely _to win_ the race. _No error_
   A   B   C   D   E

24._____

25. The _only_ food the general _demanded_ _was_ _potatoes_ . _No error_
       A   B   C   D   E

25._____

KEY (CORRECT ANSWERS)

1.	C		11.	C
2.	A		12.	C
3.	B		13.	D
4.	B		14.	B
5.	C		15.	A
6.	D		16.	A
7.	B		17.	C
8.	D		18.	C
9.	B		19.	E
10.	E		20.	E

21. A
22. D
23. D
24. B
25. E

TEST 2

DIRECTIONS: In each of the sentences below, four portions are underlined and lettered. Read each sentence and decide whether any of the UNDERLINED parts contains an error in spelling, punctuation, or capitalization, or employs grammatical usage which would be inappropriate for carefully written English. If so, note the letter printed under the unacceptable form and indicate this choice in the space at the right. If all four of the underlined portions are acceptable as they stand, select the answer E. (No sentence contains more than ONE unacceptable form.)

1. A party <u>like</u> <u>that</u> <u>only</u> <u>comes</u> once a year. <u>No error</u>
       A   B   C   D   E

1._____

2. <u>Our's</u> <u>is</u> <u>a</u> <u>swift moving</u> age. <u>No error</u>
   A   B C   D   E

2._____

3. The <u>healthy</u> climate soon <u>restored</u> him <u>to</u> his <u>accustomed</u> vigor.
      A   B   C   D

   <u>No error</u>
     E

3._____

4. <u>They</u> needed six typists and hoped that <u>only</u> that <u>many</u> <u>would</u> apply for the posi-
   A   B   C   D

tion. <u>No error</u>
      E

4._____

5. He <u>interviewed</u> people <u>whom</u> he thought had <u>something</u> <u>to impart.</u>
       A   B   C   D

   <u>No error</u>
     E

5._____

6. <u>Neither</u> of his three sisters <u>is</u> older <u>than</u> <u>he.</u> <u>No error</u>
    A   B   C   D   E

6._____

7. Since he is <u>that</u> <u>kind</u> of <u>a</u> boy, he cannot be expected to cooperate with us.
   A   B   C   D

   <u>No error</u>
     E

7._____

8. <u>When passing</u> <u>through</u> the tunnel, the air pressure <u>affected</u> <u>our</u> ears. <u>No error</u>
      A   B   C   D   E

8. ____

9. <u>The story having</u> a sad ending, <u>it</u> never <u>achieved</u> popularity <u>among</u> the
         A   B   C   D

students. <u>No error</u>
       E

9. ____

10. <u>Since</u> we are both hungry, <u>shall</u> we go <u>somewhere</u> for lunch <u>?</u> <u>No error</u>
     A   B   C   D   E

10. ____

11. <u>Will</u> you please <u>bring</u> this book <u>down to</u> the library and give it to my friend <u>,</u> who
    A   B   C   D
is waiting for it? <u>No error</u>
                E

11. ____

12. You <u>may</u> <u>have</u> the book; I <u>am</u> finished <u>with</u> it. <u>No error</u>
       A   B   C   D   E

12. ____

13. I <u>don't know</u> <u>if</u> I <u>should</u> mention <u>it</u> to her or not. <u>No error</u>
      A   B   C   D   E

13. ____

14. Philosophy is not <u>a subject</u> <u>which</u> <u>has to do</u> with philosophers and mathemat-
                          A   B   C

ics <u>only.</u> <u>No error</u>
    D   E

14. ____

15. The thoughts of the scholar <u>in his library</u> are little different <u>than</u> the old woman who
                             A   B

first said, <u>"It's</u> no use crying over spilt milk <u>."</u> <u>No error</u>
        C   D   E

15. ____

16. A complete <u>system</u> of philosophical ideas <u>are</u> <u>implied</u> in many simple <u>utterances.</u>
            A   B   C   D
<u>No error</u>
  E

16. ____

17. Even <u>if</u> one has never put <u>them</u> into words, <u>his</u> ideas <u>compose</u> a kind of a
        A   B   C   D

philosophy. <u>No error</u>
           E

17.____

18. Perhaps it <u>is</u> <u>well enough</u> that most <u>people</u> do not attempt this <u>formulation.</u>
         A   B   C   D

<u>No error</u>
  E

18.____

19. <u>Leading their</u> ordered lives, this <u>confused</u> <u>body</u> of ideas and feelings <u>is</u>
      A   B   C   D

sufficient. <u>No error</u>
          E

19.____

20. Why <u>should</u> we <u>insist upon</u> <u>them</u> <u>formulating</u> it? <u>No error</u>
      A   B   C   D   E

20.____

21. <u>Since</u> it includes <u>something</u> of the wisdom of the ages, it is <u>adequate</u> for the
    A   B   C

<u>purposes</u> of ordinary life. <u>No error</u>
  D   E

21.____

22. Therefore, I <u>have sought</u> to make a pattern <u>of mine,</u> <u>and so</u> there were, early
             A   B   C

moments of <u>my trying</u> to find out what were the elements with which I had to deal;
            D

<u>No error</u>
  E

22.____

23. I <u>wanted</u> <u>to get</u> <u>what</u> knowledge I <u>could</u> about the general structure of the
   A   B   C   D

universe. <u>No error</u>
        E

23.____

24. I wanted to <u>know</u> <u>if</u> life <u>per se</u> had any meaning or <u>whether</u> I must strive to
            A   B   C   D

give it one. <u>No error</u>
            E

24.____

25. <u>So,</u> in a <u>desultory</u> way, I <u>began</u> <u>to read.</u> <u>No error</u>
   A   B   C   D   E

25.____

KEY (CORRECT ANSWERS)

1.	C		11.	B
2.	A		12.	C
3.	A		13.	B
4.	C		14.	D
5.	B		15.	B
6.	A		16.	B
7.	D		17.	A
8.	A		18.	C
9.	A		19.	A
10.	E		20.	C

21.	E
22.	C
23.	C
24.	B
25.	E

English Expression

EXAMINATION SECTION
TEST

DIRECTIONS: Each question or incomplete statement is followed by several suggested answers or completions. Select the one that *BEST* answers the question or completes the statement. *PRINT THE LETTER OF THE CORRECT ANSWER IN THE SPACE AT THE RIGHT.*

Questions 1-9.

DIRECTIONS: The following sentences contain problems in grammar, usage diction (choice of words), and idiom.
Some sentences are correct.
No sentence contains more than one error.
You will find that the error, if there is one, is underlined and lettered. Assume that all other elements of the sentence are correct and cannot be changed. In choosing answers, follow the requirements of standard written English. If there is an error, select the *one underlined part* that must be changed in order to make the sentence correct. If there is no error, mark answer space E.

1. <u>In planning</u> your future, as honest with your self as possible, make careful decisions
        A
    about the best course a particular purpose, and, above all, have the courage deci-
    sions. <u>No error</u>.
            E

    1.____

2. <u>Even though</u> history does not actually repeat itself, knowledge history current problems
        A
    a familiar, <u>less</u> formidable look. <u>No Error</u>.
               D   E

    2.____

3. The Curies <u>had almost exhausted</u> their resources, and would find the
                        A
    <u>solvent to their financial problems</u> <u>No error</u>.
                    D   E

    3.____

4. <u>If the rumors are</u> correct, Deane <u>will not be convicted</u>, for each of the officers on the
            A   B
    court realizes that Colson and Holdman may be that testimony is not completely trust-
    worthy. <u>No error</u>.
                E

    4.____

149

5. The citizens of Washington, prefer to commute by automobile, even though motor vehi-   5.____
cles contribute contaminants to the air <u>as do all other</u> sources <u>combined.</u> . <u>No error.</u>
                                               C   D   E

6. <u>By the time Robert Vasco completes</u>his testimony, every major executive of our com-   6.____
                                A

  pany but Ray Ashurst complicity in the stock swindle.<u>No error.</u>
                                              E

7. <u>Within six months</u> he store was operating shelves goods were selling rapidly, and the   7.____
             A

  cash register <u>was ringing constantly.</u> <u>No error.</u>
                  D   E

8. Shakespeare's comedies have an advantage were to entertain and argue for a   8.____
  cause. <u>No error.</u>
         E

9. Any true insomniac <u>is well aware of</u> the futility of <u>such measures as</u> drinking hot milk,   9.____
                        A   B

  <u>regular hours, deep breathing</u>, counting sheep, and <u>concentrating on</u> black velvet
                 C   D

  <u>No error.</u>
     E

Questions 10-15.

DIRECTIONS: In each of the following sentences, some part of the sentence or the entire
sentence is underlined. Beneath each sentence you will find five ways of
phrasing the underlined part. The first of these repeats the original; the other
four are different. If you think the original is better than any of the alternatives,
choose, answer A; otherwise choose one of the others. Select the best version
and print the letter of the correct answer in the space at the right. This is a test
of correctness and effectiveness of expression. In choosing answers, follow
the requirements of standard written English; that is, pay attention to grammar,
choice of words, sentence con-struction, and punctuation. Choose the answer
that produces the most effective sentence - clear and exact, without awkwardness or ambiguity. Do not make a choice that changes the meaning of the original sentence.

10. The tribe of warriors believed that boys and girls should be <u>reared separate, and, as</u>   10.____
<u>soon as he was weaned, the boys were taken from their mothers.</u>

    A.   reared separate, and, as soon as he was weaned, the boys were taken from their
          mothers

    B.   reared separate, and, as soon as he was weaned, a boy was taken from his mother

    C.   reared separately, and, as soon as he was weaned, the boys were taken from their mothers

    D.   reared separately, and, as soon as a boy was weaned, they were taken from their mothers

    E.   reared separately, and, as soon as a boy was weaned, he was taken from his mother

11.   <u>Despite Vesta being only the third largest, it is by far the brightest of the known asteroids.</u>   11._____

    A.   Despite Vesta being only the third largest, it is by far the brightest of the known asteroids.

    B.   Vesta, though only the third largest asteroid, is by far the brightest of the known ones.

    C.   Being only the third largest, yet Vesta is by far the brightest of the known asteroids.

    D.   Vesta, though only the third largest of the known asteroids, is by far the brightest.

    E.   Vesta is only the third largest of the asteroids, it being, however, the brightest one.

12.   As a result of the discovery of the Dead Sea Scrolls, our understanding of the roots of   12._____ Christianity <u>has had to be revised considerably.</u>

    A.   has had to be revised considerably

    B.   have had to be revised considerably

    C.   has had to undergo revision to a considerable degree

    D.   have had to be subjected to considerable revision

    E.   has had to be revised in a considerable way

13.   Because <u>it is imminently suitable to</u> dry climates, adobe has been a traditional building   13._____ material throughout the southwestern states.

    A.   it is imminently suitable to

    B.   it is eminently suitable for

    C.   it is eminently suitable when in

    D.   of its eminent suitability with

    E.   of being imminently suitable in

14.   <u>Martell is more concerned with demonstrating that racial prejudice exists than preventing it from doing harm, which explains</u> why his work is not always highly regarded.   14._____

    A.   Martell is more concerned with demonstrating that racial prejudice exists than preventing it from doing harm, which explains

    B.   Martell is more concerned with demonstrating that racial prejudice exists than with preventing it from doing harm, and this explains

    C.   Martell is more concerned with demonstrating that racial prejudice exists than with preventing it from doing harm, an explanation of

    D.   Martell's greater concern for demonstrating that racial prejudice exists than preventing it from doing harm – this explains

    E.   Martell's greater concern for demonstrating that racial prejudice exists than for preventing it from doing harm explains

15.   <u>Throughout this history of the American West there runs a steady commentary on the deception and mistreatment of the Indians.</u>   15._____

A. Throughout this history of the American West there runs a steady commentary on the deception and mistreatment of the Indians.
B. There is a steady commentary provided on the deception and mistreatment of the Indians and it runs throughout this history of the American West.
C. The deception and mistreatment of the Indians provide a steady comment that runs throughout this history of the American West.
D. Comment on the deception and mistreatment of the Indians is steadily provided and runs throughout this history of the American West.
E. Running throughout this history of the American West is a steady commentary that is provided on the deception and mistreatment of the Indians.

Questions 16-20.

DIRECTIONS: In each of the following questions you are given a complete sentence to be rephrased according to the directions which follow it. You should rephrase the sentence mentally to save time, although you may make notes in your test book if you wish. Below each sentence and its directions are listed words or phrases that may occur in your revised sentence. When you have thought out a good sentence, look in the choices A through E for the word or entire phrase that is included in your revised sentence, and print the letter of the correct answer in the space at the right. The word or phrase you choose should be the most accurate and most nearly complete of all the choices given, and should be part of a sentence that meets the requirements of standard written English. Of course, a number of different sentences can be obtained if the sentence is revised according to directions, and not all of these possibilities can be included in only five choices. If you should find that you have thought of a sentence that contains none of the words or phrases listed in the choices, you should attempt to rephrase the sentence again so that it includes a word or phrase that is listed. Although the directions may at times require you to change the relationship between parts of the sentence or to make slight changes in meaning in other ways, make only those changes that the directions require; that is, keep the meaning the same, or as nearly the same as the directions permit. If you think that more than one good sentence can be made according to the directions, select the sentence that is most exact, effective, and natural in phrasing and construction.

EXAMPLES:

I. Sentence: Coming to the city as a young man, he found a job as a newspaper reporter.
Directions: Substitute He came for Coming.
A. and so he found
B. and found
C. and there he had found
D. and then finding
E. and had found

Your rephrased sentence will probably read: "He came to the city as a young man and found a job as a newspaper reporter." This sentence contains the correct answer: B. and found. A sentence which used one of the alternate phrases would change the meaning or intention of the original sentence, would be a poorly written sentence, or would be less effective than another possible revision.

II.   Sentence: Owing to her wealth, Sarah had many suitors.
      Directions: Begin with Many men courted.
      A.   so   B.   while   C.   although
      D.   because   E.   and

Your rephrased sentence will probably read: "Many men courted Sarah because she was wealthy." This new sentence contains only choice D, which is the correct answer. None of the other choices will fit into an effective, correct sentence that retains the original meaning.

16.   The archaeologists could only mark out the burial site, for then winter came.   16.____
      Begin with Winter came before.

      A.   could do nothing more   B.   could not do anything
      C.   could only do   D.   could do something
      E.   could do anything more

17.   The white reader often receives some insight into the reasons why black men are angry   17.____
      from descriptions by a black writer of the injustice they encounter in a white society.
      Begin with A black writer often gives.

      A.   when describing   B.   by describing
      C.   he has described   D.   in the descriptions
      E.   because of describing

18.   The agreement between the university officials and the dissident students provides for   18.____
      student representation on every university committee and on the board of trustees. Sub-
      stitute provides that for provides for.

      A.   be   B.   are   C.   would have   D.   would be   E.   is to be

19.   English Romanticism had its roots in German idealist philosophy, first described in Eng-   19.____
      land by Samuel Coleridge.
      Begin with Samuel Coleridge was the first in.

      A.   in which English   B.   and from it English
      C.   where English   D.   the source of English
      E.   the birth of English

20.   Four months have passed since his dismissal, during which time Alan has looked for   20.____
      work daily.
      Begin with Each day.

      A.   will have passed   B.   that have passed
      C.   that passed   D.   were to pass
      E.   had passed

153

KEY (CORRECT ANSWERS)

1.	B		11.	D
2.	E		12.	A
3.	D		13.	B
4.	C		14.	E
5.	A		15.	A
6.	B		16.	E
7.	B		17.	B
8.	A		18.	A
9.	C		19.	D
10.	E		20.	B

English Expression
CHOICE OF EXPRESSION
COMMENTARY

One special form of the English Expression multiple-choice question in current use requires the candidate to select from among five (5) versions of a particular part of a sentence (or of an entire sentence), the one version that expresses the idea of the sentence most clearly, effectively, and accurately. Thus, the candidate is required not only to recognize errors, but also to choose the best way of phrasing a particular part of the sentence.

This is a test of choice of expression, which assays the candidate's ability to express himself correctly and effectively, including his sensitivity to the subleties and nuances of the language.

SAMPLE QUESTIONS

DIRECTIONS: In each of the following sentences some part of the sentence or the entire sentence is underlined. The underlined part presents a problem in the appropriate use of language. Beneath each sentence you will find five ways of writing the underlined part. The first of these indicates no change (that is, it repeats the original), but the other four are all different. If you think the original sentence is better than any of the suggested changes, you should choose answer A; otherwise you should mark one of the other choices. Select the best answer and blacken the corresponding space on the answer sheet.

This is a test of correctness and effectiveness of expression. In choosing answers, follow the requirements of standard written English; that is, pay attention to acceptable usage in grammar, diction (choice of words), sentence construction, and punctuation. Choose the answer that produces the most effective sentence - clear and exact, without awkwardness or ambiguity. Do not make a choice that changes the meaning of the original sentence.

SAMPLE QUESTION 1
Although these states now trade actively with the West, and although they are willing to exchange technological information, their arts and thoughts and social structure <u>remains substantially similar to what it has always been</u>.
    A.   remains substantially similar to what it has always been
    B.   remain substantially unchanged
    C.   remains substantially unchanged
    D.   remain substantially similar to what they have always been
    E.   remain substantially without being changed

The purpose of questions of this type is to determine the candidate's ability to select the clearest and most effective means of expressing what the statement attempts to say. In this example, the phrasing in the statement, which is repeated in A, presents a problem of agreement between a subject and its verb (their arts and thought and social structure and remains), a problem of agreement between a pronoun and its antecedent (their arts and thought and social structure and it), and a problem of precise and concise phrasing (remains substantially similar to what it has always been for remains substantially unchanged). Each of the four remaining choices in some way corrects one or more of the faults in the sentence, but only one deals with all three problems satisfactorily. Although C presents a more careful and concise wording of the phrasing of the statement and, in the process, eliminates the problem of agreement between pronoun and antecedent, it fails to correct the problem of agreement between the subject and its verb. In D, the subject agrees with its verb and the pronoun agrees with its antecedent, but the phrasing is not so accurate as it should be. The same difficulty persists in E. Only in B are all the problems presented corrected satisfactorily. The question is not difficult.

SAMPLE QUESTION 2

Her latest novel is the largest in scope, the most accomplished in technique, and <u>it is more significant in theme than anything</u> she has written.
 A. it is more significant in theme than anything
 B. it is most significant in theme of anything
 C. more significant in theme than anything
 D. the most significant in theme than anything
 E. the most significant in theme of anything

This question is of greater difficulty than the preceding one.

The problem posed in the sentence and repeated in A, is essentially one of parallelism: Does the underlined portion of the sentence follow the pattern established by the first two elements of the series <u>(the largest</u> ... <u>the most accomplished)?</u> It does not, for it introduces a pronoun and verb <u>(it is)</u> that the second term of the series indicates should be omitted and a degree of comparison <u>(more significant)</u> that is not in keeping with the superlatives used earlier in the sentence. B uses the superlative degree of <u>significant</u> but retains the unnecessary <u>it is;</u> C removes the <u>it is.</u> but retains the faulty comparative form of the adjective. D corrects both errors in parallelism, but introduces an error in idiom <u>(the most</u> ...<u>than)</u>. Only E corrects all the problems without introducing another fault.

SAMPLE QUESTION 3

Desiring to insure the continuity of their knowledge, <u>magical lore is transmitted by the chiefs</u> to their descendants.
 A. magical lore is transmitted by the chiefs
 B. transmission of magical lore is made by the chiefs
 C. the chiefs' magical lore is transmitted
 D. the chiefs transmit magical lore
 E. the chiefs make transmission of magical lore
The CORRECT answer is D.

SAMPLE QUESTION 4

<u>As Malcolm walks quickly and confident</u> into the purser's office, the rest of the crew wondered whether he would be charged with the theft.
 A. As Malcolm walks quickly and confident
 B. As Malcolm was walking quick and confident
 C. As Malcolm walked quickly and confident
 D. As Malcolm walked quickly and confidently
 E. As Malcolm walks quickly and confidently
The CORRECT answer is D.

SAMPLE QUESTION 5

The chairman, <u>granted the power to assign any duties to whoever he </u>wished,was still unable to prevent bickering.

    A.   granted the power to assign any duties to whoever he wished
    B.   granting the power to assign any duties to whoever he wished
    C.   being granted the power to assign any duties to whoever he wished
    D.   having been granted the power to assign any duties to whosoever he wished
    E.   granted the power to assign any duties to whomever he wished

The CORRECT answer is E.

SAMPLE QUESTION 6

Certainly, well-seasoned products are more expensive, <u>but those kinds prove cheaper</u> in the end.

    A.   but those kinds prove cheaper
    B.   but these kinds prove cheaper
    C.   but that kind proves cheaper
    D.   but those kind prove cheaper
    E.   but this kind proves cheaper

The CORRECT answer is A.

SAMPLE QUESTION 7

"We shall not," he shouted, "whatever the <u>difficulties." "lose faith in the success of our </u>plan!"

    A.   difficulties," "lose faith in the success of our plan!"
    B.   difficulties, "lose faith in the success of our plan"!
    C.   "difficulties, lose faith in the success of our plan!"
    D.   difficulties, lose faith in the success of our plan"!
    E.   difficulties, lose faith in the success of our plan!"

The CORRECT answer is E.

SAMPLE QUESTION 8

<u>Climbing up the tree,</u> the lush foliage obscured the chattering monkeys.

    A.   Climbing up the tree
    B.   Having climbed up the tree
    C.   Clambering up the tree
    D.   After we had climbed up the tree
    E.   As we climbed up the tree

The CORRECT answer is E.

EXAMINATION SECTION
TEST 1

DIRECTIONS: See DIRECTIONS for Sample Questions on page 1. *PRINT THE LETTER OF THE CORRECT ANSWER IN THE SPACE AT THE RIGHT.*

1. At the opening of the story, Charles Gilbert <u>has just come</u> to make his home with his two unmarried aunts.   1.____

    A. No change   B. hadn't hardly come   C. has just came
    D. had just come   E. has hardly came

2. The sisters, who are no longer young, <u>are use to living</u> quiet lives.   2.____

    A. No change   B. are used to live
    C. are use'd to living   D. are used to living
    E. are use to live

3. They <u>willingly except</u> the child.   3.____

    A. No change   B. willingly eccepted
    C. willingly accepted   D. willingly acepted
    E. willingly accept

4. As the months pass, Charles' presence <u>affects many changes</u> in their household.   4.____

    A. No change   B. affect many changes
    C. effects many changes   D. effect many changes
    E. affected many changes

5. These changes <u>is not all together</u> to their liking.   5.____

    A. No change   B. is not altogether
    C. are not all together   D. are not altogether
    E. is not alltogether

6. In fact, they have some difficulty in adapting <u>theirselves</u> to these changes.   6.____

    A. No change   B. in adopting theirselves
    C. in adopting themselves   D. in adapting theirselves
    E. in adapting themselves

7. That is the man <u>whom I believe</u> was the driver of the car.   7.____

    A. No change   B. who I believed   C. whom I believed
    D. who to believe   E. who I believe

8. John's climb to fame was more rapid <u>than his brother's</u>.   8.____

    A. No change   B. than his brother
    C. than that of his brother's   D. than for his brother
    E. than the brother

9. We knew that he <u>had formerly swam</u> on an Olympic team.   9.____

    A. No change   B. has formerly swum
    C. did formerly swum   D. had formerly swum
    E. has formerly swam

10. Not one of us loyal supporters <u>ever get a pass</u> to a game

    10.____

    A. No change   B. ever did got a pass
    C. ever has get a pass   D. ever had get a pass
    E. ever gets a pass

11. He <u>was complemented</u> on having done a fine job.

    11.____

    A. No change   B. was compliminted
    C. was compleminted   D. was complimented
    E. did get complimented

12. This play is different from the one we <u>had seen</u> last night.

    12.____

    A. No change   B. have seen   C. had saw
    D. have saw   E. saw

13. A row of trees <u>was planted</u> in front of the house.

    13.____

    A. No change   B. was to be planted   C. were planted
    D. were to be planted   E. are planted

14. The house <u>looked its age</u> in spite of our attempts to beautify it.

    14.____

    A. No change   B. looks its age   C. looked its' age
    D. looked it's age   E. looked it age

15. I do not know <u>what to council</u> in this case.

    15.____

    A. No change   B. where to council
    C. when to councel   D. what to counsel
    E. what to counsil

16. She is more capable <u>than any other girl</u> in the office.

    16.____

    A. No change   B. than any girl
    C. than any other girls   D. than other girl
    E. than other girls

17. At the picnic the young children <u>behaved very good</u>.

    17.____

    A. No change   B. behave very good
    C. behaved better   D. behave very well
    E. behaved very well

18. I resolved <u>to go irregardless of</u> the consequences.

    18.____

    A. No change   B. to depart irregardless of
    C. to go regarding of   D. to go regardingly of
    E. to go regardless of

19. The new movie has a number of actors <u>which have been famous</u> on Broadway.

    19.____

    A. No change   B. which had been famous
    C. who had been famous   D. that are famous
    E. who have been famous

20. I am certain that these books <u>are not our's</u>.   20._____

    A. No change   B. have not been ours'
    C. have not been our's   D. are not ours
    E. are not ours'

21. <u>Each of your papers is filed</u> for future reference.   21._____

    A. No change
    B. Each of your papers are filed
    C. Each of your papers have been filed
    D. Each of your papers are to be filed
    E. Each of your paper is filed

22. I wish that <u>he would take his work more serious</u>.   22._____

    A. No change
    B. he took his work more serious
    C. he will take his work more serious
    D. he shall take his work more seriously
    E. he would take his work more seriously

23. <u>After the treasurer report had been read</u>, the chairman called for the reports of the com-   23._____
mittees.

    A. No change
    B. After the treasure's report had been read
    C. After the treasurers' report had been read
    D. After the treasurerer's report had been read
    E. After the treasurer's report had been read

24. Last night the stranger <u>lead us down the mountain</u>.   24._____

    A. No change
    B. leaded us down the mountain
    C. let us down the mountain
    D. led us down the mountain
    E. had led us down the mountain

25. It would not be safe <u>for either you or I</u> to travel in Viet Nam.   25._____

    A. No change   B. for either you or me
    C. for either I or you   D. for either of you or I
    E. for either of I or you

KEY (CORRECT ANSWERS)

1.	A		11.	D
2.	D		12.	E
3.	E		13.	A
4.	C		14.	A
5.	D		15.	D
6.	E		16.	A
7.	E		17.	E
8.	A		18.	E
9.	D		19.	E
10.	E		20.	D

21.	A
22.	E
23.	E
24.	D
25.	B

TEST 2

DIRECTIONS: See DIRECTIONS for Sample Questions on page 1. *PRINT THE LETTER OF THE CORRECT ANSWER IN THE SPACE AT THE RIGHT.*

1. Both the body and the mind <u>needs exercise</u>.

   A. No change
   C. is needful of exercise
   E. need exercise
   B. have needs of exercise
   D. needed exercise

   1.____

2. <u>It's paw injured</u>, the animal limped down the road.

   A. No change
   C. Its paw injured
   E. Its paw injure
   B. It's paw injured
   D. Its' paw injured

   2.____

3. The butter <u>tastes rancidly</u>.

   A. No change
   C. tasted rancidly
   E. taste rancid
   B. tastes rancid
   D. taste rancidly

   3.____

4. <u>Who do you think</u> has sent me a letter?

   A. No change
   C. Whome do you think
   E. Whom can you think
   B. Whom do you think
   D. Who did you think

   4.____

5. If more nations <u>would have fought</u> against tyranny, the course of history would have been different.

   A. No change
   C. could have fought
   E. had fought
   B. would fight
   D. fought

   5.____

6. Radio and television programs, along with other media of communication, <u>helps us to appreciate the arts and to keep informed</u>.

   A. No change
   B. helps us to appreciate the arts and to be informed
   C. helps us to be appreciative of the arts and to keep informed
   D. helps us to be appreciative of the arts and to be informed
   E. help us to appreciate the arts and to keep informed

   6.____

7. Music, <u>for example most always</u> has listening and viewing audiences numbering in the hundreds of thousands.

   A. No change
   C. for example, almost always
   E. for example, near always
   B. for example, most always
   D. for example nearly always

   7.____

8. When operas are performed on radio or television, <u>they effect the listener</u>.

   A. No change
   C. these effect the listeners
   E. they affect the listener
   B. they inflict the listener
   D. they affects the listeners

   8.____

9. After hearing then the listener wants to buy recordings of the music.   9.____

    A. No change
    B. After hearing them, the listener wants
    C. After hearing them, the listener want
    D. By hearing them the listener wants
    E. By hearing them, the listener wants

10. To we Americans the daily news program has become important.   10.____

    A. No change   B. To we the Americans
    C. To us Americans   D. To us the Americans
    E. To we and us Americans

11. This has resulted from it's coverage of a days' events.   11.____

    A. No change
    B. from its coverage of a days' events
    C. from it's coverage of a day's events
    D. from its' coverage of a day's events
    E. from its coverage of a day's events

12. In schools, teachers advice their students to listen to or to view certain programs.   12.____

    A. No change
    B. teachers advise there students
    C. teachers advise their students
    D. the teacher advises their students
    E. teachers advise his students

13. In these ways we are preceding toward the goal of an educated and an informed public.   13.____

    A. No change
    B. we are preeceding toward the goal
    C. we are proceeding toward the goal
    D. we are preceding toward the goal
    E. we are proceeding toward the goal

14. The cost of living is raising again.   14.____

    A. No change   B. are raising again
    C. is rising again   D. are rising again
    E. is risen again

15. We did not realize that the boys' father had forbidden them to keep there puppy.   15.____

    A. No change
    B. had forbade them to keep there puppy
    C. had forbade them to keep their puppy
    D. has forbidden them to keep their puppy
    E. had forbidden them to keep their puppy

16. Her willingness to help others' was her outstanding characteristic.   16.____

    A. No change
    B. Her willingness to help other's,

C. Her willingness to help others's
D. Her willingness to help others
E. Her willingness to help each other

17. Because he did not have an invitation, <u>the girls objected</u> to him going,   17.____

    A. No change
    B. the girls object to him going
    C. the girls objected to him's going
    D. the girls objected to his going
    E. the girls object to his going

18. Weekly dances <u>have become a popular accepted feature</u> of the summer schedule.   18.____

    A. No change
    B. have become a popular accepted feature
    C. have become a popular excepted feature
    D. have become a popularly excepted feature
    E. have become a popularly accepted feature

19. I <u>couldn't hardly believe</u> that he would desert our party.   19.____

    A. No change   B. would hardly believe
    C. didn't hardly believe   D. should hardly believe
    E. could hardly believe

20. I found the place in the book <u>more readily than she</u>.   20.____

    A. No change   B. more readily than her
    C. more ready than she   D. more quickly than her
    E. more ready than her

21. A good example of American outdoor activities <u>are sports</u>.   21.____

    A. No change   B. is sports   C. are sport
    D. are sports events   E. are to be found in sports

22. My point of view is <u>much different from your's</u>.   22.____

    A. No change
    B. much different than your's
    C. much different than yours
    D. much different from yours
    E. much different than yours'

23. The cook <u>was suppose to use two spoonfuls</u> of dressing for each serving.   23.____

    A. No change
    B. was supposed to use two spoonsful
    C. was suppose to use two spoonsful
    D. was supposed to use two spoonsfuls
    E. was supposed to use two spoonfuls

24. If anyone has any doubt about the values of the tour, <u>refer him to me</u>.   24.____

    A. No change   B. refer him to I   C. refer me to he
    D. refer them to me   E. refer he to I

25. We expect that the affects of <u>the trip will be beneficial</u>.   25.____

    A. No change
    B. the effects of the trip will be beneficial
    C. the effects of the trip should be beneficial
    D. the affects of the trip would be beneficial
    E. the effects of the trip will be benificial

KEY (CORRECT ANSWERS)

1.	E		11.	E
2.	C		12.	C
3.	B		13.	E
4.	A		14.	C
5.	E		15.	E
6.	E		16.	D
7.	C		17.	D
8.	E		18.	E
9.	B		19.	E
10.	C		20.	A

21.	B
22.	D
23.	E
24.	A
25.	B

TEST 3

DIRECTIONS: See DIRECTIONS for Sample Questions on page 1. *PRINT THE LETTER OF THE CORRECT ANSWER IN THE SPACE AT THE RIGHT.*

1. <u>That, my friend</u> is not the proper attitude.

A. No change	B. That my friend
C. That my friend,	D. That -- my friend
E. That, my friend,	

   1.____

2. The girl refused <u>to admit that the not was her's</u>.

A. No change	B. that the note were her's
C. that the note was hers'	D. that the note was hers
E. that the note might be hers	

   2.____

3. There <u>were fewer candidates that we had been lead</u> to expect.

   A. No change
   B. was fewer candidates than we had been lead
   C. were fewer candidates than we had been lead
   D. was fewer candidates than we had been led
   E. were fewer candidates than we had been led

   3.____

4. When I first saw the car, <u>its steering wheel was broke</u>.

   A. No change
   B. its' steering wheel was broken
   C. it's steering wheel had been broken
   D. its steering wheel were broken
   E. its steering wheel was broken

   4.____

5. I find that the essential spirit for <u>we beginners is missing</u>.

   A. No change
   B. we who begin are missing
   C. us beginners are missing
   D. us beginners is missing
   E. we beginners are missing

   5.____

6. I believe that <u>you had ought</u> to study harder.

A. No change	B. you should have ought
C. you had better	D. you ought to have
E. you ought	

   6.____

7. This is <u>Tom, whom I am sure</u>, will be glad to help you.

A. No change	B. Tom whom, I am sure,
C. Tom, whom I am sure,	D. Tom who I am sure,
E. Tom, who, I am sure,	

   7.____

8. His father or his mother <u>has read to him</u> every night since he was very small.

A. No change	B. did read to him
C. have been reading to him	D. had read to him
E. have read to him	

   8.____

9. He <u>become</u> an authority on the theater and its great personalities.   9.____

    A. No change   B. becomed an authority
    C. become the authority   D. became an authority
    E. becamed an authority

10. I know of no other person in the club <u>who is more kind-hearted than her</u>.   10.____

    A. No change
    B. who are more kind-hearted than they
    C. who are more kind-hearted than them
    D. whom are more kind-hearted than she
    E. who is more kind-hearted than she

11. After Bill <u>had ran the mile</u>, he was breathless.   11.____

    A. No change   B. had runned the mile
    C. has ran the mile   D. had ranned the mile
    E. had run the mile

12. Wilson <u>has scarcely no equal</u> as a pitcher.   12.____

    A. No change   B. has scarcely an equal
    C. has hardly no equal   D. had scarcely no equal
    E. has scarcely any equals

13. It <u>was the worse storm</u> that the inhabitants of the island could remember.   13.____

    A. No change   B. were the worse storm
    C. was the worst storm   D. was the worsest storm
    E. was the most worse storm

14. If only <u>we had began</u> before it was too late'.   14.____

    A. No change   B. we had began
    C. we would have begun   D. we had begun
    E. we had beginned

15. <u>Lets evaluate</u> our year's work.   15.____

    A. No change   B. Let us' evaluate
    C. Lets' evaluate   D. Lets' us evaluate
    E. Let's evaluate

16. This is an organization <u>with which I wouldn't want to be associated with</u>.   16.____

    A. No change
    B. with whom I wouldn't want to be associated with
    C. that I wouldn't want to be associated
    D. with which I would want not to be associated with
    E. with which I wouldn't want to be associated

17. The enemy fled in many directions, <u>leaving there weapons</u> on the field.   17.____

    A. No change   B. leaving its weapons
    C. letting their weapons   D. leaving alone there weapons
    E. leaving their weapons

18. I hoped that John <u>could effect a compromise between</u> the approved forces.   18._____

    A. No change
    B. could accept a compromise between
    C. could except a compromise between
    D. would have effected a compromise among
    E. could effect a compromise among

19. I was surprised to learn <u>that he has not always spoke English</u> fluently.   19._____

    A. No change
    B. that he had not always spoke English
    C. that he did not always speak English
    D. that he has not always spoken English
    E. that he could not always speak English

20. The lawyer promised <u>to notify my father and I</u> of his plans for a new trial.   20._____

    A. No change
    B. to notify I and my father
    C. to notify me and our father
    D. to notify my father and me
    E. to notify mine father and me

21. The most important feature of the series of tennis lessons <u>were the large amount</u> of   21._____
strokes taught.

    A. No change
    B. were the large number
    C. was the large amount
    D. was the largeness of the amount
    E. was the large number

22. That the prize proved to be beyond her reach <u>did not surprise him</u>.   22._____

    A. No change
    B. has not surprised him
    C. had not ought to have surprised him
    D. should not surprise him
    E. would not have surprised him

23. I am not <u>all together in agreement</u> with the author's point of view.   23._____

    A. No change   B. all together of agreement
    C. all together for agreement   D. altogether with agreement
    E. altogether in agreement

24. Windstorms have recently established a record which meteorologists hope <u>will not be</u>   24._____
<u>equal</u> for many years to come.

    A. No change   B. will be equal
    C. will not be equalized   D. will be equaled
    E. will not be equaled

25. A large number of Shakespeare's soliloquies must be considered <u>as representing thought</u>, not speech.

    25._____

    A. No change
    B. as representative of speech, not thought
    C. as represented by thought, not speech
    D. as indicating thought, not speech
    E. as representative of thought, more than speech

KEY (CORRECT ANSWERS)

1.	E		11.	E
2.	D		12.	B
3.	E		13.	C
4.	E		14.	D
5.	D		15.	E
6.	E		16.	E
7.	E		17.	E
8.	A		18.	A
9.	D		19.	D
10.	E		20.	D

21.	E
22.	A
23.	E
24.	E
25.	A

TEST 4

DIRECTIONS: See DIRECTIONS for Sample Questions on page 1. *PRINT THE LETTER OF THE CORRECT ANSWER IN THE SPACE AT THE RIGHT.*

1. A sight to inspire fear <u>are wild animals on the lose</u>.   1.____

   A. No change
   B. are wild animals on the loose
   C. is wild animals on the loose
   D. is wild animals on the lose
   E. are wild animals loose

2. For many years, the settlers <u>had been seeking to workship as they please</u>.   2.____

   A. No change
   B. had seeked to workship as they pleased
   C. sought to workship as they please
   D. sought to have worshiped as they pleased
   E. had been seeking to worship as they pleased

3. The girls stated that the dresses were <u>their's</u>.   3.____

   A. No change B. there's   C. theirs   D. theirs'   E. there own

4. <u>Please fellows</u> don't drop the ball.   4.____

   A. No change   B. Please, fellows   C. Please fellows;
   D. Please, fellows,   E. Please! fellows

5. Your sweater <u>has laid</u> on the floor for a week.   5.____

   A. No change   B. has been laying
   C. has been lying   D. laid
   E. has been lain

6. I wonder whether <u>you're sure that scheme of yours'</u> will work.   6.____

   A. No change
   B. your sure that scheme of your's
   C. you're sure that scheme of yours
   D. your sure that scheme of yours
   E. you're sure that your scheme's

7. Please let <u>her and me</u> do it.   7.____

   A. No change   B. she and I   C. she and me
   D. her and I   E. her and him

8. I expected him to be angry <u>and to scold</u> her.   8.____

   A. No change   B. and that he would scold
   C. and that he might scold   D. and that he should scold
   E. , scolding

9. Knowing little about algebra, <u>it was difficult to solve the equation</u>.   9.____

A. No change
B. the equation was difficult to solve
C. the solution to the equation was difficult to find
D. I found it difficult to solve the equation
E. it being difficult to solve the equation

10. He <u>worked more diligent</u> now that he had become vice president of the company.   10.____

    A. No change   B. works more diligent
    C. works more diligently   D. began to work more diligent
    E. worked more diligently

11. <u>Flinging himself at the barricade</u> he pounded on it furiously.   11.____

    A. No change
    B. Flinging himself at the barricade: he
    C. Flinging himself at the barricade - he
    D. Flinging himself at the barricade; he
    E. Flinging himself at the barricade, he

12. When he <u>begun to give us advise</u>, we stopped listening.   12.____

    A. No change   B. began to give us advise
    C. begun to give us advice   D. began to give us advice
    E. begin to give us advice

13. John was only one of the boys whom as you know was not eligible.   13.____

    A. No change   B. who as you know were
    C. whom as you know were   D. who as you know was
    E. who as you know is

14. Why was Jane and he permitted to go?   14.____

    A. No change   B. was Jane and him
    C. were Jane and he   D. were Jane and him
    E. weren't Jane and he

15. <u>Take courage Tom: we</u> all make mistakes.   15.____

    A. No change   B. Take courage Tom - we
    C. Take courage, Tom; we   D. Take courage, Tom we
    E. Take courage! Tom: we

16. Henderson, the president of the class and <u>who is also captain of the team</u>, will lead the   16.____
rally.

    A. No change
    B. since he is captain of the team
    C. captain of the team
    D. also being captain of the team
    E. who be also captain of the team

17. Our car has always <u>run good</u> on that kind of gasoline.   17.____

    A. No change   B. run well   C. ran good
    D. ran well   E. done good

18. There was a serious difference of opinion <u>among her and I</u>.   18._____

    A. No change   B. among she and I
    C. between her and I   D. between her and me
    E. among her and me

19. "This is most unusual," said <u>Helen, "the</u> mailman has never been this late before."   19._____

    A. No change   B. Helen, "The   C. Helen - "The
    D. Helen; "The   E. Helen." The

20. The three main characters in the story are Johnny Hobart a <u>teenager, his mother a</u>   20._____
<u>widow, and</u> the local druggist.

    A. No change
    B. teenager; his mother, a widow; and
    C. teenager; his mother a widow; and
    D. teenager, his mother, a widow and
    E. teenager, his mother, a widow; and

21. How much <u>has food costs raised</u> during the past year?   21._____

    A. No change
    B. have food costs rose
    C. have food costs risen
    D. has food costs risen
    E. have food costs been raised

22. "Will you come <u>too" she pleaded</u>?   22._____

    A. No change   B. too,?"she pleaded.
    C. too?" she pleaded.   D. too," she pleaded?
    E. too, she pleaded?"

23. If he <u>would have drank</u> more milk, his health would have been better.   23._____

    A. No change   B. would drink   C. had drank
    D. had he drunk   E. had drunk

24. Jack had <u>no sooner laid down and fallen asleep when</u> the alarm sounded.   24._____

    A. No change
    B. no sooner lain down and fallen asleep than
    C. no sooner lay down and fell asleep when
    D. no sooner laid down and fell asleep than
    E. no sooner lain down than he fell asleep when

25. Jackson is <u>one of the few Sophomores, who has</u> ever made the varsity team.   25._____

    A. No change
    B. one of the few Sophomores, who have
    C. one of the few sophomores, who has
    D. one of the few sophomores who have
    E. one of the few sophomores who has

KEY (CORRECT ANSWERS)

1.	C		11.	E
2.	E		12.	D
3.	C		13.	B
4.	D		14.	C
5.	C		15.	C
6.	C		16.	C
7.	A		17.	B
8.	A		18.	D
9.	D		19.	E
10.	E		20.	B

21.	C
22.	C
23.	E
24.	B
25.	D

———

TEST 5

1. The lieutenant had ridden almost a kilometer when the scattering shells <u>begin landing</u> uncomfortably close.

    1.____

    A. No change   B. beginning to land   C. began to land
    D. having begun to land   E. begin to land

2. <u>Having studied eight weeks</u>, he now feels sufficiently prepared for the examination.

    2.____

    A. No change
    B. For eight weeks he studies so
    C. Due to eight weeks of study
    D. After eight weeks of studying
    E. Since he's been spending the last eight weeks in study

3. <u>Coming from the Greek, and the word "democracy" means government by the people.</u>

    3.____

    A. No change
    B. "Democracy," the word which comes from the Greek, means government by the people.
    C. Meaning government by the people, the word "democracy" comes from the Greek.
    D. Its meaning being government by the people in Greek, the word is "democracy."
    E. The word "democracy" comes from the Greek and means government by the people.

4. Moslem universities were one of the chief agencies <u>in the development</u> and spreading Arabic civilization.

    4.____

    A. No change   B. in the development of
    C. to develop   D. in developing
    E. for the developing of

5. The water of Bering Strait <u>were closing</u> to navigation by ice early in the fall.

    5.____

    A. No change   B. has closed   C. have closed
    D. had been closed   E. closed

6. The man, <u>since he grew up</u> on the block, felt sentimental when returning to it.

    6.____

    A. No change   B. having grown up
    C. growing up   D. since he had grown up
    E. whose growth had been

7. <u>Jack and Jill watched the canoe to take their parents out of sight round the bend of the creek.</u>

    7.____

    A. No change
    B. The canoe, taking their parents out of sight, rounds the bend as Jack and Jill watch.
    C. Jack and Jill watched the canoe round the bend of the creek, taking their parents out of sight.

    D.   The canoe rounded the bend of the creek as it took their parents out of sight, Jack and Jill watching.

    E.   Jack and Jill watching,the canoe is rounding the bend of the creek to take their parents out of sight.

8. Chaucer's best-known work is THE CANTERBURY TALES, a collection of stories <u>which he tells</u> with a group of pilgrims as they travel to the town of Canterbury.   8.____

    A. No change   B. which he tells through   C. who tell
    D. told by   E. told through

9. The Estates-General, the old feudal assembly of France, <u>had not met</u> for one hundred and seventy-five years when it convened in 1789.   9.____

    A. No change   B. has not met   C. has not been meeting
    D. had no meeting   E. has no meeting

10. Just forty years ago, <u>there had been</u> fewer than one hundred symphony orchestras in the United States.   10.____

    A. No change   B. there had   C. there were
    D. there was   E. there existed

11. Mrs. Smith complained that her son's temper tantrums <u>aggragravated her</u> and caused her to have a headache.   11.____

    A. No change   B. gave her aggravation
    C. were aggravating to her   D. aggravated her condition
    E. instigated

12. A girl <u>like I</u> would never be seen in a place like that.   12.____

    A. No change B. as I   C. as me   D. like I am   E. like me

13. <u>Between you and me</u>. my opinion is that this room is certainly nicer than the first one we saw.   13.____

    A. No change   B. between you and I   C. among you and me
    D. betwixt you and I   E. between we

14. It is important to know for <u>what kind of a person you are working</u>.   14.____

    A. No change
    B. what kind of a person for whom you are working
    C. what kind of person you are working
    D. what kind of person you are working for
    E. what kind of a person you are working for

15. I had <u>all ready</u> finished the book before you came in.   15.____

    A. No change B. already   C. previously D. allready   E. all

16. <u>Ask not for who the bell tolls, it tolls for thee.</u>   16.____

    A. No change
    B. Ask not for whom the bell tolls, it tolls for thee.
    C. Ask not whom the bell tolls for; it tolls for thee.

D. Ask not for whom the bell tolls; it tolls for thee.
E. Ask not who the bell tolls for: It tolls for thee.

17. It is a far better thing I do, than <u>ever I did</u> before.

    A. No change   B. never I did   C. I have ever did
    D. I have ever been done E. ever have I done

17.____

18. <u>Ending a sentence with a preposition is something up with which I will not put.</u>

    A. No change
    B. Ending a sentence with a preposition is something with which I will not put up.
    C. To end a sentence with a preposition is that which I will not put up with.
    D. Ending a sentence with a preposition is something of which I will not put up.
    E. Something I will not put up with is ending a sentence with a preposition.

18.____

19. Everyone <u>took off their hats and stand up</u> to sing the national anthem.

    A. No change
    B. took off their hats and stood up
    C. take off their hats and stand up
    D. took off his hat and stood up
    E. have taken off their hats and standing up

19.____

20. <u>She promised me that if she had the opportunity she would have came irregardless of the weather.</u>

    A. No change
    B. She promised me that if she had the opportunity she would have come regardless of the weather.
    C. She assured me that had she had the opportunity she would have come regardless of the weather.
    D. She assured me that if she would have had the opportunity she would have come regardless of the weather.
    E. She promised me that if she had had the opportunity she would have came irregardless of the weather.

20.____

21. The man decided it would be advisable to marry a girl <u>somewhat younger than him</u>.

    A. No change   B. somehow younger than him
    C. some younger than him   D. somewhat younger from him
    E. somewhat younger than he

21.____

22. Sitting near the campfire, the old man told <u>John and I about many exciting adventures he had had</u>.

    A. No change
    B. John and me about many exciting adventures he had.
    C. John and I about much exciting adventure which he'd had.
    D. John and me about many exciting adventures he had had.
    E. John and me about many exciting adventures he has had.

22.____

23. If you had stood at home and done your homework, you would not have failed the course.

23._____

    A. No change
    B. If you had stood at home and done you're homework,
    C. If you had staid at home and done your homework,
    D. Had you stayed at home and done your homework,
    E. Had you stood at home and done your homework,

24. The children didn't, as a rule, do anything beyond what they were told to do.

24._____

    A. No change   B. do hardly anything beyond
    C. do anything except   D. do hardly anything except for
    E. do nothing beyond

25. Either the girls or him is right.

25._____

    A. No change
    B. Either the girls or he is
    C. Either the girls or him are
    D. Either the girls or he are
    E. Either the girls nor he is

KEY (CORRECT ANSWERS)

1.	C		11.	D
2.	A		12.	E
3.	E		13.	A
4.	D		14.	C
5.	D		15.	B
6.	B		16.	D
7.	C		17.	E
8.	D		18.	E
9.	A		19.	D
10.	C		20.	C

21.	E
22.	D
23.	D
24.	A
25.	B

READING COMPREHENSION
UNDERSTANDING AND INTERPRETING WRITTEN MATERIAL
EXAMINATION SECTION
TEST 1

DIRECTIONS: Each question has five suggested answers, lettered A to E. Decide which one is the BEST answer. *PRINT THE LETTER OF THE CORRECT ANSWER IN THE SPACE AT THE RIGHT.*

1. Some specialists are willing to give their services to the Government entirely free of charge; some feel that a nominal salary, such as will cover traveling expenses, is sufficient for a position that is recognized as being somewhat honorary in nature; many other specialists value their time so highly that they will not devote any of it to public service that does not repay them at a rate commensurate with the fees that they can obtain from a good private clientele.
The paragraph BEST supports the statement that the use of specialists by the Government

    A.   is rare because of the high cost of securing such persons
    B.   may be influenced by the willingness of specialists to serve
    C.   enables them to secure higher salaries in private fields
    D.   has become increasingly common during the past few years
    E.   always conflicts with private demands for their services

1.____

2. The fact must not be overlooked that only about one-half of the international trade of the world crosses the oceans. The other half is merely exchanges of merchandise between countries lying alongside each other or at least within the same continent.
The paragraph BEST supports the statement that

    A.   the most important part of any country's trade is transoceanic
    B.   domestic trade is insignificant when compared with foreign trade
    C.   the exchange of goods between neighborhing countries is not considerd international trade
    D.   foreign commerce is not necessarily carried on by water
    E.   about one-half of the trade of the world is international

2.____

3. Individual differences in mental traits assume importance in fitting workers to jobs because such personal characteristics are persistent and are relatively little influenced by training and experience.
The paragraph BEST supports the statement that training and experience

    A.   are limited in their effectiveness in fitting workers to jobs
    B.   do not increase a worker's fitness for a job
    C.   have no effect upon a person's mental traits
    D.   have relatively little effect upon the individual's chances for success
    E.   should be based on the mental traits of an individual

3.____

4. The competition of buyers tends to keep prices up, the competition of sellers to send 4.____
them down. Normally the pressure of competition among sellers is stronger than that
among buyers since the seller has his article to sell and must get rid of it, whereas the
buyer is not committed to anything.
The paragraph BEST supports the statement that low prices are caused by

   A. buyer competition
   B. competition of buyers with sellers
   C. fluctuations in demand
   D. greater competition among sellers than among buyers
   E. more sellers than buyers

5. In seventeen states, every lawyer is automatically a member of the American Bar Associ- 5.____
ation. In some other states and localities, truly representative organizations of the Bar
have not yet come into being, but are greatly needed.
The paragraph IMPLIES that

   A. representative Bar Associations are necessary in states where they do not now
exist
   B. every lawyer is required by law to become a member of the Bar
   C. the Bar Association is a democratic organization
   D. some states have more lawyers than others
   E. every member of the American Bar Association is automatically a lawyer in seven-
teen states.

―――――――

KEY (CORRECT ANSWERS)

1. B
2. D
3. A
4. D
5. A

―――――――

TEST 2

DIRECTIONS: Each question has five suggested answers, lettered A to E. Decide which one is the BEST answer. *PRINT THE LETTER OF THE CORRECT ANSWER IN THE SPACE AT THE RIGHT.*

1. We hear a great deal about the new education, and see a great deal of it in action. But the school house, though prodigiously magnified in scale, is still very much the same old school house.
   The paragraph IMPLIES that

   A. the old education was, after all, better than the new
   B. although the modern school buildings are larger than the old ones, they have not changed very much in other respects
   C. the old school houses do not fit in with modern educational theories
   D. a fine school building does not make up for poor teachers
   E. schools will be schools

   1.____

2. No two human beings are of the same pattern — not even twins and the method of bringing out the best in each one necessarily varies according to the nature of the child.
   The paragraph IMPLIES that

   A. individual differences should be considered in dealing with children
   B. twins should be treated impartially
   C. it is an easy matter to determine the special abilities of children
   D. a child's nature varies from year to year
   E. we must discover the general technique of dealing with children

   2.____

3. Man inhabits today a world very different from that which encompassed even his parents and grandparents. It is a world geared to modern machinery—automobiles, airplanes, power plants; it is linked together and served by electricity.
   The paragraph IMPLIES that

   A. the world has not changed much during the last few generations
   B. modern inventions and discoveries have brought about many changes in man's way of living
   C. the world is run more efficiently today than it was in our grandparents' time
   D. man is much happier today than he was a hundred years ago
   E. we must learn to see man as he truly is, underneath the veneers of man's contrivances

   3.____

4. Success in any study depends largely upon the interest taken in that particular subject by the student. This being the case, each teacher earnestly hopes that her students will realize at the very outset that shorthand can be made an intensely fascinating study.
   The paragraph IMPLIES that

   A. everyone is interested in shorthand
   B. success in a study is entirely impossible unless the student finds the study very interesting
   C. if a student is eager to study shorthand, he is likely to succeed in it
   D. shorthand is necessary for success
   E. anyone who is not interested in shorthand will not succeed in business

   4.____

5. The primary purpose of all business English is to move the reader to agreeable and   5.____
   mutually profitable action. This action may be indirect or direct, but in either case a highly
   competitive appeal for business should be clothed with incisive diction tending to replace
   vagueness and doubt with clarity, confidence, and appropriate action.
   The paragraph IMPLIES that the

   A. ideal business letter uses words to conform to the reader's language level
   B. business correspondent should strive for conciseness in letter writing
   C. keen competition of today has lessened the value of the letter as an appeal for
       business
   D. writer of a business letter should employ incisive diction to move the reader to com-
       pliant and gainful action
   E. the writer of a business letter should be himself clear, confident, and Forceful

---

KEY (CORRECT ANSWERS)

1. B
2. A
3. B
4. C
5. D

TEST 3

Each question has five suggested answers, lettered A to E. Decide which one is the BEST answer. *PRINT THE LETTER OF THE CORRECT ANSWER IN THE SPACE AT THE RIGHT.*

1. To serve the community best, a comprehensive city plan must coordinate all physical improvements, even at the possible expense of subordinating individual desires, to the end that a city may grow in a more orderly way and provide adequate facilities for its people.
The paragraph IMPLIES that

    A. city planning provides adequate facilities for recreation
    B. a comprehensive city plan provides the means for a city to grow in a more orderly fashion
    C. individual desires must always be subordinated to civic changes
    D. the only way to serve a community is to adopt a comprehensive city plan
    E. city planning is the most important function of city government

1.____

2. Facility in writing letters, the knack of putting into these quickly written letters the same personal impression that would mark an interview, and the ability to boil down to a one-page letter the gist of what might be called a five- or ten-minute conversation—all these are essential to effective work under conditions of modern business organization.
The paragraph IMPLIES that

    A. letters are of more importance in modern business activities than ever before
    B. letters should be used in place of interviews
    C. the ability to write good letters is essential to effective work in modern business organization
    D. business letters should never be more than one page in length
    E. the person who can write a letter with great skill will get ahead more readily than others

2.____

3. The general rule is that it is the city council which determines the amount to be raised by taxation and which therefore determines, within the law, the tax rates. As has been pointed out, however, no city council or city authority has the power to determine what kinds of taxes should be levied.
The paragraph IMPLIES that

    A. the city council has more authority than any other municipal body
    B. while the city council has a great deal of authority in the levying of taxes, its power is not absolute
    C. the kinds of taxes levied in different cities vary greatly
    D. the city council appoints the tax collectors
    E. the mayor determines the kinds of taxes to be levied

3.____

4. The growth of modern business has made necessary mass production, mass distribution, and mass selling. As a result, the problems of personnel and industrial relations have increased so rapidly that grave injustices in the handling of personal relationships have frequently occurred. Personnel administration is complex because, as in all human problems, many intangible elements are involved. Therefore a thorough, systematic, and continuous study of the psychology of human behavior is essential to the intelligent handling of personnel.
The paragraph IMPLIES that

4.____

A. complex modern industry makes impossible the personal relationships which formerly existed between employer and employee
B. mass decisions are successfully applied to personnel problems
C. the human element in personnel administration makes continuous study necessary to its intelligent application
D. personnel problems are less important than the problems of mass production and mass distribution
E. since personnel administration is so complex and costly, it should be sub-ordinated to the needs of good industrial relations

5. The Social Security Act is striving toward the attainment of economic security for the individual and for his family. It was stated, in outlining this program, that security for the individual and for the family concerns itself with three factors: (1) decent homes to live in; (2) development of the natural resources of the country so as to afford the fullest opportunity to engage in productive work; and (3) safeguards against the major misfortunes of life. The Social Security Act is concerned with the third of these factors – "safeguards against misfortunes which cannot be wholly eliminated in this man-made world of ours."
The paragraph IMPLIES that the

5.____

A. Social Security Act is concerned primarily with supplying to families decent homes in which to live
B. development of natural resources is the only means of offering employment to the
C. masses of the unemployed
   Social Security Act has attained absolute economic security for the individual and his family
D. Social Security Act deals with the first (1) factor as stated in the paragraph above
E. Social Security Act deals with the third (3) factor as stated in the paragraph above

---

KEY (CORRECT ANSWERS)

1. B
2. C
3. B
4. C
5. E

TEST 4

PASSAGE 1

Free unrhymed verse has been practiced for some thousands of years and reaches back to the incantation which linked verse with the ritual dance. It provided a communal emotion; the aim of the cadenced phrases was to create a state of mind. The general coloring of free rhythms in the poetry of today is that of speech rhythm, composed in the sequence of the musical phrase, not in the sequence of the metronome, the regular beat. In the twenties, conventional rhyme fell into almost complete disuse. This liberation from rhyme became as well a liberation of rhyme. Freed of its exacting task of supporting lame verse, it would be applied with greater effect where wanted for some special effect. Such break in the tradition of rhymed verse had the healthy effect of giving it a fresh start, released from the hampering convention of too familiar cadences. This refreshing and subtilizing of the use of rhyme can be seen everywhere in the poetry today.

1. The title below that BEST expresses the ideas of this paragraph is: 1.____

    A. Primitive Poetry
    B. The Origin of Poetry
    C. Rhyme and Rhythm in Modern Verse
    D. Classification of Poetry
    E. Purposes in All Poetry

2. Free verse had its origin in primitive   2.____

    A. fairytales   B. literature   C. warfare
    D. chants   E. courtship

3. The object of early free verse was to   3.____

    A. influence the mood of the people   B. convey ideas
    C. produce mental pictures   D. create pleasing sounds
    E. provide enjoyment

PASSAGE 2

Control of the Mississippi had always been goals of nations having ambitions in the New World. La Salle claimed it for France in 1682. Iberville appropriated it to France when he colonized Louisiana in 1700. Bienville founded New Orleans, its principal port, as a French city in 1718. The fleur-de-lis were the blazon of the delta country until 1762. Then Spain claimed all of Louisiana. The Spanish were easy neighbors. American products from western Pennsylvania and the North west Territory were barged down the Ohio and Mississippi to New Orleans, here they were reloaded on ocean-going vessels that cleared for the great seaports of the world.

1. The title below that BEST expresses the ideas of this paragraph is: 1.____

    A. Importance of seaports
    B. France and Spain in the New World
    C. Early control of the Mississippi
    D. Claims of European nations
    E. American trade on the Mississippi

2. Until 1762 the lower Mississippi area was held by   2.____

   A. England   B. Spain   C. the United States
   D. France   E. Indians

3. In doing business with Americans the Spaniards were   3.____

   A. easy to outsmart
   B. friendly to trade
   C. inclined to charge high prices for use of their ports
   D. shrewd
   E. suspicious

PASSAGE 3

Our humanity is by no means so materialistic as foolish talk is continually asserting it to be. Judging by what I have learned about men and women, I am convinced that there is far more in them of idealistic willpower than ever comes to the surface of the world. Just as the water of streams is small in amount compared to that which flows underground, so the idealism which becomes visible is small in amount compared with that which men and women bear locked in their hearts, unreleased or scarcely released. To unbind what is bound, to bring the underground waters to the surface — mankind is waiting and longing for men who can do that.

1. The title below that BEST expresses the ideas of this paragraph is   1.____

   A. Releasing Underground Riches
   B. The Good and Bad in Man
   C. Materialism in Humanity
   D. The Surface and the Depths of Idealism
   E. Unreleased Energy

2. Human beings are more idealistic than   2.____

   A. the water in underground streams
   B. their waiting and longing proves
   C. outward evidence shows
   D. the world
   E. other living creatures

PASSAGE 4

The total impression made by any work of fiction cannot be rightly understood without a sympathetic perception of the artistic aims of the writer. Consciously or unconsciouly, he has accepted certain facts, and rejected or suppressed other facts, in order to give unity to the particular aspect of human life which he is depicting. No novelist possesses the impartiality, the indifference, the infinite tolerance of nature. Nature displays to use, with complete unconcern, the beautiful and the ugly, the precious and the trivial, the pure and the impure. But a writer must select the aspects of nature and human nature which are demanded by the work in hand. He is forced to select, to combine, to create.

1. The title below that BEST expresses the ideas of this paragraph is: 1._____

    A. Impressionists in Literature
    B. Nature as an Artist
    C. The Novelist as an Imitator
    D. Creative Technic of the Novelist
    E. Aspects of Nature

2. A novelist rejects some facts because they   2._____

    A. are impure and ugly
    B. would show he is not impartial
    C. are unrelated to human nature
    D. would make a bad impression
    E. mar the unity of his story

3. It is important for a reader to know   3._____

    A. the purpose of the author
    B. what facts the author omits
    C. both the ugly and the beautiful
    D. something about nature
    E. what the author thinks of human nature

PASSAGE 5

If you watch a lamp which is turned very rapidly on and off, and you keep your eyes open, "persistence of vision" will bridge the gaps of darkness between the flashes of light, and the lamp will seem to be continuously lit. This "topical afterglow" explains the magic produced by the stroboscope, a new instrument which seems to freeze the swiftest motions while they are still going on, and to stop time itself dead in its tracks. The "magic" is all in the eye of the beholder.

1. The "magic" of the stroboscope is due to   1._____

    A. continuous lighting   B. intense cold
    C. slow motion   D. behavior of the human eye
    E. a lapse of time

2. "Persistence of vision" is explained by   2._____

    A. darkness   B. winking   C. rapid flashes
    D. gaps   E. after impression

KEY (CORRECT ANSWERS)

<u>PASSAGE 1</u>

1. C
2. D
3. A

<u>PASSAGE 2</u>

1. C
2. D
3. B

<u>PASSAGE 3</u>

1. D
2. C

<u>PASSAGE 4</u>

1. D
2. E
3. A

<u>PASSAGE 5</u>

1. D
2. E

TEST 5

During the past fourteen years, thousands of top-lofty United States elms have been marked for death by the activities of the tiny European elm bark beetle. The beetles, however, do not do fatal damage. Death is caused by another importation, Dutch elm disease, a fungus infection which the beetles carry from tree to tree. Up to 1941, quarantine and tree-sanitation measures kept the beetles and the disease pretty well confined within 510 miles around metropolitan New York. War curtailed these measures and made Dutch elm disease a wider menace. Every house hold and village that prizes an elm-shaded lawn or commons must now watch for it. Since there is as yet no cure for it, the infected trees must be pruned or felled, and the wood must be burned in order to protect other healthy trees.

1. The title below that BEST expresses the ideas of this paragraph is: 1._____

    A. A Menace to Our Elms   B. Pests and Diseases of the Elm
    C. Our Vanishing Elms   D. The Need to Protect Dutch Elms
    E. How Elms are Protected

2. The danger of spreading the Dutch elm disease was increased by   2._____

    A. destroying infected trees   B. the war
    C. the lack of a cure   D. a fungus infection
    E. quarantine measures

3. The European elm bark beetle is a serious threat to our elms because it   3._____

    A. chews the bark
    B. kills the trees
    C. is particularly active on the eastern seaboard
    D. carries infection
    E. cannot be controlled

It is elemental that the greater the development of man, the greater the problems he has to concern him. When he lived in a cave with stone implements, his mind no less than his actions was grooved into simple channels. Every new invention, every new way of doing things posed fresh problems for him. And, as he moved along the road, he questioned each step, as indeed he should, for he trod upon the beliefs of his ancestors. It is equally elemental to say that each step upon this later road posed more questions than the earlier ones. It is only the edcated man who realizes the results of his actions; it is only the thoughtful one who questions his own decisions.

1. The title below that BEST expresses the ideas of this paragraph is: 1._____

    A. Channels of Civilization
    B. The Mark of a Thoughtful Man
    C. The Cave Man in Contrast with Man Today
    D. The Price of Early Progress
    E. Man's Never-Ending Challenge

PASSAGE 3

Spring is one of those things that man has no hand in, any more than he has a part in sunrise or the phases of the moon. Spring came before man was here to enjoy it, and it will go right on coming even if man isn't here some time in the future. It is a matter of solar mechanics and celestial order. And for all our knowledge of astronomy and terrestrial mechanics, we haven't yet been able to do more than bounce a radar beam off the moon. We couldn't alter the arrival of the spring equinox by as much as one second, if we tried.

Spring is a matter of growth, of chlorophyll, of bud and blossom. We can alter growth and change the time of blossoming in individual plants; but the forests still grow in nature's way, and the grass of the plains hasn't altered its nature in a thousand years. Spring is a magnificent phase of the cycle of nature; but man really hasn't any guiding or controlling hand in it. He is here to enjoy it and benefit by it. And April is a good time to realize it; by May perhaps we will want to take full credit.

1. The title below that BEST expresses the ideas of this passage is: 1.____

    A. The Marvels of the Spring Equinox
    B. Nature's Dependence on Mankind
    C. The Weakness of Man Opposed to Nature
    D. The Glories of the World
    E. Eternal Growth

2. The author of the passage states that   2.____

    A. man has a part in the phases of the moon
    B. April is a time for taking full-credit
    C. April is a good time to enjoy nature
    D. man has a guiding hand in spring
    E. spring will cease to be if civilization ends

PASSAGE 4

The walled medieval town was as characteristic of its period as the cut of a robber baron's beard. It sprang out of the exigencies of war, and it was not without its architectural charm, whatever its hygienic deficiencies may have been. Behind its high, thick walls not only the normal inhabitants but the whole countryside fought and cowered in an hour of need. The capitals of Europe now forsake the city when the sirens scream and death from the sky seems imminent. Will the fear of bombs accelerate the slow decentralization which began with the automobile and the wide distribution of electrical energy and thus reverse the medieval flow to the city?

1. The title below that BEST expresses the ideas in this paragraph is.   1.____

    A. A Changing Function of the Town   B. The Walled Medieval Town
    C. The Automobile's Influence on City   D. Forsaking the City
        Life
    E. Bombs Today and Yesterday

2. Conditions in the Middle Ages made the walled town   2.____

    A. a natural development   B. the most dangerous of all places
    C. a victim of fires   D. lacking in architectural charm
    E. healthful

3. Modern conditions may

    A. make cities larger
    B. make cities more hygienic
    C. protect against floods
    D. cause people to move from population centers
    E. encourage good architecture

3.____

PASSAGE 5

The literary history of this nation began when the first settler from abroad of sensitive mind paused in his adventure long enough to feel that he was under a different sky, breathing new air, and that a New World was all before him with only his strength and Providence for guides. With him began a new emphasis upon an old theme in literature, the theme of cutting loose and faring forth, renewed, under the powerful influence of a fresh continent for civilized man. It has provided, ever since those first days, a strong current in our native literature, whose other flow has come from a nostalgia for the rich culture of Europe, so much of which was perforce left behind.

1. The title below that BEST expresses the ideas of this paragraph is:

    A. America's Distinctive Literature
    B. Pioneer Authors
    C. The Dead Hand of the Past
    D. Europe's Literary Grandchild
    E. America Comes of Age

1.____

2. American writers, according to the author, because of their colonial experiences

    A. were antagonistic to European writers
    B. cut loose from Old World influences
    C. wrote only on New World events and characters
    D. created new literary themes
    E. gave fresh interpretation to an old literary idea

2.____

KEY (CORRECT ANSWERS)

PASSAGE 1

1. A
2. B
3. D

PASSAGE 2

1. E

PASSAGE 3

1. C
2. C

PASSAGE 4

1. A
2. A
3. D

PASSAGE 5

1. A
2. E

TEST 6

1. Any business not provided with capable substitutes to fill all important positions is a weak business. Therefore a foreman should train each man not only to perform his own particular duties but also to do those of two or three positions.
The paragraph BEST supports the statement that

   A. dependence on substitutes is a sign of weak organization
   B. training will improve the strongest organization
   C. the foreman should be the most expert at any particular job under him
   D. every employee can be trained to perform efficiently work other than his own
   E. vacancies in vital positions should be provided for in advance

2. The coloration of textile fabrics composed of cotton and wool generally requires two processes, as the process used in dyeing wool is seldom capable of fixing the color upon cotton. The usual method is to immerse the fabric in the requisite baths to dye the wool and then to treat the partially dyed material in the manner found suitable for cotton.
The paragraph BEST supports the statement that the dyeing of textile fabrics composed of cotton and wool

   A. is less complicated than the dyeing of wool alone
   B. is more successful when the material contains more cotton than wool
   C. is not satisfactory when solid colors are desired
   D. is restricted to two colors for any one fabric
   E. is usually based upon the methods required for dyeing the different materials

3. The serious investigator must direct his whole effort toward. success in his work. If he wishes to succeed in each investigation, his work will be by no means easy, smooth, or peaceful; on the contrary, he will have to devote himself completely and continuously to a task that requires all his ability.
The paragraph BEST supports the statement that an investigator's success depends most upon

   A. ambition to advance rapidly in the service
   B. persistence in the face of difficulty
   C. training and experience
   D. willingness to obey orders without delay
   E. the number of investigations which he conducts

4. Honest people in one nation find it difficult to understand the viewpoint of honest people in another. State departments and their ministers exist for the purpose of explaining the viewpoints of one nation in terms understood by another. Some of their most important work lies in this direction.
The paragraph BEST supports the statement that

   A. people of different nations may not consider matters in the same light
   B. it is unusual for many people to share similar ideas
   C. suspicion prevents understanding between nations
   D. the chief work of state departments is to guide relations between nations united by a common cause
   E. the people of one nation must sympathize with the view points of others

5. Economy once in a while is just not enough. I expect to find it at every level of responsi-   5.____
bility, from cabinet member to the newest and youngest recruit. Controlling waste is
something like bailing a boat; you have to keep at it. I have no intention of easing up on
my insistence on getting a dollar of value for each dollar we spend.
The paragraph BEST supports the statement that

    A.   we need not be concerned about items which cost less than a dollar
    B.   it is advisable to buy the cheaper of two items
    C.   the responsibility of economy is greater at high levels than at low levels
    D.   economy becomes easy with practice
    E.   economy is a continuing responsibility

KEY (CORRECT ANSWERS)

1. E
2. E
3. B
4. A
5. E

TEST 7

1. On all permit imprint mail the charge for postage has been printed by the mailer before he presents it for mailing and pays the postage. Such mail of any class is mailable only at the post office that issued a permit covering it. Since the postage receipts for such mail represent only the amount of permit imprint mail detected and verified, employees in receiving, handling, and outgoing sections must be alert constantly to route such mail to the weighing section before it is handled or dispatched.
   The paragraph BEST supports the statement that, at post offices where permit mail is received for dispatch,

   A. dispatching units make a final check on the amount of postage payable on permit imprint mail
   B. employees are to check the postage chargeable on mail received under permit
   C. neither more nor less postage is to be collected than the amount printed on permit imprint mail
   D. the weighing section is primarily responsible for failure to collect postage on such mail
   E. unusual measures are taken to prevent unstamped mail from being accepted

   1.____

2. Education should not stop when the individual has been prepared to make a livelihood and to live in modern society. Living would be mere existence were there no appreciation and enjoyment of the riches of art, literature, and science.
   The paragraph BEST supports the statement that true education

   A. is focused on the routine problems of life
   B. prepares one for full enjoyment of life
   C. deals chiefly with art, literature and science
   D. is not possible for one who does not enjoy scientific literature
   E. disregards practical ends

   2.____

3. Insured and c.o.d. air and surface mail is accepted with the understanding that the sender guarantees any necessary forwarding or return postage. When such mail is forwarded or returned, it shall be rated up for collection of postage; except that insured or c.o.d. air mail weighing 8 ounces or less and subject to the 40 cents an ounce rate shall be forwarded by air if delivery will be advanced, and returned by surface means, without additional postage.
   The paragraph BEST supports the statement that the return postage for undeliverable insured mail is

   A. included in the original prepayment on air mail parcels
   B. computed but not collected before dispatching surface patrol post mail to sender
   C. not computed or charged for any air mail that is returned by surface transportation
   D. included in the amount collected when the sender mails parcel post
   E. collected before dispatching for return if any amount due has been guaranteed

   3.____

4. All undeliverable first-class mail, except first-class parcels and parcel post paid with first-class postage, which cannot be returned to the sender, is sent to a dead-letter branch. Undeliverable matter of the third-and fourth-classes of obvious value for which the sender does not furnish return postage and undeliverable first-class parcels and parcel-post matter bearing postage of the first-class, which cannot be returned, is sent to a dead parcel-post branch.

   4.____

The paragraph BEST supports the statement that matter that is sent to a dead parcel-post branch includes all undeliverable

A. mail, except first-class letter mail, that appears to be valuable
B. mail, except that of the first-class, on which the sender failed to prepay the original mailing costs
C. parcels on which the mailer prepaid the first-class rate of postage
D. third-and fourth-class matter on which the required return postage has not been paid
E. parcels on which first-class postage has been prepaid, when the sender's address is not known

5. Civilization started to move rapidly when man freed himself of the shackles that restricted his search for truth.   5.____
   The paragraph BEST supports the statement that the progress of civilization

A. came as a result of man's dislike for obstacles
B. did not begin until restrictions on learning were removed
C. has been aided by man's efforts to find the truth
D. is based on continually increasing efforts
E. continues at a constantly increasing rate

———————

KEY (CORRECT ANSWERS)

1. B
2. B
3. B
4. E
5. C

———————

TEST 8

1. E-mails should be clear, concise, and brief. Omit all unnecessary words. The parts of speech most often used in e-mails are nouns, verbs, adjectives, and adverbs. If possible, do without pronouns, prepositions, articles, and copulative verbs. Use simple sentences, rather than complex and compound.
    The paragraph BEST supports the statement that in writing e-mails one should always use

    A.   common and simple words
    B.   only nouns, verbs, adjectives, and adverbs
    C.   incomplete sentences
    D.   only words essential to the meaning
    E.   the present tense of verbs

1._____

2. The function of business is to increase the wealth of the country and the value and happiness of life. It does this by supplying the material needs of men and women. When the nation's business is successfully carried on, it renders public service of the highest value.
    The paragraph BEST supports the statement that

    A.   all businesses which render public service are successful
    B.   human happiness is enhanced only by the increase of material wants
    C.   the value of life is increased only by the increase of wealth
    D.   the material needs of men and women are supplied by welt-conducted business
    E.   business is the only field of activity which increases happiness

2._____

3. In almost every community, fortunately, there are certain men and women known to be public-spirited. Others, however, may be selfish and act only as their private interests seem to require.
    The paragraph BEST supports the statement that those citizens who disregard others are

    A.   fortunate   B.   needed
    C.   found only in small communities   D.   not known
    E.   not public-spirited

3._____

KEY (CORRECT ANSWERS)

1. D
2. D
3. E

READING COMPREHENSION
UNDERSTANDING AND INTERPRETING WRITTEN MATERIAL
EXAMINATION SECTION
TEST 1

DIRECTIONS: Each question or incomplete statement is followed by several suggested answers or completions. Select the one that BEST answers the question or completes the statement. *PRINT THE LETTER OF THE CORRECT ANSWER IN THE SPACE AT THE RIGHT.*

1. The National Assessment of Educational Progress recently released the results of the first statistically valid national sampling of young adult reading skills in the United States. According to the survey, ninety-five percent of United States young adults (aged 21-25) can read at a fourth-grade level or better. This means they can read well enough to apply for a job, understand a movie guide or join the Army. This is a higher literacy rate than the eighty to eighty-five percent usually estimated for all adults. The study also found that ninety-nine percent can write their names, eighty percent can read a map or write a check for a bill, seventy per cent can understand an appliance warranty or write a letter about a billing error, twenty-five percent can calculate the amount of a tip correctly, and fewer than ten percent can correctly figure the cost of a catalog order or understand a complex bus schedule.
Which statement about the study is BEST supported by the above passage?

    A. United States literacy rates among young adults are at an all-time high.
    B. Forty percent of young people in the United States cannot write a letter about a billing error.
    C. Twenty percent of United States teenagers cannot read a map.
    D. More than ninety percent of United States young adults cannot correctly calculate the cost of a catalog order.

1.____

2. It is now widely recognized that salaries, benefits, and working conditions have more of an impact on job satisfaction than on motivation. If they aren't satisfactory, work performance and morale will suffer. But even when they are high, employees will not necessarily be motivated to work well. For example, THE WALL STREET JOURNAL recently reported that as many as forty or fifty percent of newly hired Wall Street lawyers (whose salaries start at upwards of $50,000) quit within the first three years, citing long hours, pressures, and monotony as the prime offenders. It seems there's just not enough of an intellectual challenge in their jobs. An up and coming money-market executive concluded: *Whether it was $1 million or $100 million, the procedure was the same: Except for the tension, a baboon could do my job.* When money and benefits are: adequate, the most important additional determinants of job satisfaction are: more responsibility, a sense of achievement, recognition, and a chance to advance. All of these factors have a more significant influence on employee motivation and performance. As a footnote, several studies have found that the absence of these non-monetary factors can lead to serious stress-related illnesses.
Which statement is BEST supported by the above passage?

    A. A worker's motivation to perform well is most affected by salaries, benefits, and working conditions.

2.____

B. Low pay can lead to high levels of job stress.
C. Work performance will suffer if workers feel they are not paid well.
D. After satisfaction with pay and benefits, the next most important factor is more responsibility.

3. The establishment of joint labor-management production committees occurred in the United States during World War I and again during World War II. Their use was greatly encouraged by the National War Labor Board in World War I and the War Production Board in 1942. Because of the war, labor-management cooperation was especially desired to produce enough goods for the war effort, to reduce conflict, and to control inflation. The committees focused on how to achieve greater efficiency, and consulted on health and safety, training, absenteeism, and people issues in general. During the second world war, there were approximately five thousand labor-management committees in factories, affecting over six million workers. While research has found that only a few hundred committees made significant contributions to productivity, there were additional benefits in many cases. It became obvious to many that workers had ideas to contribute to the running of the organization, and that efficient enterprises could become even more so. Labor-management cooperation was also extended to industries that had never experienced it before. Directly after each war, however, few United States labor-management committees were in operation.
Which statement is BEST supported by the above passage?   3.____

A. The majority of United States labor-management committees during the second world war accomplished little.
B. A major goal of United States labor-management committees during the first and second world wars was to increase productivity.
C. There were more United States labor-management committees during the second world war than during the first world war.
D. There are few United States labor-management committees in operation today.

4. Studies have found that stress levels among employees who have a great deal of customer contact or a great deal of contact with the public can be very high. There are many reasons for this. Sometimes stress results when the employee is caught in the middle — an organization wants things done one way, but the customer wants them done another way. The situation becomes even worse for the employee's stress levels when he or she knows ways to more effectively provide the service, but isn't allowed to, by the organization. An example is the bank teller who is required to ask a customer for two forms of identification before he or she can cash a check, even though the teller knows the customer well. If organizational mishaps occur or if there are problems with job design, the employee may be powerless to satisfy the customer, and also powerless to protect himself or herself from the customer's wrath. An example of this is the waitress who is forced to serve poorly prepared food. Studies have also found, however, that if the organization and the employee design the positions and the service encounter well, and encourage the use of effective stress management techniques, stress can be reduced to levels that are well below average.
Which statement is BEST supported by the above passage?   4.____

A. It is likely that knowledgeable employees will experience greater levels of job-related stress.

B. The highest levels of occupational stress are found among those employees who have a great deal of customer contact.

C. Organizations can contribute to the stress levels of their employees by poorly designing customer contact situations.

D. Stress levels are generally higher in banks and restaurants.

5. It is estimated that approximately half of the United States population suffers from varying degrees of adrenal malfunction. When under stress for long periods of time, the adrenals produce extra cortisol and norepinephrine. By producing more hormones than they were designed to comfortably manufacture and secrete, the adrenals can *burn out over* time and then decrease their secretion. When this happens, the body loses its capacity to cope with stress, and the individual becomes sicker more easily and for longer periods of time. A result of adrenal malfunction may be a diminished output of cortisol. Symptoms of diminished cortisol output include any of the following: craving substances that will temporarily raise serum glucose levels such as caffeine, sweets, soda, juice, or tobacco; becoming dizzy when standing up too quickly; irritability; headaches; and erratic energy levels. Since cortisol is an anti-inflammatory hormone, a decreased output over extended periods of time can make one prone to inflammatory diseases such as arthritis, bursitis, colitis, and allergies. (Many food and pollen allergies disappear when adrenal function is restored to normal.) The patient will have no reserve energy, and infections can spread quickly. Excessive cortisol production, on the other hand, can decrease immunity, leading to frequent and prolonged illnesses.
Which statement is BEST supported by the above passage?

5._____

A. Those who suffer from adrenal malfunction are most likely to be prone to inflammatory diseases such as arthritis and allergies.

B. The majority of Americans suffer from varying degrees of adrenal malfunction.

C. It is better for the health of the adrenals to drink juice instead of soda.

D. Too much cortisol can inhibit the body's ability to resist disease.

6. Psychologist B.F. Skinner pointed out long ago that gambling is reinforced either by design or accidentally, by what he called a variable ratio schedule. A slot machine, for example, is cleverly designed to provide a payoff after it has been played a variable number of times. Although the person who plays it and wins while playing receives a great deal of monetary reinforcement, over the long run the machine will take in much more money than it pays out. Research on both animals and humans has consistently found that such variable reward schedules maintain a very high rate of repeat behavior, and that this behavior is particularly resistant to extinction.
Which statement is BEST supported by the above passage?

6._____

A. Gambling, because it is reinforced by the variable ratio schedule, is more difficult to eliminate than most addictions.

B. If someone is rewarded or wins consistently, even if it is not that often, he or she is likely to continue that behavior.

C. Playing slot machines is the safest form of gambling because they are designed so that eventually the player will indeed win.

D. A cat is likely to come when called if its owner has trained it correctly.

7. Paper entrepreneurialism is an offshoot of scientific management that has become so extreme that it has lost all connection to the actual workplace. It generates profits by cleverly manipulating rules and numbers that only in theory represent real products and real assets. At its worst, paper entrepreneurialism involves very little more than imposing losses on others for the sake of short-term profits. The others may be taxpayers, share holders who end up indirectly subsidizing other share holders, consumers, or investors. Paper entrepreneurialism has replaced product entrepreneurialism, is seriously threatening the United States economy, and is hurting our necessary attempts to transform the nation's industrial and productive economic base. An example is the United States company that complained loudly in 1979 that it did not have the $200 million needed to develop a video-cassette recorder, though demand for them had been very high. The company, however, did not hesitate to spend $1.2 billion that same year to buy a mediocre finance company. The video recorder market was handed over to other countries, who did not hesitate to manufacture them.
Which statement is BEST supported by the above passage?

    A. Paper entrepreneurialism involves very little more than imposing losses on others for the sake of short-term profits.
    B. Shareholders are likely to benefit most from paper entrepreneurialism.
    C. Paper entrepreneurialism is hurting the United States economy.
    D. The United States could have made better video-cassette recorders than the Japanese but we ceded the market to them in 1979.

7.____

8. *The prisoner's dilemma* is an almost 40-year-old game-theory model psychologists, biologists, economists, and political scientists use to try to understand the dynamics of competition and cooperation. Participants in the basic version of the experiment are told that they and their *accomplice* have been caught red-handed. Together, their best strategy is to cooperate by remaining silent. If they do this, each will get off with a 30-day sentence. But either person can do better for himself or herself. If you double-cross your partner, you will go scott free while he or she serves ten years. The problem is, if you each betray the other, you will both go to prison for eight years, not thirty days. No matter what your partner chooses, you are logically better off choosing betrayal. Unfortunately, your partner realizes this too, and so the odds are good that you will both get eight years. That's the dilemma. (The length of the prison sentences is always the same for each variation.) Participants at a recent symposium on behavioral economics at Harvard University discussed the many variations on the game that have been used over the years. In one standard version, subjects are paired with a supervisor who pays them a dollar for each point they score. Over the long run, both subjects will do best if they cooperate every time. Yet in each round, there is a great temptation to betray the other because no one knows what the other will do. The best overall strategy for this variation was found to be *tit for tat*, doing unto your opponent as he or she has just done unto you. It is a simple strategy, but very effective. The partner can easily recognize it and respond. It is retaliatory enough not to be easily exploited, but forgiving enough to allow a pattern of mutual cooperation to develop.
Which statement is BEST supported by the above passage?

    A. The best strategy for playing *prisoner's dilemma* is to cooperate and remain silent.
    B. If you double-cross your partner, and he or she does not double-cross you, your partner will receive a sentence of eight years.

8.____

C. When playing *prisoner's dilemma*, it is best to double-cross your partner.
D. If you double-cross your partner, and he or she double-crosses you, you will receive an eight-year sentence.

9. After many years of experience as the vice president and general manager of a large company, I feel that I know what I'm looking for in a good manager. First, the manager has to be comfortable with himself or herself, and not be arrogant or defensive. Secondly, he or she has to have a genuine interest in people. There are some managers who love ideas — and that's fine — but to be a manager, you must love people, and you must make a hobby of understanding them, believing in them and trusting them. Third, I look for a willingness and a facility to manage conflict. Gandhi defined conflict as a way of getting at the truth. Each person brings his or her own grain of truth and the conflict washes away the illusion and fantasy. Finally, a manager has to have a vision, and the ability and charisma to articulate it. A manager should be seen as a little bit crazy. Some eccentricity is an asset. People don't want to follow vanilla leaders. They want to follow chocolate-fudge-ripple leaders.
Which statement is BEST supported by the above passage?

9.____

A. It is very important that a good manager spend time studying people.
B. It is critical for good managers to love ideas.
C. Managers should try to minimize or avoid conflict.
D. Managers should be familiar with people's reactions to different flavors of ice cream.

10. Most societies maintain a certain set of values and assumptions that make their members feel either good or bad about themselves, and either better or worse than other people. In most developed countries, these values are based on the assumption that we are all free to be what we want to be, and that differences in income, work, and education are a result of our own efforts. This may make us believe that people with more income work that is more skilled, more education, and more power are somehow *better* people. We may view their achievements as proof that they have more intelligence, more motivation, and more initiative than those with lower status. The myth tells us that power, income, and education are freely and equally available to all, and that our failure to achieve them is due to our own personal inadequacy. This simply is not the case.

10.____

The possessions we own may also seem to point to our real worth as individuals. The more we own, the more worthy of respect we may feel we are. Or, the acquisition of possessions may be a way of trying to fulfill ourselves, to make up for the loss of community and/or purpose. It is a futile pursuit because lost community and purpose can never be compensated for by better cars or fancier houses. And too often, when these things fail to satisfy, we believe it is only because we don't have enough money to buy better quality items, or more items. We feel bad that we haven't been successful enough to get all that we think we need. No matter how much we do have, goods never really satisfy for long. There is always something else to acquire, and true satisfaction eludes many, many of us.
Which statement is BEST supported by the above passage?

A. The author would agree with the theory of *survival of the fittest.*
B. The possessions an individual owns are not a proper measure of his or her real worth.

C. Many countries make a sincere attempt to ensure equal access to quality education for their citizens.

D. The effect a society's value system has on the lives of its members is greatly exaggerated.

11. *De nihilo nihil* is Latin *for nothing comes from nothing*. In the first century, the Roman poet Persius advised that if anything is to be produced of value, effort must be expended. He also said, *In nihilum nil posse revorti* - anything once produced cannot become nothing again. It is thought that Persius was parodying Lucretius, who expounded the 500-year-old physical theories of Epicurus. *De nihilo nihil* can also be used as a cynical comment, to negatively comment on something that is of poor quality produced by a person of little talent. The implication here is: *What can you expect from such a source?*
Which statement is BEST supported by the above passage?

A. *In nihilum nil posse revorti* can be interpreted as meaning *if anything is to be produced of value, then effort must be expended.*
B. *De nihilo nihil* can be understood in two different ways.
C. Lucretius was a great physicist.
D. Persius felt that Epicurus put in little effort while developing his theories.

11.____

12. A Cornell University study has found that less than one percent of the billion pounds of pesticides used in this country annually strike their intended targets. The study found that the pesticides, which are somewhat haphazardly applied to 370 million acres, or about sixteen percent of the nation's total land area, end up polluting the environment and contaminating almost all 200,000 species of plants and animals, including humans. While the effect of indirect contamination on human cancer rates was not estimated, the study found that approximately 45,000 human pesticide poisonings occur annually, including about 3,000 cases admitted to hospitals and approximately 200 fatalities.
Which statement is BEST supported by the above passage?

A. It is likely that indirect pesticide contamination affects human health.
B. Pesticides are applied to over one-quarter of the total United States land area.
C. If pesticides were applied more carefully, fewer pesticide-resistant strains of pests would develop.
D. Human cancer rates in this country would drop considerably if pesticide use was cut in half.

12.____

13. The new conservative philosophy presents a unified, coherent approach to the world. It offers to explain much of our experience since the turbulent 1960s, and it shows what we've learned since about the dangers of indulgence and permissiveness. But it also warns that the world has become more ruthless, and that as individuals and as a nation, we must struggle for survival. It is necessary to impose responsibility and discipline in order to defeat those forces that threaten us. This lesson is dramatically clear, and can be applied to a wide range of issues.
Which statement is BEST supported by the above passage?

A. The 1970s were a time of permissiveness and indulgence.
B. The new conservative philosophy may help in imposing discipline and a sense of responsibility in order to meet the difficult challenges facing this country.
C. The world faced greater challenges during the second world war than it faces at the present time.
D. More people identify themselves today as conservative in their political philosophy.

13.____

14. One of the most puzzling questions in management in recent years has been how usu-   14.____
ally honest, compassionate, intelligent managers can sometimes act in ways that are dis-
honest, uncaring, and unethical. How could top-level managers at the Manville
Corporation, for example, suppress evidence for decades that proved beyond all doubt
that asbestos inhalation was killing their own employees? What drove the managers of a
midwest bank to continue to act in a way that threatened to bankrupt the institution, ruin
its reputation, and cost thousands of employees and investors their jobs and their savings? It's been estimated that about two out of three of America's five hundred largest
corporations have been involved in some form of illegal behavior. There are, of course,
some common rationalizations used to justify unethical conduct: believing that the activity is in the organization's or the individual's best interest, believing that the activity is not
really immoral or illegal, believing that no one will ever know, or believing that the organization will sanction the behavior because it helps the organization. Ambition can distort
one's sense of *duty*.
Which statement is BEST supported by the above passage?

   A.   Top-level managers of corporations are currently involved in a plan to increase eth-
ical behavior among their employees.
   B.   There are many good reasons why a manager may act unethically.
   C.   Some managers allow their ambitions to override their sense of ethics.
   D.   In order to successfully compete, some organizations may have to indulge in
unethical or illegal behavior from time to time.

15. Some managers and supervisors believe that they are leaders because they occupy   15.____
positions of responsibility and authority. But leadership is more than holding a position. It
is often defined in management literature as *the ability to influence the opinions attitudes
and behaviors of others.* Obviously, there are some managers that would not qualify as
leaders, and some leaders that are not *technically* managers. Research has found that
many people overrate their own leadership abilities. In one recent study, seventy percent
of those surveyed rated themselves in the top quartile in leadership abilities, and only
two percent felt they were below average as leaders.
Which statement is BEST supported by the above passage?

   A.   In a recent study, the majority of people surveyed rated themselves in the top
twenty-five percent in leadership abilities.
   B.   Ninety-eight percent of the people surveyed in a recent study had average or
above-average leadership skills.
   C.   In order to be a leader, one should hold a management position.
   D.   Leadership is best defined as the ability to be liked by those one must lead.

KEY (CORRECT ANSWERS)

1.	D	6.	B	11.	B
2.	C	7.	C	12.	A
3.	B	8.	D	13.	B
4.	C	9.	A	14.	C
5.	D	10.	B	15.	A

EXAMINATION SECTION
TEST 1

DIRECTIONS: Each question or incomplete statement is followed by several suggested answers or completions. Select the one that BEST answers the question or completes the statement. *PRINT THE LETTER OF THE CORRECT ANSWER IN THE SPACE AT THE RIGHT.*

1. Which of the following fractions is the SMALLEST?　　1.____

    A.　2/3　　　　　B.　4/5　　　　　C.　5/7　　　　　D.　5/11

2. 40% is equivalent to which of the following?　　2.____

    A.　4/5　　　　　B.　4/6　　　　　C.　2/5　　　　　D.　4/100

3. How many 100's are in 10,000?　　3.____

    A.　10　　　　　B.　100　　　　　C.　10,000　　　　　D.　100,000

4. $\frac{6}{7}+\frac{11}{12}$ is approximately　　4.____

    A.　1　　　　　B.　2　　　　　C.　17　　　　　D.　19

5. The time required to heat water to a certain temperature is directly proportional to the volume of water being heated.　　5.____
If it takes 12 minutes to heat 1 1/2 gallons of water, how many minutes will it take to heat 2 gallons of water?

    A.　12　　　　　B.　16　　　　　C.　18　　　　　D.　24

6. The cost of an item increased by 25%.　　6.____
If the original cost was C dollars, identify the expression which gives the new cost of that item.

    A.　C + 0.25　　　　　B.　1/4 C　　　　　C.　25C　　　　　D.　1.25C

7. Given the formula PV = nRT, all of the following are true EXCEPT　　7.____

    A.　T = PV/nR　　　B.　P = nRT/V　　　C.　V = P/nRT　　　D.　n = PV/RT

8. If a Fahrenheit (F) temperature reading is 104, find its Celsius (C) equivalent, given that C = i(F-32)　　8.____

    A.　36　　　　　B.　40　　　　　C.　72　　　　　D.　76

9. If 40% of a graduating class plans to go directly to work after graduation, which of the following must be TRUE?　　9.____

    A.　Less than half of the class plans to go directly to work.
    B.　Forty members of the class plan to enter the job market.
    C.　Most of the class plans to go directly to work.
    D.　Six in ten members of the class are expected not to graduate.

10. Given a multiple-choice test item which has 5 choices, what is the probability of guessing the correct answer if you know nothing about the item content?

    A. 5%   B. 10%   C. 20%   D. 25%

10.____

11. Which graph BEST represents the data shown in the table at the right?

11.____

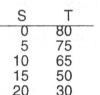

S	T
0	80
5	75
10	65
15	50
20	30
25	5

A.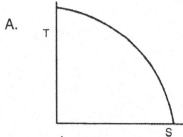

B.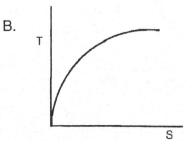

C.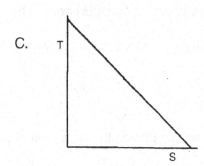

D.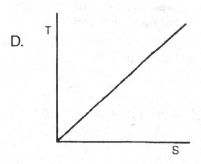

12. If 3(X + 5Y) = 24, find Y when X = 3.

    A. 1   B. 3   C. 33/5   D. 7

12.____

13. The payroll of a grocery store for its 23 clerks is $395,421. Which expression below shows the average salary of a clerk?

    A. 395,421 x 23   B. 23 ÷ 395,421

    C. (395,421x14) ÷ 23   D. 395,421 ÷ 23

13.____

14. If 12.8 pounds of coffee cost $50.80, what is the APPROXIMATE price per pound?

    A. $2.00   B. $3.00   C. $4.00   D. $5.00

14.____

15. A road map has a scale where 1 inch corresponds to 150 miles. A distance of 3 3/4 inches on the map corresponds to what actual distance?
    _____ miles

    A. 153.75   B. 375   C. 525   D. 562.5

15.____

16. How many square feet of plywood are needed to construct the back and 4 adjacent sides of the box shown at the right?
_____ square feet.

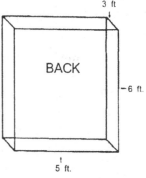

A. 63
B. 90
C. 96
D. 126

16._____

17. One thirty pound bag of lawn fertilizer costs $20.00 and will cover 600 square feet of lawn. Terry's lawn is a 96 foot by 75 foot rectangle. How much will it cost Terry to buy enough bags of fertilizer for her lawn?
Which of the following do you NOT need in order to solve this problem?
The

A. product of 96 and 75
B. fact that one bag weighs 30 pounds
C. fact that one bag covers 600 square feet
D. fact that one bag costs $20.00

17._____

18. On the graph shown at the right, between which hours was the drop in temperature GREATEST?

A. 11:00 - Noon
B. Noon - 1:00
C. 1:00 - 2:00
D. 2:00 - 3:00

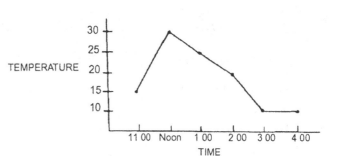

18._____

19. If on a typical railroad track, the distance from the center of one railroad tie to the next is 30 inches, approximately how many ties would be needed for one mile of track?

A. 180   B. 2,110   C. 6,340   D. 63,360

19._____

20. Which of the following is MOST likely to be the volume of a wine bottle?

A. 750 milliliters   B. 7 kilograms
C. 7 milligrams   D. 7 liters

20._____

21. What is the reading on the gauge shown at the right?

A. -7
B. -3
C. 1
D. 3

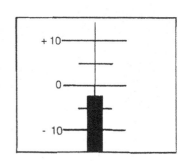

21._____

22. Which statement below disproves the assertion, *All students in Mrs. Marino's 10th grade geometry class are planning to go to college?*   22.____

    A.   Albert is in Mrs, Marino's class, but he is not planning to take mathematics next year.
    B.   Jorge is not in Mrs. Marino's class, but he is still planning to go to college.
    C.   Pierre is in Mrs. Marino's class but says he will not be attending school anymore after this year.
    D.   Crystal is in Mrs. Marino's class and plans to attend Yale University when she graduates.

23. A store advertisement reads, *Buy now while our prices are low. There will never be a better time to buy.* The customer reading this advertisement should assume that   23.____

    A.   the prices at the store will probably never be lower
    B.   right now, this store has the best prices in town
    C.   prices are higher at other stores
    D.   prices are always lowest at this store

24. *Given any positive integer A, there is always a positive number B such that A x B is less than 1.*   24.____
    Which statement below supports this generalization?

    A. $8 \times 1/16 = 1/2$ B. $8 \times 1/2 = 4$
    C. $5/2 \times 1/10 = 1/4$ D. $1/2 \times 1/2 = 1/2$

25. Of the following expressions, which is equivalent to $4C + D = 12E$?   25.____

    A. $C = 4(12E - D)$ B. $4 + D = 12E - C$

    C. $4C + 12E = -D$ D. $C = \dfrac{12E - D}{4}$

KEY (CORRECT ANSWERS)

1.	D		11.	A
2.	C		12.	A
3.	B		13.	D
4.	B		14.	C
5.	B		15.	D
6.	D		16.	C
7.	C		17.	B
8.	B		18.	D
9.	A		19.	B
10.	C		20.	A

21.	B
22.	C
23.	A
24.	A
25.	D

SOLUTIONS TO PROBLEMS

1. Converting to decimals, we get $.\overline{6}$, $.8$, $.714$ (approx), $.\overline{45}$. The smallest is $.\overline{45}$ corresponding to 5/11.

2. 40% = 40/100 = 2/5

3. 10,000 ÷ 100 = 100

4. $\dfrac{6}{7} + \dfrac{11}{12} = (72 + 77) \div 84 = \dfrac{149}{84} \approx 1.77 \approx 2$

5. Let x = required minutes. Then, 12/1 1/2 = x/2 This reduces to 1 1/2x = 24. Solving, x = 16

6. New cost is C + .25C = 1.25C

7. For PV = nRT, V = nRT/P

8. C = 5/9 (104-32) = 5/9 (72) = 40

9. Since 40% is less than 50% (or half), we conclude that less than half of the class plans to go to work directly after graduation.

10. The probability of guessing right is 1/5 or 20%.

11. Curve A is most accurate since as S increases, we see that T decreases. Note, however, that the relationship is NOT linear. Although S increases in equal amounts, the decrease in T is NOT in equal amounts.

12. 3(3+5Y) = 24. This simplifies to 9 + 15Y = 24 Solving, Y = 1

13. The average salary is $395,421 ÷ 23

14. The price per pound is $50.80 ÷ 12.8 = $3.96875 or approximately $4.

15. Actual distance is (3 3/4)(150) = 562.5 miles

16. The area of the back = (6)(5) = 30 sq.ft. The combined area of the two vertical sides is (2)(6)(3) = 36 sq.ft. The combined area of the horizontal sides is (2)(5)(3) = 30 sq.ft. Total area = 30 + 36 + 30 = 96 square feet.

17. Choice B is not relevant to solving the problem since the cost will be [(96)(75) / 600][$20] = $240. So, the weight per bag is not needed.

18. For the graph, the largest temperature drop was from 2:00 P.M. to 3:00 P.M. The temperature dropped 20 - 10 = 10 degrees.

19. 1 mile = 5280 feet = 63,360 inches. Then, 63,360 ÷ 30 = 2112 or about 2110 ties are needed.

20. Since 1 liter = 1.06 quarts, 750 milliliters = (750/1000)(1.06) = .795 quarts. This is a reasonable volume for a wine bottle.

21. The reading is -3.

22. Statement C contradicts the given information, since Pierre is in Mrs. Marino's class. Then he should plan to go to college.

23. Since there will never be a better time to buy at this particular store, the customer can assume the current prices will probably never be lower.

24. Statement A illustrates this concept. Note that in general, if n is a positive integer, then

$$(n) \left(\frac{1}{n+1} \right) < 1$$

Example: (100)(1/100)< 1

TEST 2

DIRECTIONS: Each question or incomplete statement is followed by several suggested answers or completions. Select the one that BEST answers the question or completes the statement. *PRINT THE LETTER OF THE CORRECT ANSWER IN THE SPACE AT THE RIGHT.*

1. Which of the following lists numbers in INCREASING order?

   A. 0.4, 0.04, 0.004
   C. 0.7, 0.77, 0.777
   B. 2.71, 3.15, 2.996
   D. 0.06, 0.5, 0.073

   1.____

2. $\dfrac{4}{10} + \dfrac{7}{100} + \dfrac{5}{1000} =$

   A. 4.75
   B. 0.475
   C. 0.0475
   D. 0.00475

   2.____

3. 700 times what number equals 7?

   A. 10
   B. 0.1
   C. 0.01
   D. 0.001

   3.____

4. 943 - 251 is approximately

   A. 600
   B. 650
   C. 700
   D. 1200

   4.____

5. The time needed to set up a complicated piece of machinery is inversely proportional to the number of years' experience of the worker.
   If a worker with 10 years' experience needs 6 hours to do the job, how long will it take a worker with 15 years' experience?

   A. 4
   B. 5
   C. 9
   D. 25

   5.____

6. Let W represent the number of waiters and D, the number of diners in a particular restaurant.
   Identify the expression which represents the statement: There are 10 times as many diners as waiters.

   A. 10W = D
   C. 10D + 10W
   B. 10D = W
   D. 10 = D + W

   6.____

7. Which of the following is equivalent to the formula F = XC + Y?

   A. F-C=X+Y
   B. Y = F + XC
   C. $C = \dfrac{F \; Y}{X}$
   D. $C = \dfrac{F \; X}{Y}$

   7.____

8. Given the formula A = BC / D, if A = 12, B = 6, and D = 3, what is the value of C?

   A. 2/3
   B. 6
   C. 18
   D. 24

   8.____

9. 5 is to 7 as X is to 35. X =

   A. 7
   B. 12
   C. 25
   D. 49

   9.____

10. Kramer Middle School has 5 seventh grade mathematics teachers: two of the math
    teachers are women and three are men.
    If you are assigned a teacher at random, what is the probability of getting a female
    teacher?

    A. 0.2   B. 0.4   C. 0.6   D. 0.8

10.____

11. Which statement BEST describes the graph shown at
    the right? Temperature

    A. and time decrease at the same rate
    B. and time increase at the same rate
    C. increases over time
    D. decreases over time

11.____

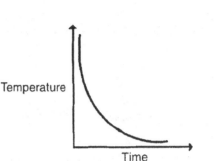

12. If 3X + 4 = 2Y, find Y when X = 2.

    A. 0   B. 3   C. 4 1/2   D. 5

12.____

13. A car goes 243 miles on 8.7 gallons of gas. Which numeric expression should be used to
    determine the car's miles per gallon?

    A. 243 x 87   B. 8.7 ÷ 243
    C. 243 ÷ 8.7   D. 243 - 8.7

13.____

14. What is the average cost per book if you buy six books at $4.00 each and four books at
    $5.00 each?

    A. $4.40   B. $4.50   C. $4.60   D. $5.40

14.____

15. A publisher's sale offers a 15% discount to anyone buying more than 100 workbooks.
    What will be the discount on 200 workbooks selling at $2.25 each?

    A. $15.00   B. $30.00   C. $33.75   D. $67.50

15.____

16. A road crew erects 125 meters of fencing in one workday. How many workdays are
    required to erect a kilometer of fencing?

    A. 0.8   B. 8   C. 80   D. 800

16.____

17. Last month Kim made several telephone calls to New York City totaling 45 minutes in all.
    What does Kim need in order to calculate the average duration of her New York City
    calls?
    The

    A. total number of calls she made to New York City
    B. cost per minute of a call to New York City
    C. total cost of her telephone bill last month
    D. days of the week on which the calls were made

17.____

18.

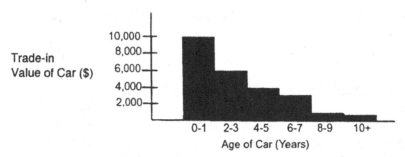

Trade-in
Value of Car ($)

Age of Car (Years)

18.____

The chart above relates a car's age to its trade-in value. Based on the chart, which of the following is TRUE?

A. A 4- to 5-year old car has a trade-in value of about $2,000.
B. The trade-in value of an 8- to 9-year old car is about 1/3 that of a 2- to 3-year old car.
C. A 6- to 7-year old car has no trade-in value.
D. A 4- to 5-year old car's trade-in value is about $2,000 less than that of a 2- to 3-year old car.

19. Which of the following expressions could be used to determine how many seconds are in a 24-hour day?

19.____

A. 60 x 60 x 24   B. 60 x 12 x 24
C. 60 x 2 x 24   D. 60 x 24

20. For measuring milk, we could use each of the following EXCEPT

20.____

A. liters   B. kilograms
C. millimeters   D. cubic centimeters

21. What is the reading on the gauge shown at the right?

21.____

A. 51
B. 60
C. 62.5
D. 70

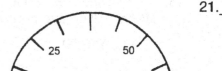

22. Bill is taller than Yvonne. Yvonne is shorter than Sue. Sue is 5'4" tall.
Which of the following conclusions must be TRUE?

22.____

A. Bill is taller than Sue.
B. Yvonne is taller than 5'4".
C. Sue is taller than Bill.
D. Yvonne is the shortest.

23. The Bass family traveled 268 miles during the first day of their vacation and another 300 miles on the next day. Maria Bass said they were 568 miles from home.
Which of the following facts did Maria assume?

23.____

A. They traveled faster on the first day and slower on the second.
B. If she plotted the vacation route on a map, it would be a straight line.
C. Their car used more gasoline on the second day.
D. They traveled faster on the second day than they did on the first.

24. *The word LEFT in a mathematics problem indicates that it is a subtraction problem.*   24.____
Which of the following mathematics problems proves this statement FALSE?

    A. I want to put 150 bottles into cartons which hold 8 bottles each. After I completely fill as many cartons as I can, how many bottles will be left?

    B. Sarah had 5 books but gave one to John. How many books did Sarah have left?

    C. Carlos had $4.25 but spent $3.75. How much did he have left?

    D. We had 38 models in stock but after yesterday's sale, only 12 are left. How many did we sell?

25. Let Q represent the number of miles Dave can jog in 15 minutes.   25.____
Identify the expression which represents the number of miles Dave can jog between 3:00 PM and 4:45 PM?

    A. 1 3/4 Q   B. 7Q

    C. $15 \times 1\frac{3}{4} \times Q$ D. Q/7

––––––––

KEY (CORRECT ANSWERS)

1.	C		11.	D
2.	B		12.	D
3.	C		13.	C
4.	C		14.	A
5.	A		15.	D
6.	A		16.	B
7.	C		17.	A
8.	B		18.	D
9.	C		19.	A
10.	B		20.	C

21.	C
22.	D
23.	B
24.	A
25.	B

––––––––

SOLUTIONS TO PROBLEMS

1. Choice C is in ascending order since .7 < .77 < .777

2. Rewrite in decimal form: .4 + .07 + .005 = .475

3. Let x = missing number. Then, 700x = 7. Solving, x = 7/700 = .01

4. 943 - 251 = 692 $\approx$ 700

5. Let x = hours needed. Then, 10/15 = x/6. Solving, x = 4

6. The number of diners (D) is 10 times as many waiters (10W). So, D = 10W or 10W = D

7. Given F = XC + Y, subtract Y from each side to get F - Y = XC. Finally, dividing by X, we get (F-Y)/X = C

8. 12 = 6C/3. Then, 12 = 2C, so C = 6

9. 5/7 = X/35 Then, 7x = 175, so x = 25

10. Probability of a female teacher = 2/5 = .4

11. Statement D is best, since as time increases, the temperature decreases

12. (3)(2) + 4 = 2Y. Then, 10 = 2Y, so Y = 5

13. Miles per gallon = 243 / 8.7

14. Total purchase is (6)($4) + (4)($5) = $44. The average cost per book is $44 ÷ 10 = $4.40

15. (220)($2.25) = $450. The discount is (.15)($450) = $67.50

16. The number of workdays is 1000 ÷ 125 = 8

17. Choice A is correct because the average duration of the phone calls = total time ÷ total number of calls

18. Statement D is correct since a 4-5 year-old car's value is $4,000, whereas a 2-3 year-old car's value is $6000.

19. 60 seconds = 1 minute and 60 minutes = 1 hour. Thus, 24 hours = (24)(60)(60) or (60)(60)(24) seconds

20. We can't use millimeters in measuring milk since millimeters is a linear measurement

21. The reading shows the average of 50 and 75 = 62.5

22. Since Yvonne is shorter than both Bill and Sue, Yvonne is the shortest.

23. Statement B is assumed correct since 568 = 268 + 300 could only be true if the mileage traveled represents a straight line

24. To find the number of bottles left, we look only for the remainder when 150 is divided by 8 (which happens to be 6)

EXAMINATION SECTION
TEST 1

DIRECTIONS   Each question or incomplete statement is followed by several suggested answers or completions. Select the one that BEST answers the question or completes the statement. *PRINT THE LETTER OF THE CORRECT ANSWER IN THE SPACE AT THE RIGHT.*

1. A solid which has a point at one end and a circle at the other end is a   1._____

   A. cone   B. sphere   C. cylinder   D. prism

2. $(5 \times 10^2) + (3 \times 10^1) + (4 \times 1) =$ 2._____

   A. 84   B. 534   C. 5034   D. (5+3-4)10

3. All members of R are members of T, but no members of T are members of V. Therefore, you know that   3._____

   A. some members of R are members of V
   B. no members of V are members of R
   C. some members of V are members of T
   D. no members of T are members of R

4. The multiplication of 6x48 can be distributed as   4._____

   A. (6x40) + (8x8)   B. (6x20) + (20x8)
   C. (6x20) + (6x20) + (6x8)   D. (6x6) + (6x8)

5. Which of these could be used as a divisor and NOT change a dividend?   5._____

   A. 0   B. 1
   C. The dividend itself   D. There is no such number

6. Through any one point, there can be   6._____

   A. an unlimited number of lines
   B. only one line
   C. only one set of parallel lines
   D. only two lines

7. Ten girls have an average of 25 points on a test.
   If 5 points are added to each girl's number, what will the average then be?   7._____

   A. 3   B. 25.5   C. 27   D. 30

8. E + A =   8._____

   A. 2EA   B. AE   C. A+E   D. A-E

9. A number that indicates how many times a base number is used as a factor is a(n)   9._____

   A. prime number   B. rational number
   C. reciprocal   D. exponent

10. Some of the multiples of a certain number are w, k, m, p, and z. Some of the multiples of another number are k, p, z, and r.
A common multiple of the two numbers is

    A. r   B. w   C. m   D. k

10.____

11. Which is another way to multiply a×b×c?

    A. (a+b)×c   B. c×a×b
    C. b×(a+c)   D. (a×b) + (a×c)

11.____

12. The set of any two points on a line and all points between them is a

    A. ray   B. bisector of an angle
    C. half line   D. line segment

12.____

13. What is the area of this rectangular region?
    A. 12 sq. ft.
    B. 20 sq. ft.
    C. 24 sq. ft.
    D. 36 sq. ft.

13.____

14. In the numeral (6568, the 6 that is underlined stands for how many times as many as the other 6?

    A. 10   B. 100   C. 1000   D. the same

14.____

15. According to the distributive principle, one third of 6 ft. 9 in. would be

    A. 23 in.   B. 3 ft. 3 in.
    C. 2 ft. + 3 in.   D. 1 yd. + 3 in.

15.____

16. Two names for the same thing are USUALLY indicated by which sign?

    A. ε   B. =   C. ~   D. u

16.____

17. Mary has 60¢ saved to buy three hairbows which cost 250 each.
Which sentence can be used to find out how many cents more (n) she needs?

    A. 60 ÷ n = 3 x 25   B. 3 x 25 = 60n
    C. 60 ÷ 3 - n = 25   D. 3 x 25 = 60 - n

17.____

18. Which of these is a prime number?

    A. 43   B. 68   C. 87   D. 165

18.____

19. Which means 24 divided by a number equals twice the number?

19.____

    A. $\dfrac{24}{n} = \dfrac{2n}{24}$ B. $24 \div n = \dfrac{n}{2}$

    C. $2 \times \dfrac{24}{n} = n$ D. $\dfrac{24}{n} = 2n$

20. Which of these numerals can you be sure is NOT correctly written?   20.____

    A. 257_{eight} B. 362_{seven} C. 421_{four} D. 453_{six}

21. What is 3754 rounded to the nearest 500?   21.____

    A. 3500   B. 3700   C. 3750   D. 4000

22. When a person measures, he ALWAYS   22.____

    A. tallies   B. compares   C. marks   D. weighs

23. Four is what percent of 37?   23.____
To find the percent, a person may use the equation

    A. $\dfrac{4}{37} = \dfrac{n}{100}$ B. $\dfrac{4}{100} = \dfrac{37}{n}$

    C. $\dfrac{(100 \times 37)}{4} = n$ D. $\dfrac{37}{100} = \dfrac{n}{4}$

24. Angle a is a right angle.   24.____
Therefore, the sum of the measurements of angles b and c is

    A. 45°

    B. 90°

    C. 180°

    D. 270°

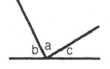

25. If 2 pencils cost 5¢, how many cents will 6 pencils cost at the same rate?   25.____
The solution equation is

    A. $\dfrac{2}{6} = \dfrac{n}{5}$ B. $\dfrac{2}{5} = \dfrac{n}{6}$ C. $\dfrac{2}{5} = \dfrac{6}{n}$ D. $\dfrac{2}{n} = \dfrac{5}{6}$

26. a(b+c) = ab + ac illustrates the _____ principle.   26.____

    A. commutative   B. associative
    C. distributive   D. binary

27. If the measurement of angle a is 130°, the measurement of angle b   27.____
is

    A. 30°

    B. 40°

    C. 50°

    D. 70°

28. In which of these will the product be LESS than m when m is a positive number and not   28.____
0?

    A. $m \times \dfrac{2}{3}$ B. $1\dfrac{1}{4} \times m$ C. $1.0 \times m$ D. $m \times \dfrac{5}{4}$

29. 15.94 x 0.5 is APPROXIMATELY   29._____

    A. 0.08   B. 0.8   C. 8   D. 80

30. If X = |2, 4, 6, 8| and Y = |3, 6, 9, 12|, then   30._____

    A. $X \cap Y = |2,3,4,6,8,9,12|$ B. $X \cup Y = |6|$

    C. $X \cup Y = |2,3,4,6,8,9,12|$ D. $X \cap Y = |2,3|$

31. If the measurement of angle b is 65 and of angle c is also 65, then the   31._____
measurement of angle a is

    A. 60°

    B. 50°

    C. 40°

    D. 20°

32. What is the area within triangle JKL? _____ sq. ft.   32._____

    A. 48

    B. 50

    C. 95

    D. 100

33. The place holder, or the unknown, in an equation is called   33._____

    A. the empty set   B. a variable

    C. an equality   D. an inequality

34. If part of K is all of W, and all of K is part of M, you can be sure that   34._____

    A. all of W is part of M

    B. all of K is all of W

    C. K is less than M - W

    D. W + K is less than M

35.   35._____

    -3   -2   -1   0   1   2   3

On the number line above, all points to the right of zero, whether marked or not, represent numbers that are

    A. positive   B. whole

    C. fractions (rationals)   D. in base ten

36. $\sqrt{5^6}$ 36._____

    A. 5^2 B. 5^3 C. 5^4 D. 5^{12}

37. Identify the rational number or numbers among the expressions 1/4, 3/4, 4/4, and 5/4.   37._____

    A. 1/4, 3/4   B. 1/4 *only*

    C. 5/4   D. all of them

38. The MOST precise of these measurements of length is   38.____

    A. 2 ft.   B. 3.25 ft.   C. 4 1/2 ft.   D. 29 in.

39. A circle graph showing that a person spends 25 percent of his budget for clothes will   39.____
have an angle whose measurement is

    A. 22 1/2°   B. 25°   C. 45°   D. 90°

40. In Figure _____ , you do NOT see a vertex.   40.____

    A.   B.   C.   D.

41. The chart at the right demonstrates   41.____
    A. addition facts for the binary base
    B. addition facts for base three
    C. multiplication facts in a non-decimal base
    D. a magic square

	0	1	2
0	0	1	2
1	1	2	10
2	2	10	11

42. Which of these numerals indicates that 4 has been used as a factor twice?   42.____

    A. 4 + 4   B. 4/2   C. 4 x 2   D. 16

43. All the pupils in an elementary class who are each over 7 ft. 8 in. tall may be described   43.____
as the

    A. odd numbers   B. solution set
    C. empty set   D. unique domain

44. 6784.65 is APPROXIMATELY 6.8 x   44.____

    A. 10^4 B. 10^2 C. 10^1 D. 10^3

45. If X is less than Y, and Z is greater than Y, then   45.____

    A. $\dfrac{z}{2} > \dfrac{y}{2}$ B. X+Y < Z

    C. Y > Z   D. $X = \dfrac{1}{2}y = \dfrac{1}{2}z$

46. If the length of each side of a square is doubled, the area of the square would be multi-   46.____
plied by

    A. 1   B. 2   C. 4   D. 8

47. -2 x -3 =   47.____

    A. 6   B. -1   C. -3   D. -6

48. Bob has laid out these right triangles to measure the distance across the river at AB. How wide is the river at AB?

    A. 60'
    B. 67 1/2'
    C. 75'
    D. 90'

48.____

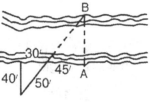

49. Which mathematical sentence below would you use to find the rate of interest earned on an investment of $1000 which earns $45 annually?

49.____

    A. $45 \div 1000 = \dfrac{100}{n}$

    B. $\dfrac{45}{100} = \dfrac{n}{1000}$

    C. $1000 \div 45 = \dfrac{100}{n}$

    D. $\dfrac{n}{100} = \dfrac{45}{1000}$

50. $5^6 \div 5^2 =$

50.____

    A. 1^3 B. 5^3 C. 5^4 D. 5^{12}

51. Suppose you were taking the 5 marbles from this box one at a time without looking until they are all gone. You draw one which is black. Now, what are the chances that you will draw a black marble the second time?

51.____

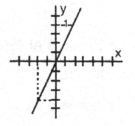

    A. 1/3   B. 1/4   C. 1/5   D. 2/5

52. This is a graph of the solution set for

    A. $y = 2 + x$
    B. $x = 2 + y$
    C. $y = 2x$
    D. $x = 2y$

52.____

53. A square, a rhombus, a rectangle, and a trapezoid are ALL

53.____

    A. pentagons   B. prisms
    C. parallelograms   D. quadrilaterals

54. A multiple of a number is

54.____

    A. a common denominator of that number and a greater number
    B. a multiplier
    C. one of two factors in a multiplication
    D. a product of that number and another factor

55. $\sqrt{13} \times \sqrt{13} =$

55.____

    A. 3.4   B. 13   C. $\sqrt{13}$ D. $\sqrt{26}$

56.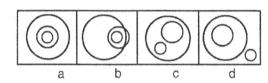

$\overline{PR} \cap \overline{ST} =$

56.____

A. $\varnothing$
B. $\overline{RS}$
C. $\overline{PT}$
D. $\overline{RT}$

57. In this group of symbols ($\perp$, =, +, ~, $\cong$, $\equiv$), there is no symbol that means

57.____

A. plus or minus
B. is equal to
C. is similar to
D. is perpendicular to

58. The numeral in base ten for a certain number has four digits.
The numeral in base four for the same number will have _____ digits.

58.____

A. four
B. more than four
C. less than 4
D. One can't tell without knowing what the number is

59. Some integers are positive numbers and some integers are negative numbers, but no positive numbers are negative numbers.
Which diagram illustrates these facts?

59.____

a   b   c   d

60. If A < B - C and all three are positive whole numbers greater than zero, then

60.____

A. A < B
B. A + C > B
C. $A < \dfrac{B+C}{2}$
D. B < C

61. If the sum of the digits of a numeral is 36, you can be sure that the number is divisible, without a remainder, by

61.____

A. 2
B. 4
C. 6
D. 9

62. A car goes one mile in 75 seconds.
To find the equivalent speed in miles per hour, which equation can be used?

62.____

A. $\dfrac{60}{75} = \dfrac{60}{n}$
B. $\dfrac{n}{60} = \dfrac{75}{60}$
C. $\dfrac{1}{75} = \dfrac{n}{60 \times 60}$
D. $75 \div 60 \times 60 = n$

63. The prime factors of three numbers are, respectively,
|2,2,3,5|, |2,3,3|, and |3,3,2,5|.
The GREATEST common factor of the three numbers is

63.____

A. 6
B. 12
C. 30
D. 90

64. Each square represents a digit in the numeral 3☐☐☐ 144. Even though you do NOT know what digits the squares represent, you can be sure that 3☐☐☐ 144 is divisible by

64.____

    A. 3   B. 6   C. 8   D. 9

65. Which fraction is the LARGEST?

65.____

    A. 9/8   B. 7/8   C. 6/7   D. 5/4

KEY (CORRECT ANSWERS)

1.	A	16.	B	31.	B	46.	C	61.	D
2.	B	17.	A	32.	A	47.	A	62.	C
3.	B	18.	A	33.	B	48.	A	63.	A
4.	C	19.	D	34.	A	49.	D	64.	C
5.	B	20.	C	35.	A	50.	C	65.	D
6.	A	21.	D	36.	B	51.	B		
7.	D	22.	B	37.	D	52.	C		
8.	C	23.	A	38.	B	53.	D		
9.	D	24.	B	39.	D	54.	D		
10.	D	25.	C	40.	C	55.	B		
11.	B	26.	C	41.	B	56.	A		
12.	D	27.	C	42.	D	57.	A		
13.	C	28.	A	43.	C	58.	B		
14.	B	29.	C	44.	D	59.	C		
15.	C	30.	C	45.	A	60.	A		

SOLUTIONS TO PROBLEMS

1. A cone has a point at one end and a circle at the other end.

2. $5 \times 10^2 + 3 \times 10^1 + 4 \times 1 = 500 + 30 + 4 = 534$

3. The appropriate diagram would look like this:

    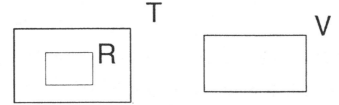

    Thus, no members of V are members of R.

4. Since $40 = 20 + 20 + 8$, $6 \times 48 = (6 \times 20) + (6 \times 20) + (6 \times 8)$

5. Any number divided by 1 remains unchanged.

6. An unlimited number of lines can pass through a given point.

7. Adding 5 points to each score will also raise the average 5 points to a new average of 30.

8. $E + A = A + E$ by the commutative law in algebra.

9. An exponent describes the number of times a base is used as a factor. Example, $n^3 =$ n.n.n

10. A multiple in both lists is K (p,z were also in both lists)

11. $a \times b \times c = c \times a \times b$ always

12. A line segment is a portion of a line with endpoints.

13. Area $= (6)(4) = 24$ sq.ft.

14. The underlined 6 means thousands whereas the other 6 means tens. The first 6 is 100 times the other 6.

15. $\dfrac{1}{3}$ (6 ft. 9 in.) = 2 ft. 3 in. or 2 ft. + 3 in.

16. $=$ means two things are the same.

17. Let n = additional cents needed. Then, $60 + n = (3)(25)$

18. 43 is a prime since it can only be divided evenly by itself and 1 (negative numbers excluded).

19. Let n = number. Then, $\dfrac{24}{n} = 2n$

20. 421_{four} has no meaning since only 0, 1, 2, 3 may be used in base four.

21. 3754 is closer to 4000 than to 3500, so rounded to the nearest 500, 3754 becomes 4000.

22. Measuring means comparing with some reference like a scale or a ruler, for example.

23. $\dfrac{4}{37} = \dfrac{n}{100}$ will yield what percent of 37 is 4.

24. $\angle a + \angle b + \angle c = 180^\circ$. Since $\angle a = 90^\circ$, $\angle b + \angle c = 90^\circ$

25. Using a proportion, 2/5 = 6/n will yield the correct cost.

26. a(b+c) = ab + ac is the distributive property.

27. $\angle a + \angle b = 180^\circ$. If $\angle a = 130^\circ$, Then $\angle b = 50^\circ$

28. $m x \dfrac{2}{3} = \dfrac{2}{3} m$ which is less than m if m > 0.

29. $(15.94)(.5) = 7.975 \simeq 8$

30. XVY means the set of elements in X or Y or both = |2, 3, 4, 6, 8, 9, 12].

31. $\angle a + 65^\circ + 65^\circ = 180^\circ$. Thus, $\angle a = 50^\circ$

32. Area = ($\dfrac{1}{2}$)(16)(6) = 48 sq.ft.

33. A variable will represent the unknown in an equation.

34. The appropriate diagram appears as:

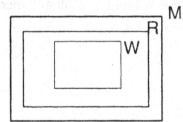

Thus, all of W is part of M.

35. All points to the right of zero represent positive numbers.

36. $\sqrt{5^6} = 5^3$ since $5^3 \cdot 5^3 = 5^6$

37. Any fraction with an integer in both numerator and denominator is a rational number.

228

38. 3.25 ft. is more precise than the other choices because the accuracy is in hundredths, and the others are whole numbers or contain accuracy only to one decimal place.

39. $(.25)(360^\circ) = 90^\circ$

40. A sphere does not contain a vertex, since there does not exist an intersection of line segments.

41. The given chart shows addition for base 3, where the only allowable digits are 0, 1, 2.

42. Since 16 = 4 x 4, the number 4 is a factor twice.

43. A set with no elements is called an empty set.

44. $6784.65 = 6.78465 \times 10^3$ or about 6.8×10^3

45. Since Z is greater than Y, then dividing by 2 yields Z/2 is greater than Y/2. Symbolically, Z/2 > Y/2.

46. Let x = original side of a square so that area = x^2.
Doubling each side to 2x makes the area $(2x)^2 = 4x^2$.
Now, $4x^2$ is 4 times as big as x^2.

47. $(-2) \times (-3) = 6$. Two negatives multiplied yield a positive.

48. By similar triangles, 45'/AB = 30'/40'. Solving, AB = 60'

49. 45/1000 = n/100 will yield the annual rate of interest.

50. $5^6 \; 5^2 = 5^4$. When dividing, subtract exponents.
Note   Bases must be the same.

51. Since only 1 black marble exists out of 4 marbles, the probability is 1/4.

52. The line contains the points (0,0) and (2,4). The related equation is y = 2x.

53. A quadrilateral is any enclosed 4-sided figure.

54. A multiple of a number includes a product of that number and another factor. Example: 8 is a multiple of 4, since 8=4x2.

55. $\sqrt{13} \times \sqrt{13} = \sqrt{169} = 13$

56. $\overline{PR} \cap \overline{ST} = \varnothing$ since there are no points in common.

57. The missing symbol is $\pm$, which means plus or minus.

58. In base four, the placeholders are 1, 4, 16, 64, 256, 1024, 4096, etc. If the number is 1000 in base ten, it would correspond to a 5-digit number in base four. If the number is 9999 in base ten, it would correspond to a 7-digit number in base four. Thus, any 4-digit number in base ten would require more than 4 digits in base four.

59. Diagram C is correct, where the 2 smaller circles represent positive and negative numbers, respectively.

60. Since A < B - C, A + C < B. Now, A < A + C because A, B, C are all positive. Finally, A < A + C < B, so A < B.

61. The rule for divisibility of 9 is that the sum of the digits must divide (with no remainder) by 9. Of course, 36 is one such number.

62. 1 mile in 75 seconds = n miles in 3600 seconds.
    This can also be written as 1/75 = n/60 X 60.

63. The factors in common are 2 and 3 and (2)(3) = 6

64. For a number to be divisible by 8, the portion of the number named by the last three digits (on the right) must be divisible by 8. Of course, 144 ÷ 8 = 18, which is a whole number.

65. Converting each fraction to a decimal, we get: 1.125, .875, .857 (approx.), 1.25. By inspection, 1.25 = 5/4 is the largest in this group.

———————

EXAMINATION SECTION
TEST 1

DIRECTIONS: Each question or incomplete statement is followed by several suggested answers or completions. Select the one that BEST answers the question or completes the statement. *PRINT THE LETTER OF THE CORRECT ANSWER IN THE SPACE AT THE RIGHT.*

1. At 7:00 A.M., a student leaves his home in his automobile to drive to school 28 miles away. He averages 50 mph until 7:30 A.M., when his car breaks down. The student has to walk and run the rest of the way.
   If he wants to arrive at school at 8:00 A.M., how fast, in mph, must he travel on foot?

   1.____

   A. 3   B. 4   C. 5   D. 6   E. 7

2. Express $1+\dfrac{1}{2+\dfrac{1}{3+\dfrac{1}{4}}}$ in simplest terms.

   2.____

   A. 27/28   B. 30/43   C. 1 1/9   D. 1 1/27   E. 1 13/30

3. A theater charges $5.00 admission for adults and $2.50 for children. At one showing, 240 admissions brought in a total of $800.
   How many adults attended the showing?

   3.____

   A. 40   B. 80   C. 120   D. 160   E. 266

4. $\sqrt{25+?}=5+8$

   4.____

   A. 8   B. 12   C. 64   D. 144   E. 169

5. The perimeter of a square is 20.
   Which of the following represents the area?

   5.____

   A. 5   B. 10   C. 20   D. 25   E. 100

6. Evaluate the expression $\dfrac{1}{4}+\dfrac{3}{8}-\dfrac{6}{16}-\dfrac{8}{32}$

   6.____

   A. 7/16   B. 1/32   C. 1/8   D. 1/4   E. 0

7. Bill spent 20% of the money he initially had in his wallet on groceries and 25% on gas. He had $66.00 left. How much money did he have before he shopped?

   7.____

   A. $85   B. $100   C. $110   D. $111   E. $120

8. Express the product $(2x + 5y)^2$ in simple form.

   8.____

   A. $4x^2 + 25y^2$ B. $4x^2 + 20xy + 25y^2$
   C. $4x^2 + 10y + 25y^2$ D. $4x^2 - 20xy + 25y^2$
   E. $4x + 25y$

9. A student received test grades of 83, 90, and 88.
   What was her grade on a fourth test if the average for the four tests is 84?

   A. 85   B. 80   C. 75   D. 70   E. 65

   9.____

10. A rectangular room is 3 meters wide, 4 meters long, and 2 meters high.
    How far is it from the northeast corner at the floor to the southwest corner at the ceiling?
    _____ members.

    A. $\sqrt{29}$ B. $\sqrt{11}$ C. $\sqrt{9}$ D. 9   E. 5

    10.____

11. If an electron has a mass of 9.109×10^{-31} kg. and a proton has a mass of 1.672×10^{-27} kg., approximately how many electrons are required to have the same mass as one proton?

    A. 150,000   B. 1,800   C. 5.4×10^4
    D. 5.4×10^{-4} E. 15×10^{-58}

    11.____

12. The introduction of a new manufacturing process will affect a saving of $1,450 per week over the initial 8-week production period. New equipment, however, will cost 1/4 of the total savings.
    How much did the equipment cost?

    A. $11,600.00   B. $2,900.00   C. $725.00
    D. $362.50   E. $181.25

    12.____

13. If P dollars is invested at r percent compounded annually, at the end of n years it will have grown to $A = P(1 + r)^n$. An investment made at 16% compounded annually. It grows to $1,740 at the end of one year.
    How much was originally invested?

    A. $150   B. $278.40   C. $1,461.60
    D. $1,500   E. $1,700

    13.____

14. What is 1/4% of 200?

    A. 0.05   B. 0.5   C. 5   D. 12.5   E. 50

    14.____

15. Which of the following is .5% of .95?

    A. .000475   B. .00475   C. .0475   D. .475   E. 4.75

    15.____

16. What is the value of (5 lbs. 1 oz)/(3 lbs. 6 oz.) in ounces?

    A. 22   B. 1.66   C. 1.5   D. 0.66   E. 0.28

    16.____

17. If 1 inch = 2.54 centimeters, 3/8 centimeter equals which of the following in inches?

    A. 6.77   B. .95   C. .39   D. .38   E. .15

    17.____

18. If $2x + y = 7$ and $x - 4y = 4$, then x equals which of the following?

    A. -15/9   B. - 1/9   C. 7/16   D. 11/9   E. 32/9

    18.____

19. What part of an hour is 6 seconds?

    A. 1/600   B. 1/10   C. 1/360   D. 1/60   E. 1/5

    19.____

20. If 1/3 + 5(x-1) = 8, then which of the following is the value of x?   20._____

    A. 8/13   B. 8/5   C. 38/25   D. 38/15   E. 38

21. Which line is perpendicular to the x-axis?   21._____

    A. x = 3   B. y = 3   C. x = y
    D. x = y/3   E. y = x/3

22. If a dental hygienist at a certain office is paid H dollars a week, the dental assistant works   22._____
36 hours a week at A dollars per hour, and the receptionist works 40 hours a week and
receives R dollars every other week, which of the following represents the weekly payroll
for these three employees?

    A. H/3 + 36A + 40R/3   B. H + 36A + R/2
    C. H/3 + 12A + R/6   D. 5H + 36 + 20R
    E. H/3 + 12A + 40R

23. Company A ordered five units of anesthetic at $12.00 per unit. Company B ordered 10   23._____
units at $13.00 per unit, and Company C ordered 4 at $10.00 per unit. Since all these
companies were at one address, the three orders were put on one bill.
Approximately what percent of the total bill did Company A have to pay?

    A. 5   B. 18   C. 26   D. 36   E. 55

24. Which of the following is the value of A, if $50(A/100) = 2A^2$?   24._____

    A. 25   B. 1   C. 5/2   D. 1/4   E. 1/2

25. Five-eighths of the employees in a certain company are male. One-fifth of these males   25._____
are single.
What percentage of the employees in the company are single males?

    A. 12.5   B. 20.0   C. 25.0   D. 32.0   E. 62.5

26. If x = 20% of y, and z = 35% of x, then z = _____% of y.   26._____

    A. 70   B. 57   C. 7   D. 1.75   E. .07

27. Which of the following is the value of the expression $\dfrac{|14-3|-|7-16|}{3|(-2)+1|}$?   27._____

    A. -20/3   B. -2/3   C. 0   D. 2/3   E. 20/3

28. A tank can be filled by a pipe in 30 minutes and emptied by another pipe in 50 minutes.   28._____
How many minutes will it take to fill the tank if both pipes are open?

    A. 45   B. 60   C. 75   D. 80   E. 100

29. If (4/5)x = (2/5)y, then which of the following is equal to y/x?   29._____

    A. 1/2   B. 2/5   C. 25/8   D. 2   E. 3

30. Which of the following would NOT result in a straight line?   30._____
    x =

    A. 1/y   B. 2y + 5   C. (y+6)/(2)
    D. 5 - y   E. 4(x+3y)

31. $\dfrac{5}{4} + \dfrac{4}{5} + \dfrac{3}{2} -$ _____ = a positive integer.   31. _____

    A. 10/20   B. 11/20   C. 71/20   D. 3/20   E. 4/20

32. If $\dfrac{2}{x} + \dfrac{3}{5} = \dfrac{4}{3}$, then which of the following is the value of x?   32. _____

    A. 30/11   B. 30/29   C. 11/30   D. -11/6   E. -5/2

33. Optometry school applicants decreased by 25% during a 4-year period. During the same   33. _____
time, the number of first-year openings in optometry school increased by 12%. If the ratio
of applicants to first-year student openings had been 3 to 1, then which of the following
would be the APPROXIMATE ratio at the end of the 4-year period?

    A. 1.5 to 1   B. 2 to 1   C. 3 to 2
    D. 4 to 3   E. 6 to 5

34. If then which of the following is the value of x?   34. _____

    A. 4   B. 27   C. 29   D. 49   E. 729

35. Two cars start at the same point and travel north and west at the rate of 24 and 32 mph,   35. _____
respectively.
How far apart are they at the end of 2 hours?

    A. 64   B. 80   C. 112   D. 116   E. 100

36. Right triangle ABC with right angle C and AB = 6, BC = 3, find AC.   36. _____

    A. 3   B. 6   C. 27   D. 33   E. $3\sqrt{3}$

37. When each of the sides of a square is increased by 1 yard, the area of the new square is   37. _____
53 square yards more than that of the original square.
What is the length of the sides of the original square?

    A. 25   B. 26   C. 27   D. 52   E. 54

38. Evaluate: $3(2)^2 + \sqrt{25} - (-2)^3$.   38. _____

    A. 9   B. 24   C. 25   D. 33   E. 76

39. Which of the following is the length of the   39. _____
line segment BC if AB = 14, AD = 5, and
angle BAD = 30°?

    A. $\sqrt{221}$

    B. $\sqrt{171}$

    C. $7\sqrt{3}$

    D. 7

    E. 9

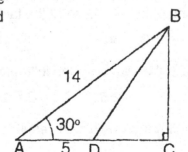

40. A bowl contains 7 green and 3 red marbles.
    What is the probability that two marbles selected at random from this bowl without
    replacement are both red?

    A. 1/15   B. 9/100   C. 21/100   D. 47/90   E. 6/10   40._____

41. If x pens cost 75 cents and y pencils cost 57 cents, then which equation below can be
    used to find the cost of 2 pens and 3 pencils?   41._____

    A. 2(75/x) + 3(57/y)   B. 3x/75 + 2y/57
    C. 75/2x + 57/3y   D. 2(x/75) + 3(y/57)
    E. 3(75/x) + 2(57/y)

42. Maria has a number of dimes and quarters whose total value is less than $9.00. There
    are twice as many dimes as quarters.   42._____
    At most, how many quarters could she have?

    A. 14   B. 15   C. 19   D. 20   E. 35

43. The number (1, 2, 3, 6) have an average (arithmetic mean) of 3 and a variance of 3.5.
    What is the average (arithmetic mean) and variance of the set of numbers (3, 6, 9, 18)?   43._____

    A. 9, 31.5   B. 3, 10.5   C. 3, 31.5
    D. 6, 7.5   E. 9, 27.5

44. A fence encloses a triangular-shaped region whose sides are 20 feet, 20 feet, and 10
    feet in length.   44._____
    If the number of inches between fence posts (centers) is 30 inches, how many posts
    will be needed?

    A. 17   B. 20   C. 21   D. 22   E. 23

45. A ceiling 6 feet by 7 feet can be painted for $52. Find the cost of painting a ceiling 18 feet
    by 21 feet, all things being equal except the dimensions.   45._____

    A. $104   B. $126   C. $156   D. $378   E. $468

46. Three consecutive odd numbers have a sum of 51.
    What is the LARGEST of these numbers?   46._____

    A. 15   B. 17   C. 18   D. 19   E. 21

47. It takes 5 hours for a qualified typist to complete a report. Coffee break begins at 10:15
    A.M. It is now 9:55 A.M.   47._____
    How much of the task can the typist be expected to complete by coffee break?

    A. 1/8   B. 1/25   C. 1/3   D. 1/5   E. 1/15

48. A container in the form of a rectangular solid is 10 feet long, 9 feet wide, and 2 feet deep.
    The container is filled with a liquid weighing 100 pounds per cubic foot.   48._____
    What is the weight of the liquid in the container in pounds?

    A. 90   B. 180   C. 1,800   D. 9,000   E. 18,000

49. The value of cos(π /3) equals the value of

    A. - cos(2 π /3)   B. cos(2 π /3)   C. cos(6 π /3)

    D. - cos(5 π /3)   E. cos(4 π /3)

49.____

50. If 5 $\leq$ x $\leq$ 12 and -2 y 9, then is as large as possible when x = _____ and y = _____.

    A. 12; 9   B. 12; 0   C. 12; -2   D. 0; 9   E. 0; 0

50.____

KEY (CORRECT ANSWERS)

1.	D	11.	B	21.	A	31.	B	41.	A
2.	E	12.	B	22.	B	32.	A	42.	C
3.	B	13.	D	23.	C	33.	B	43.	A
4.	D	14.	B	24.	D	34.	C	44.	B
5.	D	15.	B	25.	A	35.	B	45.	E
6.	E	16.	C	26.	C	36.	E	46.	D
7.	E	17.	E	27.	D	37.	B	47.	E
8.	B	18.	E	28.	C	38.	C	48.	E
9.	C	19.	A	29.	D	39.	D	49.	A
10.	A	20.	D	30.	A	40.	A	50.	B

SOLUTIONS TO PROBLEMS

1. Let x = rate of walking/running. Then, (50)(1/2) + (x)(1/2) = 28 Simplifying, 1/2x = 3. Solving, x = 6.

2. $3 + \dfrac{1}{4} = 3\dfrac{1}{4}$, $1/3\dfrac{1}{4} = \dfrac{4}{13}$, $2 + \dfrac{4}{13} = 2\dfrac{4}{13}$, $1/2\dfrac{4}{13} = \dfrac{13}{30}$.

   Finally, $1 + \dfrac{13}{30} = 1\dfrac{13}{30}$.

3. Let x = number of adults, 240-x = number of children.
   Then, 5x + 2.50(240-x) = 800. Simplifying, we get 5x + 600 - 2.50x = 800. This reduces to 2.50x = 200. Solving, x = 80.

4. $\sqrt{25+x} = 13$ Squaring both sides, 25 + x = 169. So, x = 144.

5. If the perimeter of a square is 20, each side must be 5.
   The area is $5^2 = 25$

6. Changing to a denominator of 32, we get 8/32 + 12/32 - 12/32 - 8/32 = 0/32 = 0

7. Let x = original amount. 100% - 20% - 25% = 55%
   Then, $66 = .55x. Solving, x = $120

8. $(2x+5y)^2 = 4x^2 + 10xy + 10xy + 25y^2 = 4x^2 + 20xy + 25y^2$

9. Let x = grade on her 4th test. Then, (83+90+88+x)/4 = 84 This becomes (261+x)/4 = 84. Further reduction leads to 261 + x = 336, so x = 75

10. The required distance is $\sqrt{3^2 + 4^2 + 2^2} = \sqrt{9+16+4} = \sqrt{29}$

11. $(1.672 \times 10^{-27}) \div (9.109 \times 10^{-31})$ .1836 x 10^4 ≈ 1800

12. Total savings is ($1450)(8) = $11,600.
    Equipment costs (1/4)($11,600) = $2900

13. $1740 = P(I + .16)'. Then, P = $1740 ÷ 1.16 = $1500

14. 1/4% of 200 is (.0025)(200) = .5

15. .5% of .95 is (.005)(.95) = .00475

16. 5 lbs. 1 oz. = 81 oz. and 3 lbs. 6 oz. = 54 oz.
    Then, 81 oz. ÷ 54 oz. = 1.5

17. 3/8 cm = 3/8 ÷ 2.54 = .375 ÷ 2.54 ≈ .1476 ≈ .15 inch

18. From equation 1, y = 7 - 2x. Substituting into equation 2, x - 4(7-2x) = 4. Simplifying, x - 28 + 8x = 4.
    This reduces to 9x = 32, so x = 32/9

19. Since there are 3600 seconds in 1 hour, 6 seconds would represent 6/3600 = 1/600 of an hour

20. 1/3 + 5(x-1) = 8. Simplify to 1/3 + 5x - 5 = 8.
This will reduce to 5x = 12 2/3, so x = 38/15

21. A line perpendicular to the x-axis must have an undefined slope. The equation must be x = constant. The only choice fitting this format is x = 3

22. The receptionist works 40 hours at R/2 dollars per week.
Thus, the weekly payroll for all three workers is H + 36A + R/2
(The 40 hours is not used in computing.)

23. The total bill was (5)($12) + (10)($13) + (4)($10) = $230. Company A's bill was $60.
Thus, $60/$230 ≈ 26.1% ≈ 26%

24. $50(A/100) = 2A^2$ becomes $A/2 = 2A^2$. Simplifying further, we get $A = 4A^2$ or $A(4A-1) = 0$.
The two values of A are 0 and 1/4.

25. The number of single males is represented as (5/8) (1/5)(100)% = 12.5%

26. z = .35x and x = .20y. Thus, z = (.35)(.20)y = .07y.
Then, z is 7% of y.

27. The numerator is |11|-|-9| = 11 - 9 = 2. The denominator is 3|-1| = 3. Thus, the fraction = 2/3

28. Let x = required number of minutes. Then, 1/30 x - 1/50 x = 1 Multiplying by 150, 5x - 3x = 150. Solving, x = 75

29. $\frac{4}{5}x = \frac{2}{5}y$. Then, $\frac{y}{x} = \frac{4}{5} \div \frac{2}{5} = 2$

30. $x = \frac{1}{y}$ becomes xy = 1, which represents a hyperbola.

31. $\frac{5}{4} + \frac{4}{5} + \frac{3}{2}$ = (25+16+30)/20 = 71/20 . If 71/20 - x = a positive integer, then the only correct values of x are 11/20, 31/20, 51/20.

32. Multiplying the equation by 15x, we get 30 + 9x = 20x. Then, 30 = 11x, so x = 30/11

33. Let 3x = number of applicants, x = 1st year student openings. Over the 4-year period, the number of applicants dropped to .75(3x) = 2.25x and the number of openings rose to 1.12x. Now, 2.25x ÷ 1.12x ≈ 2 to 1

34. $\sqrt{x-25} = 2$. Squaring both sides, x - 25 = 4, so x = 29

35. At the end of 2 hours, their individual <u>distances</u> are 48 miles and 64 miles. Their distance apart is = 80 miles

36. $AC^2 + 3^2 = 6^2$. This simplifies to $AC^2 = 27$.

    Thus, $AC = \sqrt{27} = 3\sqrt{3}$

37. Let x = original length of each side, so that x + 1 = new length of each side of the square. Then, $(x+1)^2 = x^2 + 53$. This simplifies to $x^2 + 2x + 1 = x^2 + 53$. Then, 2x + 1 = 53, so x = 26

38. $3(2)^2 + \sqrt{25} - (-2)^3 = 12 + 5 + 8 = 25$

39. Sine 30° = BC/14 1/2 = BC/14, so BC = 7

40. Probability of 2 red marbles being drawn without replacement is (3/10)(2/9) = 1/15

41. Each pen costs 75/x cents and each pencil costs 57/y cents. Then, 2 pens and 3 pencils cost 2(75/x) + 3(57/y)

42. Let x = number of quarters, 2x = number of dimes.
    Then, .25x + .10(2x) < 9.00
    Solving, x < 20, so, x = 19

43. The new set of numbers is 3 times as large as the original set. Therefore, the mean is 3 times as big, which is 9, and the variance is 3^2 or 9 times as big, which is (9)(3.5) = 31.5

44. Using the diagram shown at the right, for the fence $\overline{BC}$, we'll need 5 posts whose distance from each other is 2 1/2'. (This includes a post at B and a post at C.) Now along $\overline{AB}$, since AB = 20' and $20 \div 2\frac{1}{2} =$ 8, we'll need 8 posts (including a post at A). Finally, starting at A and ending at C, we need to place only 20 ÷ 2 1/2 - 1 = 7 posts since a post already exists at A and at C. Thus, the total number of posts is 5 + 8 + 7 = 20

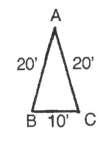

45. (6')(7') = 42 square feet costing $52, which means $52/$42 or $(26/21) per square foot. Now a ceiling 18 ft by 21 ft is 378 square feet and will cost (26/21)(378) = $468

46. Let x, x+2, x+4 represent the three odd numbers. Then, x + x+2 + x+4 = 51. This reduces to 3x + 6 = 51, from which x = 15. The three numbers are 15, 17, 19 and so the largest is 19.

47. From 9:55 AM to 10:15 AM represents 20 minutes.
    Then, 20 minutes/5 hours = 20 minutes/300 minutes, which reduces to 1/15.

48. Volume is (10)(9)(2) = 180 cu.ft. The weight of the liquid is (100)(180) = 18,000 lbs.

49. Cosine $\frac{\pi}{3}$ = .5, which is also the value of - Cosine $\frac{2\pi}{3}$

50. To make $(3x-4)/(4+5y^2)$ as large as possible, we maximize the numerator and minimize the denominator. Given the restriction $5 \le x \le 12$ use $x = 12$. Given the restriction use y = 0. (<u>Note carefully</u> that $y = 0$ yields a smaller value of $4 + 5y^2$ than $y = -2$)

———